Master The ESP32 In C:

WiFi with the ESP-IDF, FreeRTOS, LwIP & MbedTLS

**Harry Fairhead
& Mike James**

**I/O Press
I Programmer Library**

Harry Fairhead & Mike James
Master The ESP32 In C; WiFi with the ESP-IDF, FreeRTOS, LwIP & MbedTLS
First Edition
ISBN Paperback: 9781871962994
ISBN Hardback: 9781871962895
First Printing, 2025

Published by IO Press   www.iopress.info
In association with I Programmer   www.i-programmer.info
and with I o T Programmer   www.iot-programmer.com

The publisher recognizes and respects all marks used by companies and manufacturers as a means to distinguish their products. All brand names and product names mentioned in this book are trade marks or service marks of their respective companies and our omission of trade marks is not an attempt to infringe on the property of others.

For updates, errata, links to resources and the source code for the programs in this book, visit its dedicated page on the IO Press website: iopress.info.

Preface

The Espressif ESP32 has WiFi hardware built by Espressif itself as a central feature of the entire ESP32 family. The ESP-IDF (Espressif IoT Development Framework) supports the basic WiFi hardware. To make full use of it, however, you must also understand the underlying components: the Lightweight Internet Protocol (lwIP) and Mbed Transport Layer Security (mbedTLS).

Espressif has done a good job of customizing both libraries to make them easy to use with the ESP32, but understanding how they work makes it even easier. The fact that the ESP32 uses FreeRTOS as standard also makes WiFi use, and asynchronous tasks, in general much easier. It also means that we can use sockets to implement communications protocols.

Many SDKs are very difficult to get started with, but not so the ESP-IDF if you use it with VS Code. Installation and configuration are straightforward, allowing you to be developing a program within minutes of installing the necessary extension.

We start out with an examination of using FreeRTOS beyond the simple, single-task program – using cores, scheduling, locks, synchronization and interrupts. A complete chapter is dedicated to exploring the different data structures that FreeRTOS provides for inter-task communication.

Once we have mastered FreeRTOS we turn our attention to basic WiFi in station mode. Then on to using lwIP to implement TCP/IP and DHCP. Sockets are key to implementing almost any network communications and an HTTP client is used as an example. We also look at the HTTP client component provided by the IDF. After implementing a client the next challenge is how to implement a server and methods that can be used to make a client stand in for a server.

Modern communication is almost always encrypted and this can prove difficult for IoT devices with limited power and memory. Before looking at how to implement HTTPS, we take a hands-on look at practical cryptography. Next we implement an HTTPS client using the standard certificate bundle. Of course, after the client comes the server and this is a matter of supporting the appropriate encryption suites and certificates.

There is more to life than HTTP and the next four chapters introduce UDP, SNTP, SMTP and MQTT in turn. The final chapter deals with some advanced topics - implementing an AP that can be used to configure hardware; an AP that can connect its clients to the Internet; promiscuous mode packet sniffing; long range mode; ESP Now and ESP Mesh.

VS Code is our preferred IDE and is a good choice for the ESP IDF as it comes with an easy to use extension that will create projects, compile, run and debug them. These topics are covered extensively in *Programming The ESP32 In C Using The Espressif IDF*, ISBN: 9781871962918, which is also where we explore the use of the GPIO lines, cover the basics of PWM and introduce a range of sensors, servos, motors and ADCs.

None of the programs in this book are production level, as their primary goal is to clearly demonstrate how things work. Our examples are as simple as they can possibly be and they lack error handling to make sure that you can see clearly how they work. The programs are not designed to impress the reader with their complexity; they are designed to be easy to understand. You can consider them to be minimal viable programs. If you understand them then they should be easy for you to extend to more robust and general programs that do exactly what you want.

Thanks to our tireless editors Sue Gee and Kay Ewbank. who attempt to eliminate our mistakes and turn garbled text into smooth sentences. Doubtless errors remain, and we hope they are few.

For the source code for the programs in this book, together with any updates or errata and links to resources including recommendations for obtaining electronic components, visit its dedicated page on the IO Press website, iopress.info. You will find references to the folders that the complete programs are stored in at the start of each of the listings.

You can also contact us at harry.fairhead@i-programmer.info or mike.james@i-programmer.info.

Harry Fairhead
Mike James
November, 2025

Table of Contents

Chapter 9

Details of Cryptography   **143**

Chapter 10

SSL/TLS and HTTPS   **165**

Chapter 11

SSL Server   **185**

Appendix I
Advanced WiFi Configuration **273**

Chapter 1

FreeRTOS Basics

The ESP32 is a series of low-cost, low-power System on a Chip (SoC) microcontrollers primarily developed and manufactured by Espressif Systems. The ESP32 features integrated WiFi and Bluetooth and includes all the necessary networking components, such as TCP/IP, HTTP, and TLS/SSL, within its firmware. This makes it ideal for use in IoT projects where data is being collected by remote sensors.

This book explores the use of the ESP32's WiFi capabilities and assumes you are already familiar with the basics of working with the device and are confident about creating, compiling, running and debugging projects. These topics are covered extensively in *Programming The ESP32 In C Using The Espressif IDF*, ISBN: 9781871962918, which is also where we introduce working with the GPIO together with a range of sensors, servos, motors and ADCs.

At the time of writing there are seven commonly encountered ESP32 devices; the S series based on the LX6/7 processor, the C series using the RISC-V processor and the H series also using RISC-V:

The S Series:

- ◆ ESP32   (2014) LX6 using dual-core, WiFi 4 and Bluetooth
- ◆ ESP32-S2 (2019) LX7 single-core, WiFi 4 only
- ◆ ESP32-S3 (2020) LX7 dual-core, WiFi 4 and Bluetooth

The C series:

- ◆ ESP32-C3 (2020) RISC-V WiFi 4
- ◆ ESP32-C6 (2021) RISC-V WiFi 6

The H series:

- ◆ ESP32-H2 (2023) RISC-V No WiFi

The H series devices support Bluetooth, Thread and Zigbee, but not WiFi and tend to be used with other members of the ESP32 family to add Zigbee/Thread. As such it is not considered in this book.

All of the examples given work with the ESP32 and the ESP32-S3 which are the two most used devices and with the ESP32-S2 except when two cores are required. They will also work with the C series devices with some extensions to WiFi 6 and the restriction to single-core operation.

Small devices usually only have enough processing power to do one thing at a time. More powerful devices such as the ESP32, and ESP-S3 which have two cores, are capable of doing more than one thing at a time, but organizing the software to make this possible is difficult and requires a real time operating system. This is powerful, but it comes with a whole new set of challenges.

In this chapter we look at the basics of using the Free RealTime Operating System, FreeRTOS, which is used by all members of the ESP32 family. It is installed automatically and you most likely have been using it to create programs since you first started with the ESP32. For many applications the fact that there is an operating system can be ignored, but if you want to work with WiFi and data transfer in general then understanding exactly what FreeRTOS is doing and how it can help is well worth the effort.

What Is FreeRTOS?

FreeRTOS is an open-source project to make a Realtime Operating System RTOS available on a wide range of processors. The term RTOS is often used to mean any realtime operating system, not just FreeRTOS.

The basic FreeRTOS is a single-core operating system aimed at making running multiple tasks easier. The version of FreeRTOS used by the ESP32 is ESP-IDF FreeRTOS and this has been extended to work with two cores to utilize Symmetric Multi-Processing (SMP), a technique where multiple processors work together to execute tasks simultaneously. This is the version of FreeRTOS that is available as a component in ESP-IDF and the one currently used in all ESP32 programs.

As well as FreeRTOS and ESP-IDF FreeRTOS, there's also Amazon SMP FreeRTOS, which has been extended to support as many cores as you need, i.e. N-core SMP. At the time of writing this is being ported to ESP-IDF, but its status is experimental and so is best avoided until it becomes stable.

The bottom line is that you should use ESP-IDF FreeRTOS unless there's a good reason to experiment. The good news is that the basic operation and API of all FreeRTOS versions is more or less identical and you should find moving between them easy. It's worth learning ESP-IDF FreeRTOS because the skill generalizes.

From this point on the use of FreeRTOS should be taken to mean ESP-IDF FreeRTOS, but differences are few.

What Does An RTOS Do?

If you write programs for the ESP32 without making explicit use of FreeRTOS, then you are essentially working with a single "thread" of execution. That is, there is a single program running and the order in which the instructions are executed is determined exactly by the code that you write. Even this simple picture isn't quite accurate in that interrupts can occur. An interrupt stops your program running and starts an interrupt service routine (ISR) running. When the ISR is finished your program is restarted and continues almost as if nothing has happened. Of course, this isn't 100% true as the ISR will have done something and sometimes this will have an effect on your program.

Interrupts are an example of asynchronous programming. It is asynchronous in the sense that you cannot know in advance when the ISR will be running or when your program is running. The order that instructions are carried out depends on when the interrupt occurs.

The idea of asynchronous programming can be expanded beyond the idea of a simple interrupt. If a function has to wait for something to happen, the download of a file for example, then the processor has nothing to do but loop round testing for the file to be ready. A much more sensible idea is to give it something else to do while waiting. This idea leads to a basic operating system which keeps a list of programs ready to run and allocates them to the processor when it has nothing to do. This is generally called "cooperative multi-tasking", because for the system to work every process has to voluntarily give up the processor when it cannot make progress, i.e. when it is blocked.

An alternative to cooperative multi-tasking is preemptive multi-tasking . This is where at every "tick", an interrupt occurs which runs a scheduler program. This has a list of what programs are available for running and works out which one should be run next to keep the system running. If there is a candidate, the scheduler suspends the currently running program and starts a new one. If the tick happens fast enough, 1ms or less, it looks as if more than one program is running. Even in preemptive scheduling programs can yield the processor if they are blocked so as to keep the system running efficiently.

Interrupts, cooperative multi-tasking and preemptive multi-tasking are all used to manage asynchronous events and concurrent execution. A program can be suspended at any point and another program can resume from where it was suspended. True concurrency is where multiple tasks are handled simultaneously. If a processor has more than one core then more than one program can be running at the same time. This is different from single core asynchronous execution, where the illusion of parallel execution is created by rapidly switching between tasks, because now more than one thing can actually happen at a time.

Single core asynchronous has just one instruction executing at any time and this is much simpler than true concurrency, where more than one instruction can be executing at the same time.

Of course, it is standard to implement cooperative or preemptive asynchronous running of programs on more than one core making it possible to efficiently run multiple programs using the resources of multiple cores.

In practice, things are slightly more complicated than this outline suggests. You have the overhead of context switching and this means that the tick rate has to be set correctly to achieve good performance, The scheduler also has to be able to distribute the processor's time in a way that meets the requirements of the system – either total throughput or a reasonable time to respond to the outside world. Then there is the issue of allocating resources and ensuring that resources are used correctly by just one program at a time. All of these issues and more make any operating system including an RTOS more complex than you might imagine.

Tasks

ESP-IDF FreeRTOS is a preemptive SMP multi-tasking operating system that can make use of two cores if the model of the ESP32 supports them. It works in terms of tasks. A task is a function that can be run as if it was a "main" program in its own right. That is, a task is like a function call, but it doesn't block its caller until it has finished. Tasks never return to their callee and are often written as infinite loops or they complete their objective and are deleted – they never execute a return.

A task is the unit of code that is scheduled by FreeRTOS. A task shares the processor with other tasks in a way that will be explained in detail.

Creating a FreeRTOS program is all about creating and managing tasks.

The basic FreeRTOS call to create a task is:

```
xTaskCreate(pTaskFunction, pName, StackDepth, pParameters,
                                    Priority, pTaskHandle)
```

Its parameters are:

- ◆ pTaskFunction Function to run as the task
- ◆ pName   Name used to identify the task to the programmer
- ◆ StackDepth   Stack size in bytes
- ◆ pParameters   Pointer to parameters to be passed to the task
- ◆ Priority   Scheduling priority of the task
- ◆ pTaskHandle   Pointer to a task handle for managing the task. If you don't want to reference the task for management purposes you can pass NULL in place of pTaskHandle.

The function that is run as a task looks like an interrupt handler, for example:

```
void TaskFunction(void *arg)
```

The stack size should be set to be large enough to store all of the local variables that are created by the task or by any functions it calls. You can find out how close you are to running out of stack memory using uxTaskGetStackHighWaterMark, which reports the smallest free stack space since the task started running.

The memory needed for the task is allocated by FreeRTOS. If you want to control this then you can use xTaskCreateStatic() and supply pointers to memory to be used by FreeRTOS. In most situations you don't need to do this.

A simple example of running an FreeRTOS task looks little different from a standard Hello World program, (folder HelloTask):

```
#include <stdio.h>
#include "freertos/FreeRTOS.h"
void task0(void* arg) {
    for (;;) {
        printf("Hello Task World\n");
        vTaskDelay(100);
    }
}
void app_main(void)
{
    xTaskCreate(task0, "task0", 2048,  NULL, 0, NULL);
}
```

In this case, we create a single new task that runs the function task0 which simply prints Hello Task World every second. The vTaskDelay function suspends the task for the specified number of ticks and, as the default tick rate is every 10ms, suspending for 100 ticks wakes the task up every second. You can also use the predefined portTICK_PERIOD_MS to set a time to suspend in t milliseconds:

```
vTaskDelay(t / portTICK_PERIOD_MS)
```

If you run the program you will see the message displayed every second. What is less obvious is that app_main is also a task and you can see that this is true by adding a for loop that prints another message, (folder HelloTask):

```
void app_main(void)
{
    xTaskCreate(task0, "task0", 2048,  NULL, 0, NULL);
        for (;;) {
        printf("app main\n");
        vTaskDelay(100);
    }
}
```

Now you will see the messages alternating as each task gets to run.

You may have been wondering why all ESP32 programs start with `app_main` and not the usual C/C++ `main`? Normally FreeRTOS uses a standard main program to allow you to start your own tasks. Something like:

```
int main()
{
    xTaskCreate(app_main, "app_main", 2048, NULL, 0, NULL);
    vTaskStartScheduler();
}
```

The call to `vTaskStartScheduler()` gets FreeRTOS running and never returns. ESP-IDF FreeRTOS does this for you behind the scenes so you only need to create `app_main` which is a task. In this sense there is no "main" program under FreeRTOS, just tasks. The idea is that `app_main` then creates any additional tasks your app may require and returns when it is finished. If you don't create any additional tasks you can treat `app_main` as if it was just a standard C main program. Notice that `app_main` returning doesn't mark the end of your program as it may leave other tasks that it created still running, but it does delete `main`.

Core Affinity

If there are two cores, as is the case with many ESP32 devices, then the created task will run on either core and can even swap which core it is running on. In the jargon, the task is said to have no core affinity.

Usually we do want to assign a core affinity to a task as we generally want it to run on the Application CPU, known as APP_CPU or CPU1 and not interfere with the working of WiFi/Bluetooth on the Protocol CPU, PRO_CPU or CPU0. To assign a task to a particular core we can use:

```
xTaskCreatePinnedToCore( pTaskFunction, pcName,
        StackDepth,pParameters,Priority, pTaskHandle, CoreID)
```

which is the same as `xTaskCreate` but with an extra `CoreID` parameter which is 0 for CPU0 or 1 for CPU1. You can also use APP_CPU_NUM PRO_CPU_NUM if you want to. For example to specify that task0 should run on PRO_CPU you could change the main program of `HelloTask` to:

```
void app_main(void)
{
    xTaskCreatePinnedToCore( task0, "task0", 2048,  NULL, 0,
                                            NULL, PRO_CPU_NUM);

        for (;;) {
        printf("app main\n");
        vTaskDelay(100);
    }
}
```

You can also change the affinity of app_main by setting:

`#define CONFIG_ESP_MAIN_TASK_AFFINITY 0`

to one either directly or by using the SDK Configuration editor:

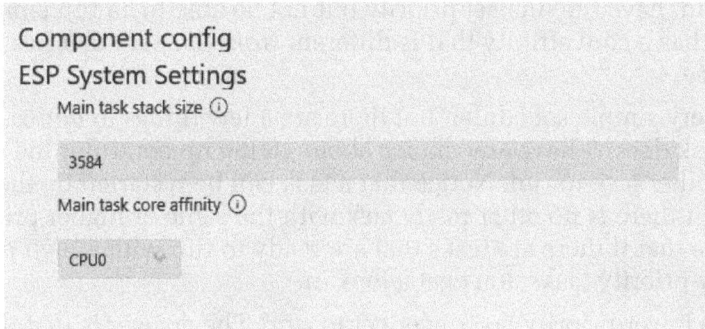

Component config
ESP System Settings
Main task stack size ⓘ

3584

Main task core affinity ⓘ

CPU0

Of course, your objective is to distribute tasks between the cores so as to maximize their use – this is not an easy problem.

For devices with just a single core the all of the tasks including the WiFi run on the same core.

Scheduling

Understanding the FreeRTOS scheduler is crucial to working out how to configure tasks to run in the way that they need to. The scheduler is a simple, fixed-priority, preemptive scheduler. Every tick, 10ms by default, the timer interrupt fires and the scheduler is run on core zero. Core one, if it exists, has a timer interrupts but doesn't perform a full scheduler run.

A task can be in one of four states: Running, Ready (to run), Blocked or Suspended. The difference between Blocked and Suspended is that a task that is Blocked is waiting on something that the system can supply, such as the time being up for a task that has called `vTaskDelay`. The system can change the status of a task from Blocked to Running on its own.

The Suspended state can only be set by another task calling `vTaskSuspend`, in which case it can only be returned to the Ready state by another task calling `vTaskResume`. The important difference is that the scheduler doesn't have to check to see if a suspended task is now able to run, that's the job of another task.

Tasks are stored in a list which the scheduler has access to. When the scheduler runs it places the current task into the queue into either the Ready, Suspended or Blocked state. It then checks to see if any blocked tasks are in fact unblocked and it converts any it finds into the Ready state.

Finally the scheduler examines the list of Ready tasks and runs the one with the highest priority able to run on the core that the interrupted task was running on. If there are multiple tasks with the same priority then they each get their turn to run in a round robin fashion. Notice that a task may be ready to run, have the highest priority but not be able to be run simply because it has a core affinity that is different from the core that has just become free.

This is a very simple scheduler, but there are a few things to notice. The first is that a task doesn't have any choice about giving up control if the system selects another task to run. Notice that a task can be restarted by the scheduler if there is no other ready task with the same or higher priority. Also notice that if there are tasks that are ready to run with a high priority, then lower-priority tasks don't get a look in.

So how do lower-priority tasks ever get to run? The answer is that they don't unless all the higher priority tasks are blocked or suspended. This makes it very important that you don't assign a lower priority to a task unless you are certain that the higher priority tasks will block or suspend often.

To summarize:

- Every task has a fixed priority assigned when it is created.
- The scheduler gets to run whenever the current task leaves the running state, either because it is suspended or is blocked. If this doesn't happen for `portTICK_PERIOD_MS` milliseconds, then the running task is interrupted and the scheduler runs anyway.
- When the scheduler runs, it first examines all tasks suspended for a time and if that time is up they are marked as Ready.
- The scheduler then looks for the task in the Ready state with the highest priority that can run on the core that has become free. If there is more than one then the tasks are run in turn, i.e. in round robin fashion.

This is a very simple scheduling algorithm and it has the advantage that you can mostly work out what is going to happen.

The `app_main` runs at priority 1 by default and this means that most of the tasks that it creates should run at priority 1 or more. The basic strategy for assigning priorities is to give the majority of the tasks the same priority so that they share the processing time and assign any task that has to be run as soon as possible after it enters the Ready state a higher priority.

The Standard Tasks

Working with the scheduling algorithm would be easy if there were only the tasks you created in the system. There are, however, five standard tasks that the system starts before your program is loaded:

Task Name	Description	Affinity	Priority
Idle Tasks (IDLEx)	An idle task (IDLEx) is created for (and pinned to) each core.	Corex	0
FreeRTOS Timer Task (Tmr Svc)	FreeRTOS will create the Timer Task if any FreeTOS Timer APIs are called	Core0	CONFIG_FREERTOS_TIMER_TASK_PRIORITY
Main Task (main)	Task that simply calls app_main. This task will self delete when app_main returns	CONFIG_ESP_MAIN_TASK_AFFINITY	1
IPC Tasks (ipcx)	IPC tasks are used to implement the Inter-processor Call (IPC) feature	Corex	24
ESP Timer Task (esp_timer)	ESP-IDF creates the ESP Timer Task used to process ESP Timer callbacks	Core0	22

These tasks aren't running all of the time, but the priorities that you assign to the tasks that you create can stop them running at all.

Notice that this implies that app_main runs at priority 1, which allows all of the standard tasks to run with the exception of IDLEx, the Idle Task. If you create a task with priority greater than 1 then you might find that app_main never gets to run.

The idle task is responsible for cleaning up memory if tasks come to an end and it resets the watchdog timer. If it doesn't run occasionally then you program will be terminated with a watchdog exception, see the following example.

For devices with just a single core the all of the tasks including the WiFi run on the same core.

A First Example

Creating a task is easy. It is how tasks behave when running together that is harder. As a simple example, consider running two tasks on the same core at the same priority. The first task sets a GPIO line high and the second sets it low. This allows you to use a logic analyzer to see when each task is running, (folder GPIO):

```
#include <stdio.h>
#include "freertos/FreeRTOS.h"
#include "driver/gpio.h"

void task1(void* arg) {
    for (;;) {
        gpio_set_level(2, 1);
    }
}
void task2(void* arg) {
    for (;;) {
        gpio_set_level(2, 0);
    }
}

void app_main(void)
{
    gpio_reset_pin(2);
    gpio_set_direction(2, GPIO_MODE_OUTPUT);

    TaskHandle_t th1;
    xTaskCreatePinnedToCore(task1, "task1", 2048,
                                    NULL, 0, &th1, 1);
    TaskHandle_t th2;
    xTaskCreatePinnedToCore(task2, "task2", 2048,
                                    NULL, 0, &th2, 1);
}
```

You can see that both tasks are run on CPU1 at priority 0. If you try this out you will see:

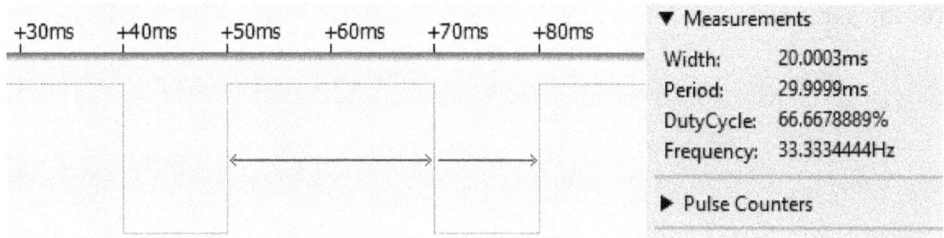

						▼ Measurements	
+30ms	+40ms	+50ms	+60ms	+70ms	+80ms	Width:	20.0003ms
						Period:	29.9999ms
						DutyCycle:	66.6678889%
						Frequency:	33.3334444Hz
						▶ Pulse Counters	

As there are two tasks with the same priority, you may expect each to run for half of the time, but it is clear that this isn't the case. While `task1` appears to run for two time slots, `task2` runs for only one. The reason for this apparent anomaly is that at Priority 0 there are three tasks – the two we created and the Idle Task. So what happens is that `task 1` starts running for one time slot. Then the idle task gets to run and this leaves the GPIO line high, even though task 1 is suspended. Then the idle task is preempted at the end of the time slot and task 2 starts running.

If you change the priority of the tasks to 1, see folder `Priority`, then you do see the tasks running for an equal time as promised, but now the idle task doesn't get to run at all and the result is a watchdog timer timeout:

```
E (135306) task_wdt: Task watchdog got triggered.
The following tasks/users did not reset the watchdog in time:
E (135306) task_wdt:    - IDLE1 (CPU 1)
E (135306) task_wdt: Tasks currently running:
E (135306) task_wdt: CPU 0: IDLE0
E (135306) task_wdt: CPU 1: task2
E (135306) task_wdt: Print CPU 1 backtrace
```

What is the solution to this? It all depends on how you are designing your system and whether or not you actually want a watchdog timer to act on your behalf. The simplest solution is to disable the watchdog timer on CPU1 using the ESP-IDF Configuration Manager.

You can turn the watchdog timer off in the Idle Task, but if you do you have to make sure that it doesn't run in this state:

```
void task1(void* arg) {
    TaskHandle_t IT= xTaskGetIdleTaskHandle();
    esp_task_wdt_delete(IT);
    for (;;) {
        gpio_set_level(2, 1);
    }
}
```

With this modification to the task, you can run it at priority 1 and you won't trigger a watchdog timeout. When you are ready to allow the Idle Task to run again, you have to reinstall the Watchdog Timer.

The Idle Task is responsible for freeing the kernel-allocated memory from tasks that have been deleted. It is therefore important that the Idle Task is not starved of microcontroller processing time if your application makes any calls to `vTaskDelete`. Memory allocated by the task code, e.g. using malloc, is not automatically freed, and should be freed before the task is deleted.

The Watchdog Problem

In many cases a better solution is to adjust the watchdog's timeout period or feed the watchdog from the task that is keeping control of the core. In practice, real applications do need a watchdog timer to restart them after a crash.

This issue with the imposed watchdog timer is typical of the way you have to compromise when any operating system is involved with a processor that has to interface with the external world. Without an operating system, you can write a program that has exact timing. This is usually more difficult, but you can program in assurances such as the output will always have a 50% duty cycle. As soon as you use an operating system, writing a system becomes easier, but making any guarantees about timing is much more difficult, if not impossible. In the previous example, we had two tasks of equal priority and in theory this should produce a 50% duty cycle, but due to the fact that the Idle Task also needs a time slot, the results are not 50%.

What should you do to force the scheduling to be what you want? The Idle Task resets the watchdog, but it also does garbage collection of the memory freed by deleting tasks. Even if you decide that the watchdog timer isn't needed, you still need to allow the Idle Task to run occasionally to ensure system stability. Then there are tasks with a higher priority that every now and then become Ready to run and are run at the next time slot. Timing in an RTOS is difficult.

As long as you are generating outputs or servicing inputs that can tolerate delays and disruption in the tens of milliseconds, then there is no problem. You can impose stricter timing limits, but only for short bursts of time because you are going to have to allow the system tasks to run at some point. Also notice that, as well as FreeRTOS interrupts every time slot, you also have to contend with interrupts from other sources.

Tasks and Interrupts

There is a particular problem when you start using tasks and interrupts. The way that an ISR, Interrupt Service Routine, is called when an interrupt happens is very similar to the way the operating system starts a task running in response to a tick interrupt, but there is a very big difference. The interrupt can happen at any time and it isn't part of the operating system's task list. The operating system doesn't manage the interrupt. Instead the interrupt stops the current task on the core and runs the ISR. What this means is that you have to be careful about how you write ISRs. They need to be short and they need to avoid accessing system resources to avoid multiple access problems.

For example, if a task is in the middle of using printf and an interrupt uses it then the results can be anything from garbled output to a full system crash.

However, interrupts often need to access FreeRTOS functions to manage tasks. For example, a good way to implement the response to an interrupt is to get the ISR to activate a task to do the job. This allows the interrupt to be handled more or less as if it was a task with an assigned priority and so with less chance of degrading the system. To allow an interrupt to interact with FreeRTOS, some FreeRTOS functions have ISR versions which work even though the calling function is not a task. The two most common ISR functions are:

- xTaskResumeFromISR(TaskToResume)
- uxTaskPriorityGetFromISR(TaskHandle)

These work in the same way as the standard FreeRTOS function, but they allow an ISR to make use of task management.

Managing Tasks

There are some simple functions that allow you to manage tasks:

- vTaskSuspend(TaskToSuspend)
- vTaskResume(TaskToResume)
- xTaskResumeFromISR(TaskToResume)
- vTaskDelete(TaskToDelete)
- vTaskSuspendAll()
- xTaskResumeAll()

where all of the parameters are task handles. A task that is suspended remains suspended until another task resumes it.

The SuspendAll function stops all tasks except for the one that called it, but leaves interrupt handlers free to operate.

Tasks run forever unless they are deleted. Deleting a task safely is subject to a range of conditions. Basically, make sure that a task that is about to be deleted has freed all of its allocated memory and resources such as heap memory, spinlocks etc. The internally-used memory is freed by the Idle Task when it next runs.

You can also delete a Suspended task from another task. A task can self-delete, assuming it has cleaned up its resources using:

vTaskDelete(Null)

In addition there is taskYield() which will put the current task into Ready state and allow the scheduler to select the next task to run – which could be the same task if there are no alternatives. You can also use vTaskDelay(0) to do the same thing.

There are several of functions that will get or set information about tasks:

- `uxTaskPriorityGet(TaskHandle)`
- `uxTaskPriorityGetFromISR(TaskHandle)`
- `vTaskPrioritySet(TaskHandle,NewPriority)`
- `eTaskState eTaskGetState(TaskHandle)`
- `string = pcTaskGetName(TaskHandle)`
- `TaskHandle = xTaskGetHandle(pcNameToQuery)`
- `TaskHandle = xTaskGetCurrentTaskHandle()`
- `TaskHandle = xTaskGetIdleTaskHandle()`
- `uxTaskGetStackHighWaterMark(TaskHandle)`
- `uxTaskGetStackHighWaterMark2(TaskHandle)`
- `vTaskGetInfo(TaskHandle, pTaskStatus,`
                       `GetFreeStackSpace,State)`

The `getInfo` function is the one that returns most information as a `TaskStatus` struct with the following fields:

`Handle`	Handle of the task
`pcTaskName`	Points to the task's name
`XtaskNumber`	Number unique to the task
`eCurrentState`	State of the current task, returns one of: `eRunning`, `eReady`, `eBlocked`, `eSuspended`, `eDeleted`, `eInvalid`
`uxCurrentPriority`	Priority at which the task is running
`uxBasePriority`	Not used
`ulRunTimeCounter`	Total run time allocated to the task so far
`pxStackBase`	Points to lowest address of the task's stack
`UsStackHighWaterMark`	Smallest amount of free stack while the task has been running
`XcoreID`	Core affinity 0, 1, or `tskNO_AFFINITY`

Notice that the stack high water mark takes a long time to compute. If you don't want it, set `GetFreeStackSpace` to `false`.

To use some of these functions you have to configure the project to activate them. For example, to use the `getInfo` function you have to set `configUSE_TRACE_FACILITY` to 1:

Component config

FreeRTOS

Kernel

✓ configUSE_TRACE_FACILITY ⓘ

KCONFIG Name: **FREERTOS_USE_TRACE_FACILITY**

Enables additional structure members and functions to assist with e: more details).

configUSE_STATS_FORMATTING_FUNCTIONS ⓘ

Here is a simple example to discover how generous our allocation of a 2kByte stack is (folder stacksize):

```
TaskHandle_t th1;
xTaskCreatePinnedToCore(task1, "task1", 2048, NULL, 1, &th1, 1);
vTaskDelay(1000 / portTICK_PERIOD_MS);
TaskStatus_t TaskStatus;
vTaskGetInfo(th1, &TaskStatus, true,true);
printf("%ld\n",TaskStatus.usStackHighWaterMark);
```

This prints 944, which means that at most 1104 bytes are used by the stack, suggesting it could be made smaller.

There are some functions concerned with tasks and time:

- ticks = xTaskGetTickCount()
- ticks = xTaskGetTickCountFromISR()
- vTaskDelay(TicksToDelay)
- xTaskDelayUntil(pPreviousWakeTime, TimeIncrement)
- xTaskAbortDelay(TaskHandle)

We have been using vTaskDelay to introduce delays into programs from our early examples, but now you can appreciate that it simply puts the task into a Blocked state and the operating system changes it back to Ready when the time is up. The task is resumed when the tick count gets to:

pPreviousWakeTime + TimeIncrement.

So, to generate an initial delay of n time slots you would use:

```
TickType_t xLastWakeTime = xTaskGetTickCount ();
xTaskDelayUntil( &xLastWakeTime, n );
```

The clever part is that xTaskDelayUntil stores the current tick count, when it is called, in xLastWakeTime, which means the next time you call it you get a delay of n time slots, irrespective of exactly when the next call occurs. In other words, a set of xTaskDelayUntil calls will result in the task being woken up again after n time slots, irrespective of how long it runs before calling the function again.

There are some functions that are helpful if you are trying to debug tasks and they are described in the documentation.

Threads and Tasks

You may already know how to write asynchronous/concurrent programs using a slightly different construct to tasks – threads. The threads model is standard in both Linux and Windows and many other operating systems. In FreeRTOS, a task rather than a thread is the basic unit of multi-tasking . A thread is a unit of execution, a data structure complete with fields to record the details of the execution. To use a thread it is first associated with a function which it executes to completion. The thread can then be reused to run another function if desired.

In a sense, a task is a function combined with a thread. What this means is that, while you can reuse threads to run other functions, you cannot reuse tasks. You can create another task using the same function and this is very similar to using another thread to run the same function.

If you already know how to use threads then there is a thread library which is built on top of the FreeRTOS task. If you don't know about threads then the only reason to use them in place of tasks is so that your program can run under another operating system such as Linux. There is no other reason for preferring threads to tasks.

One problem of using tasks as opposed to threads is that much of the jargon of asynchronous programming is cast in terms of threads. For example, we say that a function is "thread safe" which means it can be used in more than one thread at a time. This translates to "task safe" which means that a function can be used in more than one task at a time. This includes the function being used to start a new task and being called from more than one executing task.

For a function to be thread safe it has to have a state that renews itself when the function is used. In most cases, it means that all of its variables have to be local and stored on the stack and it shouldn't use any global or shared resources unless you can ensure that these can be shared safely. It isn't easy to give a recipe for creating a thread-safe function because there are so many ways a function can become non-thread safe. In the end all you can do is analyze what happens if the function is called again while it is being executed. If the function can be used without disturbing its previous use then it is thread safe. If using it again modifies a previous use it is not thread safe.

A second confusing use of the thread nomenclature is when a thread is given a name that indicates what it does, typically the UI thread or the WiFi thread and then you can only access the resource with the designated thread. For example, if a system has a UI thread then it is common to place the restriction that the UI can only be accessed by the UI thread. If another thread attempts to access a UI component then often an exception is thrown and a "cross-threaded" error reported. From the point of view of tasks, this translates to having a UI task and that no other task should access the UI components.

The point of having threads with designated tasks is to make sure that components can only be accessed by one thread at any given time. It effectively reduces the multi-tasking system to a single tasking system for that aspect, the UI for example. The same idea works if you dedicate a task to a specific subsystem like WiFi, but it raises the question of how other tasks communicate with that dedicated task.

In essence, a task is a thread plus a function.

Summary

- FreeRTOS is the standard operating system for the ESP32 range of devices. You can create programs for the ESP32 without making use of its multi-tasking features, which let you run multiple programs or tasks at the same time. but in the long run you are going to need them.

- If the device has only one core then all tasks run on it. If there are two cores a task can run on either core or it can be assigned to a particular core.

- Tasks run at different times depending on their assigned priority. FreeRTOS has a very simple fixed priority scheduler.

- The task with the highest priority which is ready to run is always run first and if there is more than one they are run one after another.

- A task can suspend itself for a set time or simply ask the scheduler to see if there is a higher priority task ready to run in its place.

- By default a watchdog timer is setup and the Idle task has to run every so often to reset it. This can make it difficult to test experimental programs that do not let the Idle task run.

- Tasks can be suspended and resumed by other tasks. A task can also suspend itself and even delete itself.

- Each task has its own stack and you have to make sure this is large enough not to cause an overflow.

- Threads are a more general way of implementing multi-tasking. While the relationship between a thread and a task isn't clear, the best way is to consider a task to be a thread with a particular function to run.

Chapter 2

Locks and Synchronization

The ESP32 and ESP32 S3 have two cores and this makes multi-tasking with true concurrency possible and slightly more challenging. The added difficulty of multi-tasking , which is controlling access to shared resources, is more difficult when there is true concurrency. For example, in a single-core system, simply disabling interrupts ensures that there is only one task running and it cannot be interrupted. As interrupts are disabled the scheduler doesn't get to run as there are no timer ticks. That is, disabling interrupts is a way of implementing a "critical section", a portion of code that has to be run to completion without interruption and without the interference of another task. In a multi-core system, however, this is not enough as, even with interrupts disabled, another task, running on another core, could try to access the same resources.

Single core members of the ESP32 still have many of the same problems as the multicore devices but as only one task can be running at any given time they are not quite as difficult to deal with.

Before we move on to look at solutions it is worth examining what the problems are.

Race Conditions

There is a fundamental problem with tasks and asynchronous/parallel programming in general. The problem is that tasks share the same memory space and indeed the two cores share the same memory space. This is convenient as it makes communication between tasks very easy, but it also makes it dangerous.

The problem is that an operation that one task is performing can be interrupted by another task performing an operation of its own. As long as the tasks are using different areas of memory, there is no problem. If they are working with the same area of memory then things can be less safe. This is a problem with tasks and with interrupt service routines. If running code can be preempted then there is scope for things to go wrong. As what goes wrong is due to the interaction of different threads of execution it is usually referred to as a race condition, but the nomenclature isn't particularly appropriate.

The most basic race condition is sometimes called "tearing". If access to data is not "atomic", i.e. it can be split by another operation, then you may not retrieve a sensible value. For example, suppose memory reads are atomic in byte access and you want to read two bytes. If the memory location is 0xFFFF and Task 1 starts to read it then the first byte it gets is 0xFF. If Task 2 now writes 0x0000 to the memory location and Task 1 reads the second byte it now has 0xFF00, which is not the original value and not the value written by Task 2. It is as if the final value is the result of tearing up the original and new value and putting them together. Notice that in a multi-core system "atomic" also means that another core cannot be doing the same thing at the same time – they have to wait until the atomic task is complete.

Another common race condition is "update loss". This occurs when two tasks update a shared resource by first making a copy of the resource. For example, consider adding one to a shared variable.

This is clearly a problem because if both tasks had added one to 42 the answer should be 44.

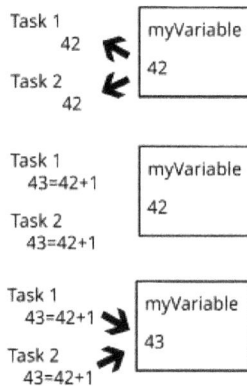

Task 1
42
Task 2
42

myVariable
42

Task 1
43=42+1
Task 2
43=42+1

myVariable
42

Task 1
43=42+1
Task 2
43=42+1

myVariable
43

You can see that the problem is that Task 1 makes a copy of the variable and then Task 2 does the same thing without waiting for Task 1 to update the variable. The final value of the variable depends on which task gets to write to the variable last. Imagine that Task 1 adds 2 to give 44 and Task 2 adds 3 to give 45 – now the final value of the variable depends on which is last to store its result.

The order of access matters to the outcome. Such problems are very difficult to debug because they occur erratically depending on timing and this makes them look like some sort of hardware problem. A race condition can make a repeated calculation give a different result each time. As the bug depends on timing, it can be difficult to reproduce reliably and it is usually the case that the problem vanishes when the program is run in a debugger due to the slower execution rate. Such bugs are often called Heisenbugs because of the way that they appear when you are not looking for them and disappear when you are.

It can be difficult to work out exactly what operations are atomic as it depends, not only on the processor, but on the compiler as well. For example, if you write x++ is this atomic and is it different from writing x=x+1? It depends on whether or not the processor has an atomic increment operator. If not, both involve retrieving a memory location into a register, incrementing the register and storing the result back into the memory location and this is clearly not atomic unless extra steps are taken to make it atomic.

Tearing – A Demonstration

Tearing does not occur with 32-bit or less access as memory is always accessed in 32-bit chunks as an atomic operation. However, you might expect tearing to occur with a 64-bit integer as two 32-bit accesses are required. Tearing does occur, but it can be difficult to capture it in action.

For example, assuming we have two cores, (program in folder Tearing):

```
#include <stdio.h>
#include "freertos/FreeRTOS.h"
uint64_t flag1 = 0;
uint64_t flag2 = 0;

void task1(void* arg) {
    for (;;) {
        flag1 = 0xFFFFFFFFFFFFFFFF;
        flag2 = 0xFFFFFFFFFFFFFFFF;
        if (flag1 != flag2) {
            printf("task 1 %llX   %llX\n", flag1, flag2);
            fflush(stdout);
            vTaskDelay(100);
        }
    }
}
void task2(void* arg) {
    for (;;) {
        flag1 = 0x0;
        flag2 = 0x0;
        if (flag1 != flag2) {
            printf("task 2 %llX   %llX\n", flag1, flag1);
            fflush(stdout);
            vTaskDelay(100);
        }
    }
}
void app_main(void)
{
    xTaskCreatePinnedToCore(task1, "task1", 4048, NULL, 0, NULL, 1);
    xTaskCreatePinnedToCore(task2, "task2", 4048, NULL, 0, NULL, 0);
}
```

If you run this with the compiler setting "debug without optimization":

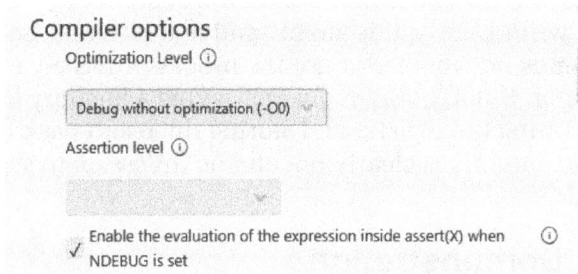

Compiler options
Optimization Level ⓘ

Debug without optimization (-O0) ⌄

Assertion level ⓘ

⌄

✓ Enable the evaluation of the expression inside assert(X) when ⓘ
NDEBUG is set

then you will find output like:

```
task 2 FFFFFFFF      FFFFFFFF
task 2 FFFFFFFF00000000      FFFFFFFF00000000
task 1 FFFFFFFF00000000      FFFFFFFFFFFFFFFF
task 2 FFFFFFFFFFFFFFFF      FFFFFFFFFFFFFFFF
```

You can see that we have values that should not occur and sometimes that are identical, which means the `if` statement shouldn't have evaluated to `true`. The only interpretation is that the values are being changed in the middle of the comparison by the other task. In addition, updates to the values are sometimes complete when the `printf` displays their values, in which case they are identical, but wrong in the context of the task doing the printing. Or the update is incomplete and we see torn values with all ones in one half of the value and all zeros in the other.

We get a similar result with a single core machine but the pattern of errors is slightly different. Now we tend to see:

```
task 2 FFFFFFFFFFFFFFFF      FFFFFFFFFFFFFFFF
task 1 0      FFFFFFFFFFFFFFFF
task 2 FFFFFFFFFFFFFFFF      FFFFFFFFFFFFFFFF
task 1 0      FFFFFFFFFFFFFFFF
task 2 FFFFFFFFFFFFFFFF      FFFFFFFFFFFFFFFF
```

and the pattern tends to repeat because of the regularities in the task switching performed by FreeRTOS.

Notice that this behavior disappears if you compile the program with optimizations selected.

Update Loss

Many programmers are lulled into a false sense of security with respect to race conditions believing that the probability that one could occur is very low. In fact, race conditions cause real effects surprisingly often. Consider, for example, update which creates two tasks that increment a shared 64-bit variable and then a third task is created which just waits for both tasks to be completed and then prints the value in the shared variable. The following example assumes two cores, program in folder Update:

```c
#include <stdio.h>
#include "freertos/FreeRTOS.h"

int64_t count = 0;
bool done0 = false;
bool done1 = false;

void task0(void *arg)
{
    for (int i = 0; i < 0xFFFFF; i++)
    {
        count = count + 1;
    }
    done0 = true;
    for (;;){}
}
void task1(void *arg)
{
    for (int i = 0; i < 0xFFFFF; i++)
    {
        count = count + 1;
    }
    done1 = true;
    for (;;) {}
}
void task2(void *arg)
{
    while (!done0 || !done1)
    {
        vTaskDelay(5);
    };
    printf("%llX\n", count);
    fflush(stdout);
    for (;;) {}
}
```

```
void app_main()
{
    xTaskCreatePinnedToCore(task0, "task0", 4000, NULL, 0, NULL, 1);
    xTaskCreatePinnedToCore(task1, "task1", 4000, NULL, 0, NULL, 0);
    xTaskCreatePinnedToCore(task2, "task2", 4000, NULL, 0, NULL, 1);
}
```

Notice the way that task2 waits for both task0 and task1 to complete. If you run this program you will discover that you don't get the same answer twice. Typically, you might see, after around 0.42 seconds:

```
144280
148402
144280
```

and so on. If you re-run the program, but with the tasks on the same core, then you get some repeated results due to the more deterministic nature of the way the tasks are run but it still doesn't reach the correct total of 0x1FFFFFE .

It can be confusing to find a deterministic program apparently producing different results each time it is run and it does feel as though a hardware problem should be responsible – but it is 100% code.

If you replace the 64-bit counter with a 32-bit counter then, with the default compiler settings, you don't see any race conditions. However, if you split the increment into two statements:

```
        temp = count + 1;
        count = temp;
```

and compile without optimization, you do get a race condition. If you compile with optimization, the use of the temp variable is removed and you don't get a race condition.

You can see from all of this that working out what is safe and what is not is very difficult and that a small change in the way an algorithm is expressed or a change to the compiler's optimization level can result in a race hazard where there was none.

Locks – Critical Sections

The solution to race hazards is to use locks to restrict access to a resource to a single task at a time. If a task needs to read, update and write a shared resource, then the resource should be locked from before the read to after the write. In the case of there being only a single core then we could ensure that access to a shared resource was exclusive to the task by simply turning off interrupts. If there are no interrupts, then the task cannot be interrupted! However, as there are two cores, this isn't enough as another task could try to access the same resource at the same time.

To cope with managing two cores we have to add a spinlock to the mix by way of modified critical region functions:

```
taskENTER_CRITICAL(pspinlock)
taskEXIT_CRITICAL(pspinlock)
```

where `pspinlock` is a `portMUX_TYPE` spinlock allocated statically or dynamically. There are also ISR versions of the `ENTER` and `EXIT` routines.

If CPU0 locks a resource with a spinlock then interrupts are disabled. When CPU1 tries to access the same resource it has to lock the same spinlock, but as CPU0 already has it locked, it has to wait in a tight loop until it is free.

Notice that there is nothing stopping CPU1 accessing the resource without trying to lock it. This is a purely cooperative locking scheme. Also notice that, while waiting on a lock, the core in question does no useful work. For this reason, critical sections should be kept as short as possible and certainly should not call any long-running blocking functions.

To protect the counting program from race conditions you could replace the two tasks with critical sections, the modified program is in folder `updateLock`:

```
static portMUX_TYPE my_spinlock = portMUX_INITIALIZER_UNLOCKED;
void task0(void *arg)
{
    for (int i = 0; i < 0xFFFFF; i++)
    {
        taskENTER_CRITICAL(&my_spinlock);
        count = count + 1;
        taskEXIT_CRITICAL(&my_spinlock);
    }
    done0 = true;
    for (;;)
    {
    }
}
void task1(void *arg)
{
    for (int i = 0; i < 0xFFFFF; i++)
    {
        taskENTER_CRITICAL(&my_spinlock);
        count = count + 1;
        taskEXIT_CRITICAL(&my_spinlock);
    }
    done1 = true;
    for (;;)
    {
    }
}
```

With these changes we get the correct result, 1F FFFE, repeatedly.

The cost of using locks is both the potential wasted time when the locked-out core simply waits, and the overhead in locking and unlocking access to a shared resource. For example, the time for the program to complete goes up from around half a second to three and a half seconds.

Even so, locking is usually the only way to make a program reliable.

The Semaphore For Flexibility

Critical sections are fine for restricting access to one task at a time but there are cases where access can be more flexible. The semaphore is a lock that keeps a count related to the number of current lock holders. A task acquires the semaphore using:

```
xSemaphoreTake(SemaphoreHandle_t xSemaphore,
                          TickType_t xTicksToWait)
```

This call waits for the specified time for the semaphore to become available. You can use `portMAX_DELAY` to wait forever. If it acquires the semaphore in the time, it returns `true`, otherwise it returns `false`. The task is blocked while it waits and hence uses no processor time.

The semaphore is released using:

```
xSemaphoreGive(SemaphoreHandle_t xSemaphore)
```

The count is set to an initial value when created and it is decremented after each `Take` and incremented after each `Give`. A `Take` succeeds only if the count is greater than zero. For example, if you set a `Semaphore` to 3 then the first three calls to `Take` will immediately return with the result `True` and the fourth will wait because the count is 0.

You create a counting semaphore, i.e. a standard semaphore, using:

```
SemaphoreHandle_t xSemaphoreCreateCounting(UBaseType_t uxMaxCount,
                              UBaseType_t uxInitialCount)
```

The amount of memory a counting semaphore takes depends on its specified `uxMaxCount` and `uxInitialCount` sets the count it is initialized to.

A binary semaphore is a restricted semaphore that has a maximum count of 1 and it is initialized to 0:

```
SemaphoreHandle_t xSemaphoreCreateBinary( void );
```

A binary semaphore is almost the same as a mutex, which is an even simpler type of locking mechanism. A mutex can be taken by a single task and after that all other tasks fail to take it until it is released.

Notice that semaphores and mutexes are purely cooperative locking schemes. If a task ignores the lock it can access the resource.

The idea of a semaphore is easy enough to understand, but it is more difficult to see what it is used for. A semaphore with an initial value of 1, i.e. a binary semaphore, can be used as a lock as only one task can take it at any one time.

A semaphore with an initial value of n can be used to restrict the number of threads that access a resource at any one time to n. This clearly isn't about avoiding a race condition because, if n threads can access a shared resource, a race condition is very likely to happen. If, however, a resource is designed to be safely shared up to a maximum user limit then you can manage it using a semaphore. You can also use a semaphore to signal when a condition has been satisfied a specific number of times. For example, suppose you have n tasks and another task needs to wait until all n tasks have finished. The solution is to set up a semaphore with an initial value of zero and have each task give the semaphore when it has finished. This means that the semaphore will eventually be incremented n times and hence it can be taken exactly n times. The monitoring task can thus wait for the n tasks to finish by attempting to take the semaphore n times:

```
for(int i=0;i<n;i++){
    xSemaphoreTake(xSemaphore,portMAX_DELAY)
}
```

While a semaphore can be used as a lock, its primary use is as a synchronization device.

To protect the counting program from race conditions, you could replace the two tasks with, (complete program in folder UpdateSemaphore):

```
SemaphoreHandle_t xSemaphore;
int64_t count = 0;
bool done0 = false;
bool done1 = false;
void task0(void *arg)
{
    for (int i = 0; i < 0xFFFFF; i++)
        if (xSemaphoreTake(xSemaphore, portMAX_DELAY) == pdTRUE)
        {
            count = count + 1;
            xSemaphoreGive(xSemaphore);
        }
    done0 = true;
    for (;;){ }
}
void task1(void *arg)
{
    for (int i = 0; i < 0xFFFFF; i++)
        if (xSemaphoreTake(xSemaphore, portMAX_DELAY) == pdTRUE)
        {
            count = count + 1;
            xSemaphoreGive(xSemaphore);
        }
    done1 = true;
    for (;;){}
}
```

```
void app_main()
{
    xSemaphore = xSemaphoreCreateBinary();
    xSemaphoreGive(xSemaphore);
    xTaskCreatePinnedToCore(task0, "task0", 4000, NULL, 0, NULL, 1);
    xTaskCreatePinnedToCore(task1, "task1", 4000, NULL, 0, NULL, 0);
    xTaskCreatePinnedToCore(task2, "task2", 4000, NULL, 0, NULL, 1);
}
```

With these changes we get the correct result, 1F FFFE, repeatedly, but it now takes 22 seconds compared to 3.5 seconds for the critical section.

The cost of using locks is both the potential waste of time when the locked-out core simply waits and the overhead in locking and unlocking access to a shared resource. For example, the counting program with locks takes three times as long to complete as the unlocked version. Even so, locking is usually the only way to make a program reliable.

Event Groups

FreeRTOS has two methods of allowing tasks to communicate state between themselves, event groups and notifications.

An event group is basically a set of bits in a special variable. Tasks can block and wait for a particular set of bits to be in a given state. Event groups can be used as locks or as synchronization primitives.

To create an event group you use:

```
EventGroupHandle_t xEventGroupCreate( void );
```

The number of bits is fixed at 24.

The returned event group bits can then be modified:

```
xEventGroupSetBits( EventGroupHandle_t xEventGroup,
                              const EventBits_t uxBitsToSet)
xEventGroupSetBitsFromISR( EventGroupHandle_t xEventGroup,
                              const EventBits_t uxBitsToSet)
xEventGroupClearBits( EventGroupHandle_t xEventGroup,
                              onst EventBits_t uxBitsToClear)
xEventGroupClearBitsFromISR( EventGroupHandle_t xEventGroup,
                              const EventBits_t uxBitsToClear)
xEventGroupGetBits( EventGroupHandle_t xEventGroup)
xEventGroupGetBitsFromISR( EventGroupHandle_t xEventGroup)
```

The bits to modify are specified as a bit mask.

Once the event group has been created, a task can test the bits for a particular pattern and enter a blocked state until the pattern is present:

```
EventBits_t xEventGroupWaitBits(
                    const EventGroupHandle_t xEventGroup,
                    const EventBits_t uxBitsToWaitFor,
                    const BaseType_t xClearOnExit,
                    const BaseType_t xWaitForAllBits,
                    TickType_t xTicksToWait );
```

The uxBitsToWaitFor parameter is a bit mask that defines the bits that have to be 1s for the task to run. You can select an AND or OR action by setting xWaitForAllBits. If xWaitForAllBits is true then all bits of the tested bits have to be set, i.e. the AND of the bits. If xWaitForAllBits is false then only one bit of the tested bits has to be set, i.e. the OR of the bits. The xTicksToWait sets the timeout for the operation and as long as it doesn't time out and xClearOnExit is true the bits are cleared before the task starts to run. The function returns the current state of the bits.

There is also:

```
EventBits_t xEventGroupSync( EventGroupHandle_t xEventGroup,
                    const EventBits_t uxBitsToSet,
                    const EventBits_t uxBitsToWaitFor,
                    TickType_t xTicksToWait );
```

Which sets the bits and waits for them as an atomic operation, i.e. it is a combination of xEventGroupSetBits and xEventGroupWaitBits. This should be used if multiple tasks are manipulating the event group to avoid race conditions. The other event group functions are atomic.

As an example of the use of event groups, we can use them to provide a binary semaphore lock on the counting program given earlier (the full program is in folder UpdateEvent. To do this we need to setup an event group with bit 0 set high to indicate that the lock is free.

```
EventGroupHandle_t event;
void app_main()
{
    event = xEventGroupCreate();
    xEventGroupSetBits(event, 0x1);
    xTaskCreatePinnedToCore(task0, "task0", 4000, NULL, 0, NULL, 1);
    xTaskCreatePinnedToCore(task1, "task1", 4000, NULL, 0, NULL, 0);
    xTaskCreatePinnedToCore(task2, "task2", 4000, NULL, 0, NULL, 1);
}
```

Next we need to test for the event group bit being 1 before proceeding:

```
void task0(void *arg)
{
    for (int i = 0; i < 0xFFF; i++)
    {
        xEventGroupWaitBits(event, 0x1, true, true, 100);
        count = count + 1;
        xEventGroupSetBits(event, 0x1);
    }

    done0 = true;
    for (;;){ }
}
```

The test is whether bit zero is a 1 and if it isn't the wait blocks for 100 ticks. If it is a 1 then the wait sets it to a 0 and returns. The final instruction in the for loop sets the bit to 1 so as to free the lock. The code for task1 is identical.

This works, but it is very, very slow compared to the semaphore version. A rough estimate is that it would take more than 18 days to complete the program counting to 0xFFFFF. This is the reason for the smaller count in this example – which still takes 102 seconds. If the tasks run on the same core, then the time drops to 47 seconds.

Clearly you should only use events for low-frequency synchronization which needs complex data.

Task Notifications

Task notifications are a more efficient way of blocking until a condition is satisfied. However, the mechanism sends the notification directly to a specified task. This means that it is only useful if you want to wake up a specific Blocked task.

The basic mechanism is that each task has notification values and it can enter a blocking mode by waiting on a value. The task is Unblocked when another task sends it a notification update, which may or may not change the notification value. The actual notification value is only used for information and what wakes the task up is the actual notification event rather than the change to the value.

Each task has an array of 32-bit notifications, but originally there was only a single value and because of this all notification functions have an Indexed version as well as a version that only works with notification[0]. By default ESP FreeRTOS supports a single array element . You can set how many using the SDK configuration to set configTASK_NOTIFICATION_ARRAY_ENTRIES.

As the zeroth element is used by other FreeRTOS functions, it is better to use notification[1] for your own functions.

The most basic notification function is:

```
BaseType_t xTaskNotifyIndexed( TaskHandle_t xTaskToNotify,
                               UBaseType_t uxIndexToNotify,
                               uint32_t ulValue,
                               eNotifyAction eAction );
```

This modifies the notification value at the given index on the specified task. How the notification value is changed depends on `eAction`:

- `eNoAction`   The value is not changed
- `eSetBits`   The value is bitwise Ored| with `ulValue`
- `eIncrement`   The value is incremented
- `eSetValueWithOverwrite`   The value is replaced by `ulValue`
- `eSetValueWithoutOverwrite`   If the task is not waiting the value is replaced by `ulValue`

The notification value is used by a task to implement a wait in a blocked state using:

```
BaseType_t xTaskNotifyWaitIndexed( UBaseType_t uxIndexToWaitOn,
                                   uint32_t ulBitsToClearOnEntry,
                                   uint32_t ulBitsToClearOnExit,
                                   uint32_t *pulNotificationValue,
                                   TickType_t xTicksToWait );
```

The task will wait on the notification value specified by the index, and unblocks when it receives a notification or it times out. You can set bits to clear on entry or exit by specifying a bit mask and you can save the original value of the notification using the `pulNotificationValue` pointer.

As already mentioned, it is the fact that the task receives a notification event that unblocks it and not the notification value. A task can only wait on one notification value at a time and any changes to any other notification value have no effect on it. The function returns `false` if it times out and `true` if it receives a notification.

There are a number of other notification functions, but they are all variations or restrictions on the two described above. For example,

```
BaseType_t xTaskNotifyAndQueryIndexed(
                           TaskHandle_t xTaskToNotify,
                           UbaseType_t uxIndexToNotify,
                           uint32_t ulValue,
                           eNotifyAction eAction,
                           uint32_t *pulPreviousNotifyValue);
```

works like `xTaskNotifyIndexed` , but has a pointer to return the initial notification value.

```
uint32_t ulTaskNotifyValueClearIndexed( TaskHandle_t xTask,
                                        UBaseType_t uxIndexToClear,
                                        uint32_t ulBitsToClear)
```

clears bits as specified by a bit mask.

There are two functions which enable the use of notification as a counting semaphore:

- ```
  BaseType_t xTaskNotifyGiveIndexed(
        TaskHandle_t xTaskToNotify, BaseType_t uxIndexToNotify)
  ```
- ```
  uint32_t ulTaskNotifyTakeIndexed(
    UbaseType_t uxIndexToWaitOn, BaseType_t xClearCountOnExit,
                                    TickType_t xTicksToWait);
  ```

The Give function increments the notification value and the Take decrements it. The Take function will place the task in a Blocked state if the notification value is zero. This makes the notification behave like a semaphore. Notice that this extends how the notification work in that it takes account of what the notification value actually is.

Finally we have:

- ```
  BaseType_t xTaskNotifyStateClearIndexed( TaskHandle_t xTask,
                            UBaseType_t uxIndexToClear );
  ```

which clears the pending state of the notification element.

There are ISR versions of some of the functions:

- ```
  vTaskNotifyGiveIndexedFromISR()
  ```
- ```
  xTaskNotifyAndQueryFromISRIndexed()
  ```
- ```
  xTaskNotifyFromISRIndexed()
  ```

And there are non-index versions of all of the functions.

All notify functions are atomic.

As an example of using notifications we can use the semaphore functions to provide locking for the update example, folder UpdateNotify:

```
TaskHandle_t th0, th1;
void task0(void *arg)
{
    for (int i = 0; i < 0xFFF; i++)
    {

        ulTaskNotifyTakeIndexed(0, true, 1000);
        count = count + 1;
        xTaskNotifyGiveIndexed(th1, 0);
    }

    done0 = true;
    for (;;)
    {
        vTaskDelay(1000);
    }
}
```

```
void task1(void *arg)
{
    for (int i = 0; i < 0xFFF; i++)
    {
        ulTaskNotifyTakeIndexed(0, true, 1000);
        count = count + 1;
        xTaskNotifyGiveIndexed(th0, 0);
    }

    done1 = true;
    for (;;)
    {
        vTaskDelay(1000);
    }
}
void app_main()
{
    xTaskCreatePinnedToCore(task0, "task0", 4000, NULL, 0, &th0, 1);
    xTaskCreatePinnedToCore(task1, "task1", 4000, NULL, 0, &th1, 0);
    xTaskCreatePinnedToCore(task2, "task2", 4000, NULL, 0, NULL, 1);
    xTaskNotifyGiveIndexed(th0, 0);
}
```

This is more subtle than using a full semaphore because the state of the
system is stored in each of the tasks rather than in a separate third party that
they both can access to discover the state. In this case the notification value
in each task is non-zero if the task is allowed to modify count. You can think
of a zero value as indicating that another task is accessing count.

The app_main program sets the notification to 1 for task0. This means that
task0 doesn't wait, but task1 does. task0 clears its own notification and
then sets that of task1 to 1. This allows task1 to update count and so on.

This program takes longer to run than the semaphore program given earlier
and so the number of repeats is reduced to 0xFFF for which it takes 123
seconds with two cores and 81 seconds with one core. To execute 0xFFFFF
loops would take just less than 22 days for two cores.

The reason for this difference is due to scheduling. In the case of the
semaphore there is just one state indicator and it is either 0 or 1 and hence
as soon as a task sets it to 1 another task can take it and move from Blocked
to Ready. In the case of the notifications, there are two state indicators and it
is possible for them both to be 0 at the same time and this allows other tasks
to run. If you measure the time between execution of each task it is more
than 15ms using both cores during which another task runs – this makes the
time to complete the loop roughly 0xFFF x 15 x 2 ms which is 122.85
seconds.

To avoid this problem you have to turn off the watchdog timer and run task0 and task1 at priority 1:

```
xTaskCreatePinnedToCore(task0, "task0", 4000, NULL, 1, &th0, 1);
xTaskCreatePinnedToCore(task1, "task1", 4000, NULL, 1, &th1, 0);
xTaskCreatePinnedToCore(task2, "task2", 4000, NULL, 0, NULL, 1);
```

With this change, the time per loop drops to around $20\mu s$ and the total time for a full 0xFFFFF count is around 40s, which is still longer than the semaphore approach.

Which Lock?

Clearly from the timings of the counter program you should prefer to use critical sections or semaphores because they are faster, despite what the documentation claims. If you are locking a single task from another task then notifications are slightly faster than semaphores, but if you are using interlocking notifications as in the earlier example, then things aren't so good due to the way other tasks get their turn in the scheduler.

If you need to lock or synchronize multiple tasks then semaphores are your only option. If you need to communicate a complicated state then events or notifications might be better.

Summary

- When tasks share resources there is the potential for race conditions, where the outcome of an operation depends on the order in which tasks access a resource to occur.

- Tearing is an example of a race condition due to two or more tasks accessing the same data in a way that results in neither task completing its update and the result being a mixture of the two.

- Update loss happens when two or more tasks attempt to update a resource with a read-modify-write cycle and only the task that performs the final write succeeds in updating the resource.

- It is necessary to control access to resources that are shared between tasks to avoid race conditions. The standard way of doing this is to identify critical sections and use locks.

- The semaphore is a very flexible lock that can be used to synchronize the behavior of multiple tasks.

- An alternative to a semaphore is to use event groups or a task notification.

Understanding how locking and synchronization primitives work is important, but at the end of the day all it really provides is a kit of parts that you can use to implement more complex solutions. In this chapter we take a look at some of the common situations and uses of tasks, locking and synchronization.

There is a dogma that FreeRTOS tasks should be written so that they never end. This is because an RTOS is usually regarded as a way of extending the polling loop at the heart of all real time applications. Instead of one big polling loop, the idea is that each task is its own polling loop. This idea is so strongly held that there are many proposed reasons for preferring it, but none are conclusive. If you want to start a task to do a job and then delete it when it is finished then this is a perfectly reasonable way to design the system as long as you are happy with the overhead of creating and deleting a task. This raises some basic questions about knowing when a task has completed its job.

Waiting For a Task

Ideally tasks should be organized so that they get on with their jobs independently of one another, but occasionally one task may need to wait for another to complete and deliver some data.

The solution is very simple. Just wait on a semaphore and arrange for the task to Give it before deleting itself, the program can be found in folder Wait1:

```
#include <stdio.h>
#include "freertos/FreeRTOS.h"

SemaphoreHandle_t xSemaphore;

void task0(void *arg)
{
    vTaskDelay(100);
    printf("task0\n");
    xSemaphoreGive(xSemaphore);
    vTaskDelete(NULL);
}
```

```
void app_main()
{
    xSemaphore = xSemaphoreCreateBinary();
    xTaskCreatePinnedToCore(task0,"task0",4000,NULL,0,NULL,1);
    xSemaphoreTake(xSemaphore, portMAX_DELAY);
    printf("task complete\n");
}
```

If you run this you will see task0 followed by task complete, demonstrating
that the app_main task has waited for task0 to complete.

The alternative is to use a notification in roughly the same way, (in folder
Wait2):

```
#include <stdio.h>
#include "freertos/FreeRTOS.h"
void task0(void *arg)
{
    vTaskDelay(100);
    printf("task0\n");
    xTaskNotifyGiveIndexed(*(TaskHandle_t*)arg, 0);
    vTaskDelete(NULL);
}
void app_main()
{
    TaskHandle_t main = xTaskGetCurrentTaskHandle();
    ulTaskNotifyTakeIndexed(0, true, 1);
    xTaskCreatePinnedToCore(task0, "task0", 4000, &main, 0,NULL, 1);
    ulTaskNotifyTakeIndexed(0, true, portMAX_DELAY);
    printf("task complete\n");
}
```

Notice that in this case we have to pass the task handle of app_main to task0
so that it can notify it. This could be extended to notify more than one task
of completion, but it would require keeping a list of who to notify. In this
situation the semaphore is preferable.

First To Finish

Another requirement is to wait for one of a group of tasks to finish. This is
very easy using a semaphore, again assuming two cores, folder First:

```
#include <stdio.h>
#include "freertos/FreeRTOS.h"
#include "esp_random.h"
SemaphoreHandle_t xSemaphore;
void task0(void *arg)
{
    uint32_t delay = (esp_random() % 500) + 1;
    vTaskDelay(delay);
    printf("task0\n");
    xSemaphoreGive(xSemaphore);
    vTaskDelete(NULL);
}
```

```
void task1(void *arg)
{
    uint32_t delay = (esp_random() % 500) + 1;
    vTaskDelay(delay);
    printf("task1\n");
    xSemaphoreGive(xSemaphore);
    vTaskDelete(NULL);
}

void app_main()
{
    xSemaphore=xSemaphoreCreateBinary();
    xTaskCreatePinnedToCore(task0,"task0", 4000, NULL, 0, NULL, 1);
    xTaskCreatePinnedToCore(task1,"task1", 4000, NULL, 0, NULL, 0);
    xSemaphoreTake(xSemaphore, portMAX_DELAY);
    printf("task complete\n");
}
```

In this case each task takes a random amount of time to complete and when
it does it signals the app_main task that it has finished. The final task
eventually completes, but it could be terminated by the app_main task.

All Finished

To detect when a set of tasks has finished is a little more complicated, but
the semaphore still does the job very well. The idea is that if you need to
wait for N tasks to complete you need to Take the semaphore N times. To
allow for all of the tasks to complete at exactly the same time the semaphore
has to be able to store a count of N. Each task simply gives the semaphore
when it has completed and the tasks waiting count the tasks off using a for
loop, assuming two cores, folder All:

```
#include <stdio.h>
#include "freertos/FreeRTOS.h"
#include "esp_random.h"

SemaphoreHandle_t xCountingSemaphore;

void task0(void *arg)
{
    uint32_t delay = (esp_random() % 500) + 1;
    vTaskDelay(delay);
    printf("task0\n");
    xSemaphoreGive(xCountingSemaphore);
    vTaskDelete(NULL);
}
```

```
void task1(void *arg)
{
    uint32_t delay = (esp_random() % 500) + 1;
    vTaskDelay(delay);
    printf("task1\n");
    xSemaphoreGive(xCountingSemaphore);
    vTaskDelete(NULL);
}

void app_main()
{
    xCountingSemaphore = xSemaphoreCreateCounting(2, 0);
    xTaskCreatePinnedToCore(task0, "task0", 4000, NULL, 0, NULL, 1);
    xTaskCreatePinnedToCore(task1, "task1", 4000, NULL, 0, NULL, 0);
    for (int i = 0; i < 2; i++)
    {
        xSemaphoreTake(xCountingSemaphore, portMAX_DELAY);
    }
    printf("task complete\n");
}
```

The semaphore is set to 0 with a maximum count of 2 as there are only two tasks to monitor.

Creating an Async Function

One of the most common requirements is to create an asynchronous function from elements that are not asynchronous. The basic idea is that you need to wait for something to complete or be ready to use and the straightforward synchronous way of doing this is to simply poll for completion using a for loop – often referred to, slightly incorrectly, as a spin loop or spin lock. The problem with the polling approach is that it keeps the core from doing anything else while waiting. If there is nothing else to do then this is not a problem, but in a multi-tasking operating system like FreeRTOS there are usually tasks that could make use of the time. To allow this to happen the function has to enter a Blocked state and the problem is that in a blocked state it cannot poll for completion.

There are two solutions to the problem and the first is very simple – use vTaskDelay to control the rate of polling while entering the Blocked state for long enough to allow other tasks to make progress. As an example, consider a button connected to a GPIO line used to toggle the state of an LED. We need to poll for the state of the GPIO often enough to make the user feel that the button and LED are connected and responsive.

The main program in this example stays the same for all modifications:

```
void app_main()
{
    gpio_reset_pin(1);
    gpio_set_direction(1, GPIO_MODE_INPUT_OUTPUT);
    gpio_reset_pin(2);
    gpio_set_direction(2, GPIO_MODE_INPUT_OUTPUT);
    gpio_reset_pin(4);
    gpio_set_direction(4, GPIO_MODE_INPUT);
    gpio_pullup_en(4);
    xTaskCreatePinnedToCore(task0, "task0", 4000, NULL, 0, NULL, 1);
    xTaskCreatePinnedToCore(task1, "task1", 4000, NULL, 0, NULL, 1);
    printf("task complete\n");
}
```

If simply sets up two GPIO pins, GPIO 2 to drive the LED and GPIO 4 for the push button. It also creates task0 which has the job of monitoring the input line and changing the LED each time it is pressed. GPIO 1 is also configured as an output and is used to show when the task is actually running.

A simple synchronous task is:

```
void task0(void *arg)
{
    while (true)
    {

        while (gpio_get_level(4) == 0)
        {
            gpio_set_level(1,!gpio_get_level(1));
        }
        gpio_set_level(2, !gpio_get_level(2));
        while (gpio_get_level(4) == 1)
        {
            gpio_set_level(1,!gpio_get_level(1));
        }
    }
}
```

This is a very simple toggle function. It first waits for GPIO 4 to go high, indicating that the button has been pressed and then toggles the state of GPIO 2. It then waits for the button to be released. The task as it stands is perfectly good and it will change the LED every time a user presses the button – however it hogs its core for as long as FreeRTOS lets it. In practice, it would use its default 10ms time slot until it was preempted and another task of the same or higher priority got a turn to run.

GPIO 1 is toggled each time GPIO line 4 is tested to show when the task is running.

If you run it at priority 0 with no other tasks what you see on a logic analyzer is:

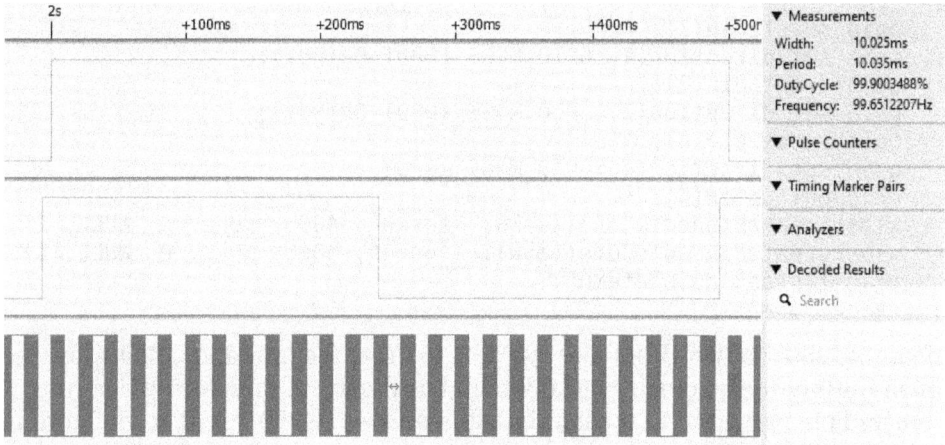

The top trace is the button, the middle is the LED and the bottom trace shows when the input is tested. You can see that this happens very often, but it is interrupted every 10ms for 10ms while another task runs. It is clear that the monitoring task has a maximum latency of 10ms and yet it uses a full 10ms time slot.

This is a big waste of processing power.

A much better solution is to make the task yield the core while waiting for the user to do something, folder GPIOasyncpoll:

```
#include <stdio.h>
#include "freertos/FreeRTOS.h"
#include "driver/gpio.h"

void task0(void *arg)
{
    while (true)
    {
        while (gpio_get_level(4) == 0)
        {
            gpio_set_level(1, !gpio_get_level(1));
            vTaskDelay(5);
        }
        gpio_set_level(2, !gpio_get_level(2));
        while (gpio_get_level(4) == 1)
        {
            gpio_set_level(1, !gpio_get_level(1));
            vTaskDelay(5);
        }
    }
}
```

```
void task1(void *arg)
{
    while (true)
    {
    };
}
void app_main()
{
    gpio_reset_pin(1);
    gpio_set_direction(1, GPIO_MODE_INPUT_OUTPUT);
    gpio_reset_pin(2);
    gpio_set_direction(2, GPIO_MODE_INPUT_OUTPUT);
    gpio_reset_pin(4);
    gpio_set_direction(4, GPIO_MODE_INPUT);
    gpio_pullup_en(4);
    xTaskCreatePinnedToCore(task0,"task0", 4000, NULL, 2, NULL, 0);
    xTaskCreatePinnedToCore(task1,"task1", 4000, NULL, 0, NULL, 0);
    xTaskCreatePinnedToCore(task1,"task2", 4000, NULL, 0, NULL, 0);
    xTaskCreatePinnedToCore(task1,"task3", 4000, NULL, 0, NULL, 0);
    printf("task complete\n");
}
```

If you try this out you will find that task0 tests the GPIO line every 50ms,
independent of how may other tasks are running at a lower priority. Notice
that in this case the lower priority tasks do get the majority of the core's
processing time as task0 only uses a few tens of microseconds every 50ms.

Of course, the big problem with this approach is that unless you modify the
tick rate the minimum latency obtainable is 10ms. A much bigger problem
is that it depends on task0 being the only task to run at that priority level or
greater. It is very easy to unwittingly disturb this arrangement.

Interrupt-Based Async

If the event that you are waiting for is not associated with an interrupt then
there isn't much you can do beyond creating a function that polls in an
asynchronous way. In this case the best latency you can achieve is
approximately the tick period, 10ms by default. However, if the event can
generate an interrupt, the latency can be reduced to less than the tick period,
a few tens of microseconds in some cases.

The basic idea is that the interrupt service routine (ISR) simply gives a
semaphore that the task that is waiting to process the data has taken and is
blocked on. This has the advantage that the task is in Blocked state until
there is work to do and, as the ISR doesn't use any processor time until it
services an interrupt, there is no wasted processor time polling the GPIO
line.

The simplest implementation is, assuming two cores, folder GPIOasyncint:

```c
#include <stdio.h>
#include "freertos/FreeRTOS.h"
#include "driver/gpio.h"
SemaphoreHandle_t xSemaphore;

void ISR4(void *arg)
{
    gpio_intr_disable(4);
    BaseType_t xHigherPriorityTaskWoken = pdFALSE;
    xSemaphoreGiveFromISR(xSemaphore, &xHigherPriorityTaskWoken);
    gpio_intr_enable(4);
}
void task0(void *arg)
{
    while (true)
    {
        xSemaphoreTake(xSemaphore, portMAX_DELAY);
        gpio_set_level(2, !gpio_get_level(2));
    }
}
void task1(void *arg)
{
    while (true){};
}
void app_main()
{
    vSemaphoreCreateBinary(xSemaphore);
    xSemaphoreTake(xSemaphore, 1);
    gpio_install_isr_service(ESP_INTR_FLAG_LOWMED |
                                        ESP_INTR_FLAG_EDGE);

    gpio_reset_pin(2);
    gpio_set_direction(2, GPIO_MODE_INPUT_OUTPUT);

    gpio_reset_pin(4);
    gpio_set_direction(4, GPIO_MODE_INPUT);
    gpio_pullup_en(4);
    gpio_intr_disable(4);
    gpio_set_intr_type(4, GPIO_INTR_POSEDGE);
    gpio_isr_handler_add(4, ISR4, NULL);

    xTaskCreatePinnedToCore(task0, "task0", 4000, NULL, 0, NULL, 0);
    xTaskCreatePinnedToCore(task1, "task1", 4000, NULL, 0, NULL, 0);
    xTaskCreatePinnedToCore(task1, "task2", 4000, NULL, 0, NULL, 0);
    xTaskCreatePinnedToCore(task1, "task3", 4000, NULL, 0, NULL, 0);
    gpio_intr_enable(4);
    printf("task complete\n");
}
```

This sets up GPIO 4 to interrupt on a positive-going edge. A binary semaphore is created and taken so as to block the task when it tries to take it. The ISR simply gives the semaphore when the interrupt happens and then lets task0 get on with toggling the GPIO line.

If you try this out you will discover that it takes 45ms from the interrupt to the toggling of the GPIO line. The reason for this very large latency is that when the ISR gives the semaphore it simply changes the state of the task0 from Blocked to Ready and then takes its turn with the scheduler. In this case it has to wait for four or so other tasks to have their 10ms time allocation before it is run. This means that the fastest pulse train that task0 can deal with is around 20Hz any faster and it misses pulses.

We can do better than this by assigning task0 a higher priority than the other tasks in the system:

```
xTaskCreatePinnedToCore(task0, "task0", 4000, NULL,2 , NULL, 0);
```

This change improves the latency to around 8ms. The problem is that when the interrupt occurs the current task still has to complete its tick before another task gets the chance to run.

To reduce the latency even further the ISR has to tell the scheduler to start a new task running. The GiveFromISR function has a parameter which it sets to true if giving the semaphore changes the state of a task that has a higher priority than the current task to Ready:

```
 BaseType_t xHigherPriorityTaskWoken = pdFALSE;
 xSemaphoreGiveFromISR(xSemaphore, &xHigherPriorityTaskWoken);
```

If this is true then the documentation suggests that the scheduler should be forced to start a new task, but there is no clue as to how to do this. However, the almost undocumented function:

```
portYIELD_FROM_ISR(xHigherPriorityTaskWoken);
```

will cause the scheduler to select a new task if the parameter is true.

So changing the ISR to:

```
void ISR4(void *arg)
{
    gpio_intr_disable(4);
    BaseType_t xHigherPriorityTaskWoken = pdFALSE;
    xSemaphoreGiveFromISR(xSemaphore, &xHigherPriorityTaskWoken);
    portYIELD_FROM_ISR(xHigherPriorityTaskWoken);
    gpio_intr_enable(4);
}
```

causes the latency to drop to 20μs and the maximum frequency that can be handled to about 30kHz.

You may have to increase the IPC stack size if the current default isn't enough.

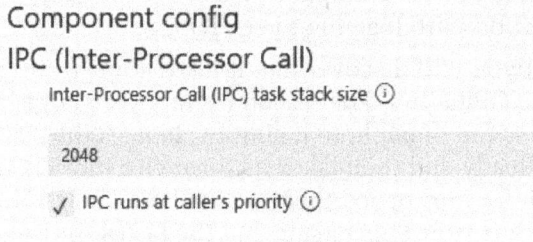

Component config
IPC (Inter-Processor Call)
Inter-Processor Call (IPC) task stack size ⓘ

2048

✓ IPC runs at caller's priority ⓘ

The full version of the program is in folder GPIOasyncint.

You can save some memory by using notifications in place of a semaphore. In this case the latency is about the same at $20\mu s$. You can see an example of using notifications in the GPIOasyncNote folder.

Clearly, if you want minimum processor load and small latency then using an interrupt is the best way, but not all events have interrupts. Even if there is an interrupt, it is dependent on the task that the ISR unblocks having a higher priority than most of the other tasks.

Summary

- Semaphore can be used to wait for another task to complete or to reach a particular point.

- When multiple tasks are all trying to achieve a result, a semaphore can be used to wait for the first of the group to complete or to wait for all of the tasks in a group to complete.

- Any function can be converted into an asynchronous function by yielding control back to FreeRTOS at regular intervals.

- A better method of converting a function into an asynchronous function is to set up an interrupt handler that is called when the function can do some work. If no such interrupt exists a periodic yield can be used to achieve the same result.

Chapter 4

Data Structures

Tasks can communicate with each other via shared memory as long as they make use of locks to avoid race conditions. The situation is more complicated if a task is producing lots of data that is intended to be processed by other tasks. This is the producer-consumer dilemma and, in general, there can be multiple producer tasks and multiple consumer tasks. The generally accepted solution to this problem is to use a shared queue of some sort. A queue is simply a data structure that can accept data to be stored until it is read. Queues differ in where they allow you to add data, at the front or back of the queue, and where they allow you to read data, again the front or back of the queue.

There are a number of different shared buffers provided by FreeRTOS and by the ESP-IDF extension, but the simplest and most useful is xQueue, which technically is closer to being a deque as you can add new items at the front or the back, but only remove items from the front. Notice that this means it is safe from race conditions by design and no further locking is needed.

Queues

To create an xQueue you can either allocate the memory statically or on the heap:

```
xQueueCreate(NumberOfItems, ItemSize)
xQueueCreateStatic(NumberOfItems, ItemSize,
                            pQueueStorage, pQueueBuffer)
```

Both return QueueHandle to be used in subsequent functions. In the case of Create the queue is created on the heap. If you want to create it in static storage you need to pass pointers to two blocks of memory:

```
StaticQueue_t QueueStorage;
uint8_t QueueBuffer[ NumberOfItems * ItemSize ];
```

You can also delete an xQueue:

```
vQueueDelete(QueueHandle)
```

Once you have an `xQueue` you can add items to it and retrieve items:

```
xQueueSendToFront(QueueHandle, pItem, TicksToWait)
xQueueSendToBack(QueueHandle, pItemTo, TicksToWait)
```

and there are `FromISR` versions of these functions. If `TicksToWait` is 0 then the functions return at once, even if the queue is full. Otherwise the functions wait for the specified time to see if the queue has space. All items are stored and retrieved by value and they all have to be the same size. If you want to work with references, you have to explicitly store a pointer. Notice that if you add items to the back of the queue you have a FIFO (First In First Out) queue and if you add items to the front of the queue you have a LIFO (Last In First Out) queue also known as a stack.

There are two functions that can be used to retrieve items:

```
xQueueReceive(QueueHandle, pBuffer, TicksToWait)
xQueuePeek(QueueHandle, pBuffer, TicksToWait)
```

The difference is that `Receive` removes the item from the queue and `Peek` doesn't. Also notice that both functions will block until `TicksToWait` times out. This means that the task is in a pending state and no processor time is wasted waiting for input. If you want to wait on multiple queues then use a `QueueSet` which blocks until one of the queues in the set has data ready to read.

There are two functions that tell you about the state of the queue:

```
number = uxQueueSpacesAvailable(QueueHandle)
number = uxQueueMessagesWaiting(QueueHandle)
```

As an `xQueue` is safe from race conditions, there is even an advantage to be had to sharing one in place of a single variable that you would have to protect with a critical section. To make this easier there is:

```
xQueueOverwrite(QueueHandle, pItem)
```

which will overwrite the item currently at the head of the queue.

Important Caveat: Crucially, this function only handles the transfer of the data. It provides no protection against the 'read-modify-write' race condition. If the item being overwritten is a complex data structure that a receiving task is currently reading or modifying, you must use a separate synchronization primitive (like a Mutex or a Semaphore) to ensure atomic access to that data.

As a very simple example, consider having one task, task1, that writes data to the queue and a second task, task2, that reads it, assuming we have two cores, folder Queue :

```
#include <stdio.h>
#include "freertos/FreeRTOS.h"
QueueHandle_t q;
int64_t count = 0;

void task1(void* arg) {
    for (;;) {
        xQueueSendToBack(q, &count, 2);
        count++;
        vTaskDelay(1);
    }
}
void task2(void* arg) {
    int64_t data;
    for (;;) {
        xQueueReceive(q, &data, 20);
        printf("%llX %d\n", data,uxQueueSpacesAvailable(q));
    }
}
void app_main(void)
{
    q = xQueueCreate(100, sizeof(int64_t));
    xTaskCreatePinnedToCore(task1,"task1", 2048, NULL, 0, NULL, 1);
    xTaskCreatePinnedToCore(task2,"task2", 4048, NULL, 0, NULL, 0);
}
```

If you run the program you will see that the reading task, task2, keeps up with task1, the writing task, and the queue is always empty after the read. This is how it has to be in that, if the rate of writing were faster than the rate of reading, then the queue would fill up and overflow.

A queue isn't magic and cannot increase the throughput of a system. All it can do is smooth out the flow to make the average write rate equal the average read rate. That is, a queue only works if the average read and write rates are the same and the burst rate is less than the size of the queue.

Stream Buffers

FreeRTOS provides stream buffers as an alternative to the queue when you need to send and receive multiple bytes at a time. They work in terms of bytes and there is no need to specify the size of an item – you simply read and write bytes by value. This is more flexible but there can only be one reader and one writer, i.e. two tasks, or an ISR and a task. When you create a stream buffer you have to specify its size in bytes and a trigger level, which sets when the receiving task is moved from a Blocked to a Ready state.

This means that the receiving task can remain Blocked until a specified number of bytes is available in the buffer. You can also specify two callbacks – one for send completed and one for receive completed. Send completed is called if the number of bytes in the buffer is more than the trigger and receive completed is called if any data is read from the buffer.

The basic function to create a stream buffer is:

```
StreamBufferHandle_t xStreamBufferCreate(
    size_t xBufferSizeBytes, size_t xTriggerLevelBytes );
```

which creates a buffer of a given size and trigger level.

There is a version of this function that creates a static buffer and specifies two callbacks.

Other important functions are:

```
void vStreamBufferDelete(
                StreamBufferHandle_t xStreamBuffer);
```

Reclaims the memory used by the stream buffer

```
size_t xStreamBufferSend(
        StreamBufferHandle_t xStreamBuffer,
        const void *pvTxData,
        size_t xDataLengthBytes,
        TickType_t xTicksToWait );
```

Sends the specified number of bytes to the buffer and blocks until there is enough space or it times out and returns the number of bytes sent

```
size_t xStreamBufferReceive(
        StreamBufferHandle_t xStreamBuffer,
        void *pvRxData,
        size_t xBufferLengthBytes,
        TickType_t xTicksToWait );
```

Receives up to the specified number of bytes into the buffer.

Important Caveat: Crucially, this function only handles the transfer of the data. It provides no protection against the 'read-modify-write' race condition. If the item being overwritten is a complex data structure that a receiving task is currently reading or modifying, you must use a separate synchronization primitive (like a Mutex or a Semaphore) to ensure atomic access to that data.

If it times out it returns however many bytes are available at the time. If the buffer is a batch buffer it waits for at least the number of bytes specified by the trigger or it times out even if the buffer has data ready to read. That is a batch buffer always works in "trigger" sized batches.

There are also some management functions;

- xStreamBufferBytesAvailable()   Returns number of bytes in buffer
- xstreamBufferSpacesAvailable()   Returns number of bytes free
- xstreamBufferIsEmpty()   Returns true if buffer empty
- xStreamBufferIsFull()   Returns true if buffer full
- xstreamBufferSetTriggerLevel()   Changes the trigger level
- xStreamBufferReset()   Discards any data and resets the buffer

The stream buffer works using notifications and there are two functions that can be used to work with the index of the notification:

- uxStreamBufferGetStreamBufferNotificationIndex()
- vStreamBufferSetStreamBufferNotificationIndex()

The stream buffer is slightly more complex than a standard buffer because of the use of the trigger level. The timeout and the trigger work together. If there is data in the buffer when the call is made then the data is returned at once. If there is no data in the buffer then the read function waits for either the timeout or until there is at least the trigger number of bytes.

As an example of using a stream buffer we can re-implement the simple count queue example, assuming two cores, folder Stream:

```
#include <stdio.h>
#include "freertos/FreeRTOS.h"
StreamBufferHandle_t sb;
uint8_t count = 0;

void task1(void *arg)
{
    for (;;)
    {
        xStreamBufferSend(sb, &count, 1, 100);
        count++;
    }
}
void task2(void *arg)
{
    uint8_t data;
    for (;;)
    {
        xStreamBufferReceive(sb, &data, 1, 100);
        printf("%d %d\n", data, xStreamBufferSpacesAvailable(sb));
    }
}
void app_main(void)
{
    sb = xStreamBufferCreate(100, 50);
    xTaskCreatePinnedToCore(task1,"task1", 2048, NULL, 0, NULL, 1);
    xTaskCreatePinnedToCore(task2,"task2", 4048, NULL, 0, NULL, 0);
}
```

`task0` repeatedly sends a single byte to the buffer while `task1` repeatedly reads a single byte. As they are running on different cores `task0` slowly fills up the buffer and then waits for `task1` to read the data. The number of free spaces is printed along with the data and you should be able to see that no data is lost.

A more realistic example is passing a struct using a stream buffer. To do this we need to set the trigger to the size of the buffer – but we still need to check that every read is a complete struct. For example, if the struct is:

```
typedef struct{
    int32_t temperature;
    int32_t pressure;
    int32_t count;
}mydata_t;
mydata_t mydata={20,75,0};
```

the stream buffer is defined as:

```
    sb = xStreamBufferCreate(sizeof mydata *50,sizeof mydata);
```

Notice that the trigger is the size of the struct. To write the struct;

```
void task1(void *arg)
{
    for (;;)
    {
      xStreamBufferSend(sb,(uint8_t *) &mydata,sizeof mydata, 100);
      mydata.count++;
    }
}
```

The read task is slightly more complicated:

```
void task2(void *arg)
{
    mydata_t data;
    for (;;)
    {
        int n = 0;
        int m = sizeof data;
        int offset = 0;
        while (n < sizeof data)
        {
            n = xStreamBufferReceive(sb, (uint8_t*)&data +
                                            offset, m, 100);
            m = m - n;
            offset = offset + n;
        }
        printf("%ld %d\n", data.count,
                        xStreamBufferSpacesAvailable(sb));
    }
}
```

You can see the complete program in folder `StreamStruct`.

Message Buffers

The FreeRTOS message buffer is built on top of the stream buffer. It adds the ability to send messages of variable length. The length is stored along with the data and this takes typically four additional bytes. As it is built on top of stream buffers it has the same restriction of a single sender and a single receiver task.

The message buffer functions are mostly the same as the stream buffer functions, but starting with xMessageBuffer. The two that are different are the send and receive functions:

- ```
  size_t xMessageBufferSend(
              MessageBufferHandle_t xMessageBuffer,
              void *pvTxData,
              size_t xDataLengthBytes,
              TickType_t xTicksToWait );
  ```

Writes the specified number of bytes to the buffer

- ```
  size_t xMessageBufferReceive(
              MessageBufferHandle_t xMessageBuffer,
              void *pvRxData,
              size_t xBufferLengthBytes,
              TickType_t xTicksToWait );
  ```

Reads up to the specified number of bytes into the buffer.

The xBufferLengthBytes parameter gives the size of the buffer the number of bytes read depends on the number of bytes written. That is, the read function first reads the number of bytes that were written

Using a message buffer it is easier to pass a struct, folder MessageStruct:

```
#include <stdio.h>
#include "freertos/FreeRTOS.h"
MessageBufferHandle_t   mb;

typedef struct{
    int32_t temperature;
    int32_t pressure;
    int32_t count;
}mydata_t;

mydata_t mydata = {20,75,0};

void task1(void *arg)
{
    for (;;)
    {
        xMessageBufferSend(mb,&mydata,sizeof mydata, 100);
        mydata.count++;
    }
}
```

```
void task2(void *arg)
{
    mydata_t data;
    for (;;)
    {
        int n = xMessageBufferReceive(mb, &data,sizeof data, 100);
        printf("%ld %d\n", data.count,
                            xMessageBufferSpacesAvailable(mb));
    }
}
void app_main(void)
{
    mb = xMessageBufferCreate(500);
    xTaskCreatePinnedToCore(task1, "task1", 2048, NULL, 0, NULL, 1);
    xTaskCreatePinnedToCore(task2, "task2", 4048, NULL, 0, NULL, 0);
}
```

In this case the message, i.e. the struct, is always the same size, but in practice the size could vary. The problem with this is working out what sort of message has just been received. The simplest solution is to include a single first item as a type indicator.

The QueueSet

The QueueSet is a way of waiting for a queue to have some data to read or a semaphore to be takeable. The idea is that a QueueSet can have any number of queues or semaphores added to it – queues being empty and semaphores set to zero. A function can then wait, in a Blocked state, in the QueueSet for either a queue to have some data to read or a semaphore being ready to take, i.e. non-zero. The QueueSet returns the handle to the queue or semaphore that is ready. If you know the Linux select you will recognize that the QueueSet is a simpler implementation of the same idea. The lwIP library also provides an implementation of select which can be used to wait for sockets to be ready in the same way, see Chapter 7.

The QueueSet functions are:

- ◆ xQueueCreateSet   Create a QueueSet
- ◆ xQueueCreateSetStatic   Create a static QueueSet
- ◆ xQueueAddToSet   Add a queue or a semaphore to the set
- ◆ xQueueRemoveFromSet   Remove a queue or semaphore from the set
- ◆ xQueueSelectFromSet   Return the elements that are ready.
- ◆ xQueueSelectFromSetFromISR Wait until one of the queues has data to be read or one of the semaphores can be taken.

As an example of how `QueueSet` works we can re-implement the first task to finish program given earlier, in folder `FirstQueueSet`:

```
#include <stdio.h>
#include "freertos/FreeRTOS.h"
#include "esp_random.h"
SemaphoreHandle_t xSemaphore0;
SemaphoreHandle_t xSemaphore1;
void task0(void *arg)
{
    uint32_t delay = (esp_random() % 500) + 1;
    vTaskDelay(delay);
    printf("task0\n");
    xSemaphoreGive(xSemaphore0);
    vTaskDelete(NULL);
}
void task1(void *arg)
{
    uint32_t delay = (esp_random() % 500) + 1;
    vTaskDelay(delay);
    printf("task1\n");
    xSemaphoreGive(xSemaphore1);
    vTaskDelete(NULL);
}
void app_main()
{
    xSemaphore0 = xSemaphoreCreateBinary();
    xSemaphoreTake(xSemaphore0, 1);
    xSemaphore1 = xSemaphoreCreateBinary();
    xSemaphoreTake(xSemaphore1, 1);
    xTaskCreatePinnedToCore(task0, "task0", 4000, NULL, 0, NULL, 1);
    xTaskCreatePinnedToCore(task1, "task1", 4000, NULL, 0, NULL, 0);

    QueueSetHandle_t xQueueSet = xQueueCreateSet(2);
    xQueueAddToSet(xSemaphore0, xQueueSet);
    xQueueAddToSet(xSemaphore1, xQueueSet);
    QueueSetMemberHandle_t xActivatedMember =
                    xQueueSelectFromSet(xQueueSet, portMAX_DELAY);
    if (xActivatedMember == xSemaphore0)
    {
        printf("Task0 Completed first\n");
    }
    if (xActivatedMember == xSemaphore1)
    {
        printf("Task1 Completed first\n");
    }
    printf("app main task complete\n");
}
```

Notice that in this case we need two semaphores and this makes the previous implementation preferable. You have to set the size of the QueueSet so that it can store the queues or semaphores.

Ring Buffer

The ESP version of FreeRTOS has an additional data structure – the ring buffer. This is used in other ESP-IDF modules such as the serial port. It isn't standard in FreeRTOS and this should be kept in mind if you want to port your programs to another platform.

Why a ring buffer?

The reason is that the FreeRTOS data structures are restricted to a single sender and a single receiver and they work by copying values into the buffer. The ring buffer is a FIFO buffer that works with arbitrary sized items, provides pointers to data in the buffer, and supports more than one reader/writer at a time. As it works with pointers to the data in the buffer it allows a ring buffer to be used with hardware that needs an address to transfer data rather than the data itself.

A ring buffer is, as its name suggests, a data structure that uses a pointer to indicate where the next item should be stored. As data is stored, the pointer is moved on until it reaches the end of the buffer when it wraps to the start of the buffer and so on – hence ring buffer. There is also a pointer to the current read position and the current data is between the read pointer and the write pointer.

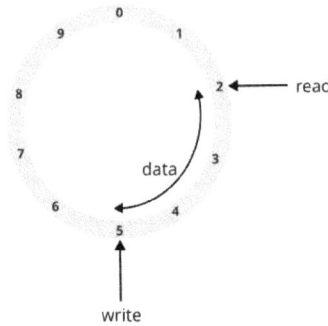

The data is stored in the ring buffer by value, but data is read from the buffer by returning the value of the read pointer.

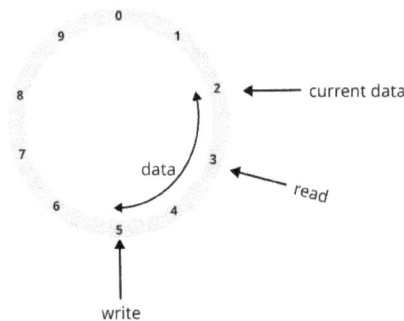

The data is accessed via this pointer and the buffer isn't freed after the read. To do this you have to call the `ReturnItem` function which frees the buffer between the current data and the read pointer. After this, you cannot rely on the current data being valid:

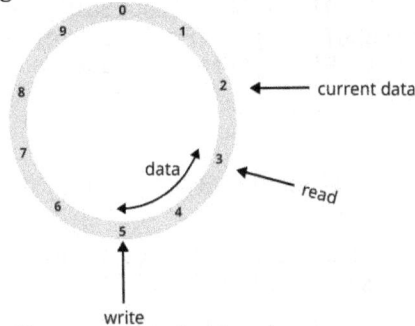

Three types of ring buffer are provided by the ESP32 SDK - no-split buffers where each item is stored in contiguous memory, allow-split buffers where an item can be split between the start and end of the buffer. and byte buffers which store data as a sequence of bytes.

All ring buffers are created using:

```
RingbufHandle_t xRingbufferCreate(
            size_t xBufferSize, RingbufferType_t xBufferType)
```

with xBufferType one of:

- ◆ `RINGBUF_TYPE_NOSPLIT`
- ◆ `RINGBUF_TYPE_ALLOWSPLIT`
- ◆ `RINGBUF_TYPE_BYTEBUF`

The way the read/write functions behave depends on the type of the buffer and these are described in the following sections.

There are also some standard utility functions:

- ◆ `void vRingbufferDelete(RingbufHandle_t xRingbuffer)`
  Deletes the ring buffer
- ◆ `size_t xRingbufferGetMaxItemSize(`
  `  RingbufHandle_t xRingbuffer)`
  Returns the maximum item size
- ◆ `size_t xRingbufferGetCurFreeSize(`
  `                  RingbufHandle_t xRingbuffer)`
  Returns number of free bytes
- ◆ `void vRingbufferGetInfo(`
  `              RingbufHandle_t xRingbuffer,`
  `              UBaseType_t *uxFree,`
  `              UBaseType_t *uxRead,`
  `              UBaseType_t *uxWrite,`
  `              UBaseType_t *uxAcquire,`
  `              UBaseType_t *uxItemsWaiting)`
  Gets the value of the pointers used by the buffer and the number of items waiting to be read

You can also use a ring buffer as a QueueSet:

- BaseType_t xRingbufferAddToQueueSetRead(
  RingbufHandle_t xRingbuffer, QueueSetHandle_t xQueueSet)
- static inline BaseType_t xRingbufferCanRead(
  RingbufHandle_t xRingbuffer,QueueSetMemberHandle_t xMember)
- BaseType_t xRingbufferRemoveFromQueueSetRead(
  RingbufHandle_t xRingbuffer, QueueSetHandle_t xQueueSet)

Byte Ring Buffer

The simplest buffer type is a byte buffer as this just reads and writes bytes. To write to a byte buffer you use

```
BaseType_t xRingbufferSend(RingbufHandle_t xRingbuffer,
  const void *pvItem, size_t xItemSize, TickType_t xTicksToWait)
```

This sends the data to the buffer and blocks if there isn't enough free space for the entire item or until the timeout is up. Notice that this is subtle as it implies that the ring buffer will never contain a partial write. The function blocks until all xItemSize bytes can be written as a single atomic operation.

This is the write function used for all buffers. It stores the data pointed to by pvItem in the buffer and moves the write pointer on by xItemSize.

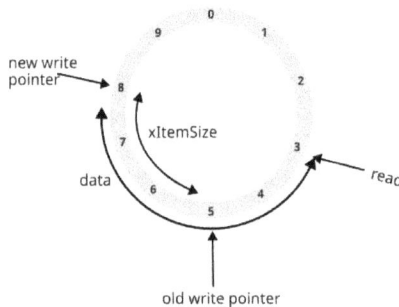

The read function is specific to the byte buffer:

```
void *xRingbufferReceiveUpTo(RingbufHandle_t xRingbuffer,
  size_t *pxItemSize, TickType_t xTicksToWait, size_t xMaxSize)
```

This returns a pointer to the ring buffer that contains the data. The xMaxSize parameter specifies the maximum number of bytes to read and the function returns the number of bytes read in pxItemSize. The current value of the read pointer is the return value and then the read pointer is moved on by pxItemSize.

If there is data in the buffer then the function returns at once with pxItemSize less than or equal to xMaxSize bytes. If the buffer is empty it blocks until there is data and returns with pxItemSize less than or equal to xMaxSize bytes or it times out.

The `ReceiveUpTo` function does not clear the buffer of data as the pointer it returns is used to access the data in the buffer. To clear the data you need to use:

```
void vRingbufferReturnItem(RingbufHandle_t xRingbuffer,
                                        void *pvItem)
```

This frees the space used by the items in the ring buffer. It frees the bytes between the `pvItem` pointer and the current position of the read pointer.

The pointer returned by the read function no longer references the data after the call returns.

Putting all this together we can easily convert the count example given earlier to use a byte ring buffer, folder `ring1`:

```
#include <stdio.h>
#include "freertos/FreeRTOS.h"
#include "freertos/ringbuf.h"

RingbufHandle_t rb;

void task1(void *arg)
{
    uint8_t count;
    for (;;)
    {
        xRingbufferSend(rb, &count, 1, 100);
        count++;
    }
}

void task2(void *arg)
{
    for (;;)
    {
        uint8_t *count;
        size_t n;
        count = xRingbufferReceiveUpTo(rb, &n, 100, 1);
        printf("%d %d\n", *count, xRingbufferGetCurFreeSize(rb));
        vRingbufferReturnItem(rb, count);
    }
}
void app_main(void)
{
    rb = xRingbufferCreate(100, RINGBUF_TYPE_BYTEBUF);
    xTaskCreatePinnedToCore(task1, "task1", 2048, NULL, 0, NULL, 1);
    xTaskCreatePinnedToCore(task2, "task2", 4048, NULL, 0, NULL, 0);
}
```

Working one byte at a time is the easiest thing to do with a byte buffer, but in most cases we need to work with multiple bytes at a time. This is more difficult than you might expect.

The reason is that, due to "wrap around", you cannot guarantee to read the number of bytes you need in a single read. Reading from the buffer stops when the end of the buffer is reached, even if the number of bytes requested haven't been read. This means that to retrieve data that is stored across the start and end of the buffer two reads are required. For example, implementing the struct example given earlier using a byte buffer is surprisingly tricky. The write function is the same, the full program is in the folder Ring2:

```
RingbufHandle_t rb;
typedef struct{
    int32_t temperature;
    int32_t pressure;
    int32_t count;
} mydata_t;
mydata_t mydata = {20, 75, 0};
void task1(void *arg)
{
    for (;;)
    {
        xRingbufferSend(rb, &mydata, sizeof mydata, 100);
        mydata.count++;
    }
}
```

The read function, however, has to transfer as many bytes are are available into a struct:

```
void task2(void *arg)
{
    uint8_t *pdata;
    union{
        mydata_t data;
        uint8_t bdata[sizeof(mydata_t)];
    } mydata;
    for (;;){
        size_t n = 0;
        int m = sizeof mydata;
        int offset = 0;
        while (m > 0)
        {
            pdata = xRingbufferReceiveUpTo(rb, &n, 100, m);
            memcpy(mydata.bdata + offset, pdata, n);
            m = m - n;
            offset = offset + n;
            vRingbufferReturnItem(rb, pdata);
        }
        printf("%ld %d\n", mydata.data.count,
                            xRingbufferGetCurFreeSize(rb));
    }
}
```

We need to be able to treat the struct that the data is being transferred to as a byte array as well as a struct. The safest way to do this is to use a union. The read of the buffer is easy:

```
pdata = xRingbufferReceiveUpTo(rb, &n, 100, m);
```

but the number of bytes read may not be the whole struct. To cope with this, we need to transfer the bytes we have into the union as a byte array:

```
 memcpy(mydata.bdata + offset, pdata, n);
```

This moves n bytes from the byte ring buffer into the byte array. Following this we have the partial data and we can return the bytes to the buffer's free space:

```
vRingbufferReturnItem(rb, pdata);
```

A second read is now possible if the data is spread across the wrap around, but this time we have to move the data into the byte array without overwriting what is already there – hence the addition of the offset. It helps to think of m as the number of bytes we still have to read, n as the number of bytes read this time and offset as the total number of bytes read so far.

You can see the full program in folder ring2.

In a production program you would also have to include a test for a malformed item being stored in the buffer, such as there not being enough bytes to fill a struct or too many.

Split Ring Buffer

The byte buffer is useful for data with little structure, but in general the split/no-split versions of the ring buffer are more useful because they store the size of each item and this makes retrieval easier. However, all ring buffers share the wrap around problem. If you simply store data at the current write pointer then eventually an item is going to be split between the end and the start of the buffer. This is no problem for the ring buffer, but it is a problem for any external access to the buffer that is expecting a pointer to a contiguous block of memory.

To cope with this "split" problem you have to use the special read function which has to be used with split ring buffers and returns two reads in one go:

```
BaseType_t xRingbufferReceiveSplit(RingbufHandle_t xRingbuffer,
                void **ppvHeadItem, void **ppvTailItem,
                size_t *pxHeadItemSize, size_t *pxTailItemSize,
                TickType_t xTicksToWait)
```

HeadItem and HeadItemSize give the location and size of the first block of data and TailItem and TailItemSize give the details of the second block. If there is no second block then the TailItem pointer is NULL and the TailItemSize variable is unchanged.

The function returns false if it times out.

Using this we can recast the previous example which stores a struct. The write function is unchanged, but the read function is, folder `Ring3`:

```
void task2(void *arg)
{
    uint8_t *pdatah, *pdatat;
    union
    {
        mydata_t data;
        uint8_t bdata[sizeof(mydata_t)];
    } mydata;

    for (;;)
    {
        size_t nh = 0;
        size_t nt = 0;
        xRingbufferReceiveSplit(rb, (void **)&pdatah,
                                (void **)&pdatat, &nh, &nt, 100);
        if (pdatah != NULL)
        {
            memcpy(mydata.bdata, pdatah, nh);
            vRingbufferReturnItem(rb, pdatah);
        }

        if (pdatat != NULL)
        {
            memcpy(mydata.bdata + nh, pdatat, nt);
            vRingbufferReturnItem(rb, pdatat);
        }
        printf("%ld %d\n", mydata.data.count,
                                xRingbufferGetCurFreeSize(rb));
    }
}
```

The `union` is used to allow the same data to be treated as an array of bytes or a struct. The data is read in one go and the head is stored in the struct. If there is a second block of data, the tail is transferred to the struct in the same way. You can see the full program in the folder `ring3`.

The advantage of using a split ring buffer is that it doesn't waste storage space.

No-Split Ring Buffer

The no-split ring buffer promises to always store an item in contiguous memory. That is, it will never store an item across the wrap around. This makes using the buffer very easy, but it achieves this by inserting padding data to move any item that would be split into the start of the buffer. This clearly wastes space, but only half the size of an item on average.

The read function for a no-split buffer is very simple:

```
void *xRingbufferReceive(RingbufHandle_t xRingbuffer,
    size_t *pxItemSize, TickType_t xTicksToWait)
```

This retrieves an item from the buffer as a returned pointer and an item size. As the write function always stores a complete item in the buffer, the read function either returns after a timeout with a NULL pointer or the pointer references the entire data that makes up the item.

As an example, we can implement the struct program again. As always there is no change to the write function, but the read function is, folder Ring4:

```
void task2(void *arg)
{
    uint8_t *pdata;
    size_t n;
    for (;;)
    {
        pdata = xRingbufferReceive(rb, &n, 100);
        printf("%ld %d\n", ((mydata_t *)pdata)->count,
                            xRingbufferGetCurFreeSize(rb));
        vRingbufferReturnItem(rb, pdata);
    }
}
```

As the returned pointer is going to be referencing a block of data the correct size for the struct, we can simply cast it to the struct and print any field we want to. Of course, in the real world you would have to check that the writer actually wrote the struct and not something else and that a timeout didn't occur. If you want to copy the data from the ring buffer you can use:

```
 memcpy(mydata, pdata, n);
```

This is a lot simpler than a split or a byte buffer and unless you have a special need to save space it is much better to use a no-split buffer.

You can see the full program in the folder ring4.

To create a no-split buffer you can use:

```
RingbufHandle_t xRingbufferCreate(size_t xBufferSize,
                                  RINGBUF_TYPE_NOSPLIT)
```

or

```
RingbufHandle_t xRingbufferCreateNoSplit(size_t xItemSize,
                                         size_t xItemNum)
```

where the size of the buffer is determined by multiplying ItemSize by xItemNum.

Ring Buffer Deferred Access

There is a particular problem that occurs in IoT applications that a ring buffer can help with. In some cases hardware connected to the ESP32 will be capable of transferring data directly into a linear buffer without the help of software. For example, a serial port might automatically store incoming data in a buffer specified by a pointer. The problem is that you cannot store data directly in a ring buffer. Instead you need to use read and write functions which the hardware knows nothing about. The solution is to use the ring buffer's deferred access functions. These allow you to reserve a block of no-split ring buffer memory which can be passed to hardware to write to as if it was just a standard buffer.

To acquire memory you use:

```
BaseType_t xRingbufferSendAcquire(RingbufHandle_t xRingbuffer,
    void **ppvItem, size_t xItemSize, TickType_t xTicksToWait)
```

This returns a pointer pvItem to a block of memory within the ring buffer that is xItemSize bytes in size. The function blocks until the specified amount of memory is available or it times out. Notice that this only works with no-split buffers.

Only after the function:

```
BaseType_t xRingbufferSendComplete(RingbufHandle_t xRingbuffer,
                                                void *pvItem)
```

is called is the data regarded as complete and made available to a reader. For example, we can use the transfer of a struct into the buffer to demonstrate the general principle. The write function is:

```
void task1(void *arg)
{
    for (;;)
    {
        mydata_t *data = NULL;
        xRingbufferSendAcquire(rb, (void **)&data,
                                    sizeof(mydata_t), 100);
        memcpy(data, &mydata, sizeof(mydata_t));
        xRingbufferSendComplete(rb, data);
        while (true)
        {
        };
    }
}
```

The SendAcquire function sets data to reference a section of the ring buffer that can be used to store the struct. memcpy then copies the struct into the buffer. In a real application the data pointer would be used to tell the hardware where to send the data. Finally SendComplete signals that the data is Ready to be read.

The read function is:

```
void task2(void *arg)
{
    uint8_t *pdata;
    size_t n;
    pdata = xRingbufferReceive(rb, &n, 100);
    printf("%ld %ld %ld    %d\n",
        ((mydata_t *)pdata)→pressure,
          ((mydata_t *)pdata)->temperature,
            ((mydata_t *)pdata)→count,
                xRingbufferGetCurFreeSize(rb));
    vRingbufferReturnItem(rb, pdata);
    for (;;)
    {
    }
}
```

The call to Receive will block until the write program calls SendComplete and only then will it read the data.

You can see the full program in folder ring5.

Summary

- An alternative to using locks is to use safe data structures that make it impossible for a race condition to occur.
- xQueue is a FreeRTOS structure which allows tasks to interact and pass data to each other.
- The stream buffer is a queue that works in terms of bytes and is more suited to passing streams of data between tasks.
- The message buffer is built on top of the stream buffer and allows tasks to pass variable-length messages.
- The QueueSet is an implementation of the Linux select function which allows you to wait until a resource is ready to be processed.
- The ESP32 IDF also has a ring buffer implementation which is designed to make working with hardware easier.
- The ring buffer may seem complicated at first, but in its no-split mode it is very easy to use.
- The ESP ring buffer is ideal if you want to create a buffer for a hardware interface.

This chapter is about getting started with WiFi and understanding its underlying IP infrastructure. When you understand this the rest of the API becomes much easier to understand. This is the basis on which the lwIP library is built and it deals with the lower-level tasks of making and managing connections.

ESP32 Architecture

You don't really need to know anything about the ESP32's WiFi hardware to make use of it. Indeed there is very little information available apart from how to use the WiFi drivers in the C development kit. Unlike other processors, the ESP 32 has its own custom WiFi hardware and a great deal of its working is exposed in the WiFi API, much of which the average app will never need to use – see Appendix I.

The ESP32 and ESP32 S3 have two processor cores, which are used to run the WiFi and applications simultaneously. This means that WiFi has little impact on the running of your application. The two cores, CPU 0 and CPU 1, are the Protocol CPU (PRO_CPU) and Application CPU (APP_CPU) respectively. The PRO_CPU processor handles the WiFi, Bluetooth and other internal peripherals like SPI, I2C, ADC etc. The APP_CPU runs the application code, including your programs.

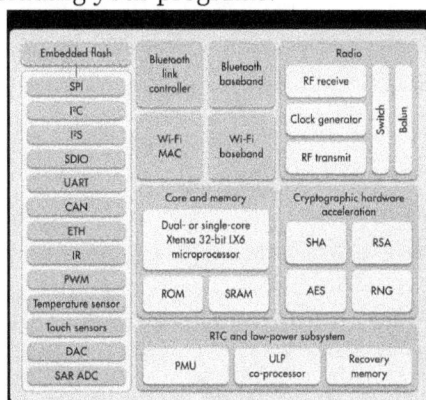

As well as the radio, the ESP32 also supports four cryptographic accelerators to make the implementation of HTTPS (Hypertext Transfer Protocol Secure) and TLS (Transport Layer Security) more efficient.

The WiFi Stack

The ESP32 has additional libraries to make it possible to work with the WiFi hardware without having to work at the level of the hardware. The two most useful are the `esp_wifi` library which provides high-level functions mostly concerned with setting up the WiFi and making connections and `esp_netif`, a set of wrapper functions around the open source lwIP (light-weight IP) stack. In principle, this is capable of using other IP stacks, and this is the advantage of using it rather than lwIP directly, but currently it only works with lwIP.

The WiFi hardware needs periodic attention and this is managed via FreeRTOS tasks using, in the case of a two core device, the one core for WiFi operations and the other for applications as described earlier. The WiFi driver makes use of the `esp_event` library to communicate with the application side of the transaction.

The `esp_event` library is a general event handling facility and isn't restricted to the WiFi – you can use it for your own events and event handlers. The event handlers are registered to an event loop which receives events and activates handlers to deal with them. An event loop can either run as a dedicated task or it can be invoked by the application by calling a function. The WiFi driver makes use of the default event loop running in a dedicated FreeRTOS task. You have to start the event loop and register event handlers for any WiFi event you want to handle.

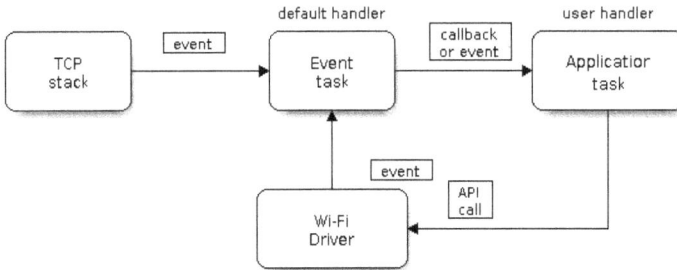

To be clear, you use `esp_wifi` to establish the connection with the AP (Access Point) or client and `esp_netif` to use that connection as an IP connection to a netif (network interface).

In particular `esp_netif` is responsible for acquiring an IP address via DHCP or manually assigning one, DNS and SNTP. Once you have an `esp_netif` you can use it to find out the IP address and configure other details of the IP connection. With `esp_netif` you can start to use the IP interface via the standard sockets API which is part of LwIP or whatever IP stack `esp_netif` is wrapping at the time.

What all this means is that using the WiFi interface as an IP interface has three general stages:

1. Connect to a WiFi AP using `esp_wifi`
2. Set up `esp_netif` which uses the WiFi connection
3. Use `esp_netif` to send and receive IP packets using sockets

In this chapter we look at the first step of configuring and initializing the WiFi.

Initialization and Connection

The function that initializes the WiFi is:

```
esp_err_t esp_wifi_init(const wifi_init_config_t *config)
```

It uses the `config` struct which mostly contains settings that you would rarely want to modify from their default values. In most cases all you need to do is set the struct to its default value and then call the init function:

```
wifi_init_config_t wificonfig = WIFI_INIT_CONFIG_DEFAULT();
esp_wifi_init(&wificonfig);
```

If you have finished with the WiFi you can use:

```
esp_err_t esp_wifi_deinit(void)
```

which release the resources used by the driver.

The initial configuration doesn't include how the WiFi hardware should be used. To set/get this you need to use:

```
esp_err_t esp_wifi_set_mode(wifi_mode_t mode)
esp_err_t esp_wifi_get_mode(wifi_mode_t *mode)
```

where mode is one of:

- `WIFI_MODE_NULL`   Loads the driver, but not the resources it needs
- `WIFI_MODE_STA`   Station mode
- `WIFI_MODE_AP`   Access point mode
- `WIFI_MODE_APSTA` Access point and station mode

Some ESP32 devices also support WiFi NAN(Neighbor Awareness Networking) but not the S3 or C3.

After configuring the WiFi you can control its use with:

- `esp_err_t esp_wifi_start(void)`
- `esp_err_t esp_wifi_stop(void)`

which start and stop the WiFi transmitting and receiving respectively.

You generally have to set the country code to make sure that your use of WiFi is compliant:

```
esp_err_t esp_wifi_set_country_code(const char *country,
                                    bool ieee80211d_enabled)
esp_err_t esp_wifi_get_country_code(char *country)
```

The country code is one of:

```
AT AU BE BG BR CA CH CN CY CZ DE DK EE ES FI FR GB GR HK HR HU IE
IN IS IT JP KR LI LT LU LV MT MX NL NO NZ PL PT RO SE SI SK TW US
```

or 01 which is the default world safe mode and legal in any country.

If you set `ieee80211d_enabled` to `true` then the country code is supplied by the AP the client connects to.

A lower-level way of setting the WiFi so that it is legal in a country is to use:

```
esp_err_t esp_wifi_set_country(const wifi_country_t *country)
esp_err_t esp_wifi_get_country(wifi_country_t *country)
```

In this case country is a pointer to a struct that specifies the characteristics of WiFi in a country:

- `char cc[3]` — Country code
- `uint8_t schan` — Start channel
- `uint8_t nchan` — Total number of channels
- `int8_t  max_tx_power` — Maximum transmitting power
- `wifi_country_policy_t` — Either `WIFI_COUNTRY_POLICY_AUTO` or `WIFI_COUNTRY_POLICY_MANUAL`

In the final field `MANUAL` uses the configuration as given and `AUTO` sets the values from a table in firmware.

All network devices have a unique MAC (Media Access Control) code and every ESP32 has a unique address programmed into it. This is the address used by the Ethernet protocol to identify a device. Sometimes it is useful to know the MAC code or set it to some other value so that the ESP 32 can emulate some other device:

```
esp_err_t esp_wifi_set_mac(wifi_interface_t ifx
                           const uint8_t mac[6])
esp_err_t esp_wifi_get_mac(wifi_interface_t ifx,
                           uint8_t mac[6])
```

The ifx parameter has to be one of:
- `WIFI_IF_STA`
- `WIFI_IF_AP`
- `WIFI_IF_NAN`

If the ESP 32 you are using supports the 5GHz band, currently only the C5, you can get/set the band using:

- `esp_err_t esp_wifi_set_protocols(wifi_interface_t ifx, wifi_protocols_t *protocols)`
- `esp_err_t esp_wifi_get_protocols(wifi_interface_t ifx, wifi_protocols_t *protocols)`

You can also select which of the many WiFi protocols you want to use. In general you can simply let the station and AP negotiate a protocol but if you need to get/set them you can use:

- `esp_err_t esp_wifi_set_protocol(wifi_interface_t ifx, uint8_t protocol_bitmap)`
- `esp_err_t esp_wifi_get_protocol(wifi_interface_t ifx, uint8_t *protocol_bitmap)`

The protocol bitmap is a bitwise OR of:

- `WIFI_PROTOCOL_11B`
- `WIFI_PROTOCOL_11G`
- `WIFI_PROTOCOL_11N`
- `WIFI_PROTOCOL_LR`
- `WIFI_PROTOCOL_11A`
- `WIFI_PROTOCOL_11AC`
- `WIFI_PROTOCOL_11AX`

You can discover what protocol is in use by calling:

```
esp_err_t esp_wifi_sta_get_negotiated_phymode(
                                wifi_phy_mode_t *phymode)
```

where `phymode` is one of the protocols listed above.

When you make a WiFi connection the details are stored for reuse during a reconnection. By default these are stored in flash memory to be reused after a power cycle. You can opt to store the details only in RAM so that they are lost on power off:

```
esp_err_t esp_wifi_set_storage(wifi_storage_t storage)
```

where storage is one of:

- `WIFI_STORAGE_FLASH`
- `WIFI_STORAGE_RAM`

If you need to put things back as the were you can use the reset function:

```
esp_err_t esp_wifi_restore(void)
```

which restores the WiFi stack's persistent settings to default values.

This function will reset settings made using the following APIs:

- `esp_wifi_set_bandwidth`
- `esp_wifi_set_protocol`
- `esp_wifi_set_config related`
- `esp_wifi_set_mode`

Basic Station Mode

Now that we have explored all of the WiFi configuration functions we can make use of them to create a basic connection to a WiFi AP. This is not supposed to be a production-ready example, it aims to show just how simple things are.

There are some additional functions that apply in station mode. The most important is the set/get configuration. This sets the credentials used to connect to the AP:

```
esp_err_t esp_wifi_set_config(wifi_interface_t interface,
                                          wifi_config_t *conf)
esp_err_t esp_wifi_get_config(wifi_interface_t interface,
                                          wifi_config_t *conf)
```

The conf structure offers many options, most of which you won't need to change. The two that are most used are the SSID (Service Set IDentifier) and password and often the authentication modes that are supported:

```
wifi_config_t staconf = {
   .sta = {
          .ssid = "AP Name",
          .password = "password",
          .threshold.authmode = WIFI_AUTH_WPA_PSK,
          }
};
```

In general authmode has to be set to any of:

- WIFI_AUTH_OPEN
- WIFI_AUTH_WEP
- WIFI_AUTH_WPA_PSK
- WIFI_AUTH_WPA2_PSK
- WIFI_AUTH_WPA_WPA2_PSK
- WIFI_AUTH_ENTERPRISE
- WIFI_AUTH_WPA2_ENTERPRISE
- WIFI_AUTH_WPA3_PSK
- WIFI_AUTH_WPA2_WPA3_PSK
- WIFI_AUTH_WAPI_PSK
- WIFI_AUTH_OWE
- WIFI_AUTH_WPA3_ENT_192

In general, you have to set authmode to make a connection. If you get it wrong you will see a repeated lost connection report.

To actually make or break the connection to the AP you use:

- esp_err_t esp_wifi_connect(void)
- esp_err_t esp_wifi_disconnect(void)

We can now put all this together and write the simplest WiFi connect program.

First we need to initialize the Non Volatile Storage (nvs) so that the station can store its credentials:

```
void app_main(void)
{
    nvs_flash_init();
```

Next we configure the driver and the hardware:

```
    wifi_init_config_t wificonfig = WIFI_INIT_CONFIG_DEFAULT();
    esp_wifi_init(&wificonfig);
```

To make the connection to an AP we need to specify its SSID and a password:

```
    wifi_config_t staconf = {
        .sta = {
            .ssid = "SSID",
            .password = "password",
            .threshold.authmode = WIFI_AUTH_WPA_PSK,
        }};
```

It is also a good idea to specify the least strong authorization mode you will accept.

Now we can set station mode:

```
    esp_wifi_set_mode(WIFI_MODE_STA);
    esp_wifi_set_config(WIFI_IF_STA, &staconf);
```

start the WiFi and connect:

```
    esp_wifi_start();
    esp_wifi_connect();
}
```

The complete app_main is, folder WiFi1:

```
#include <stdio.h>
#include "nvs_flash.h"
#include "esp_wifi.h"

void app_main(void)
{
    nvs_flash_init();
    wifi_init_config_t wificonfig = WIFI_INIT_CONFIG_DEFAULT();
    esp_wifi_init(&wificonfig);
    wifi_config_t staconf = {
        .sta = {
            .ssid = "SSID",
            .password = "password",
            .threshold.authmode = WIFI_AUTH_WPA_PSK,
        }};
    esp_wifi_set_mode(WIFI_MODE_STA);
    esp_wifi_set_config(WIFI_IF_STA, &staconf);
    esp_wifi_start();
    esp_wifi_connect();
}
```

If you run this with a debug target you will see messages from the WiFi driver in the monitor. There are some red errors on display because the driver is trying to post events that you are expected to process, but there are also a lot of green messages showing the progress of the connection. If you look carefully you will find a message announcing the connection:

```
I (516) wifi:state: auth -> assoc (0x0)
I (516) wifi:state: assoc -> run (0x10)
I (736) wifi:connected with dlink3, aid = 5, channel 13, 40D, bssid = 00:1f:1f:24:48:70
I (746) wifi:security: WPA2-PSK, phy: bgn, rssi: -40
I (746) wifi:pm start, type: 1
```

The connection has been made, but without event handling we cannot track the progress of the connection and without a esp_netif struct and the use of functions in the lwIP library there isn't much we can do with it. In particular, without the DHCP client the network doesn't supply the connection with an IP address.

We can use the function:

esp_err_t esp_wifi_sta_get_ap_info(wifi_ap_record_t *ap_info)

to find out the details of the connection. For example:

```
    vTaskDelay(500);
    wifi_ap_record_t ap_inf;
    esp_wifi_sta_get_ap_info(&ap_inf);
    printf("Channel %d\n", ap_inf.primary);
```

This prints the channel number that has been used to connect to the AP as long as the connection has been made within five seconds.

Clearly we need to handle the events that the WiFi driver generates.

Event Loops

As already mentioned, the event loop library is a general purpose event system, but it is central to the way that the WiFi driver communicates with other tasks. The event library works in terms of events and event loops. You can define your own event loops, but the WiFi uses the default loop and this is what we will concentrate on. However, custom loops work in the same way.

The basic idea of an event loop is that the event source publishes the event to the event loop. Event consumers register functions that should be called when an event occurs, the event handler, and the event loop calls the function when the event occurs. Of course, the event loop has to deal with multiple events and multiple event handlers and it does this by keeping a list of event handlers and processing them in turn.

The event loop functions for the default loop are:

- `esp_err_t esp_event_loop_create_default(void)`
- `esp_err_t esp_event_loop_delete_default(void)`

which creates and deletes the default loop respectively.

To register or unregister an event handler use:

- `esp_err_t esp_event_handler_register(esp_event_base_t event_base, int32_t event_id, esp_event_handler_t event_handler,void *event_handler_arg)`

- `esp_err_t esp_event_handler_unregister(esp_event_base_t event_base, int32_t event_id, esp_event_handler_t event_handler)`

The handler is specified by `event_handler` and is called with `event_handler_arg` as one of its parameters:

```
void wifi_event_handler(void *event_handler_arg,
  esp_event_base_t event_base, int32_t event_id, void *event_data)
```

The events that a handler is called for are specified using `esp_event_base` and `event_id`. The `base` specifies a set of possible event ids that all relate to the same thing. For example, all of the WiFi related events start at the event base given by `WIFI_EVENT` and event ids are named appropriately e.g. `WIFI_EVENT_STA_START`, `WIFI_EVENT_STA_STOP` etc.

You can register the same handler multiple times to allow it to handle multiple events but it is common to make use of `ESP_EVENT_ANY_BASE` and `ESP_EVENT_ANY_ID` to handle all events or all events in a given base. For example:

```
esp_event_handler_register(WIFI_EVENT, ESP_EVENT_ANY_ID,
                                wifi_event_handler, NULL);
```

registers a handler for all WiFi events. Notice that the event handler is passed parameters that give the event base and the event id and a custom event argument that depends on the event. This makes it possible for a single handler to work out what the event is and respond appropriately.

If you are implementing your own events then you first need to register the base event using:

- `ESP_EVENT_DECLARE_BASE(EVENT_BASE)`
- `ESP_EVENT_DEFINE_BASE(EVENT_BASE)`

where *EVENT_BASE* should be unique. You only need to use the declare if you are planning to assign your own unique value to *EVENT_BASE*. If you use the define the system will declare and initialize the base variable. The macro creates a variable of the same name as the base pointing at the location of a string the same as the base.

That is, the macro expands to:

```
esp_event_base_t const MY_CUSTOM_EVENT_BASE =
                                    "MY_CUSTOM_EVENT_BASE"
```

You can define the event ids any way you want to, but the simplest thing to do is define an enumeration.

To post an event you use the function:

```
esp_err_t esp_event_post(esp_event_base_t event_base,
                         int32_t event_id,
                         const void *event_data,
                         size_t event_data_size,
                         TickType_t ticks_to_wait)
```

This posts the event specified and the event loop will call the registered function with the event_data specified. Notice that the event handler gets two items of custom data – the arg specified when it was registered and event_data constructed when the event occurs.

WiFi Events

Now that we know how the event loop works we can add event handling to the WiFi connection example. The problem is that there are a great many WiFi events, but in general you only need to handle a few of them:

- WIFI_EVENT_STA_START
- WIFI_EVENT_STA_CONNECTED
- WIFI_EVENT_STA_DISCONNECTED

All we have to do it start the default event loop and register an event handler:

```
 esp_event_loop_create_default();
 esp_event_handler_register(WIFI_EVENT, ESP_EVENT_ANY_ID,
                                      wifi_event_handler, NULL);
```

A basic WiFi event handler is something like:

```
static void wifi_event_handler(void *event_handler_arg,
                         esp_event_base_t event_base,
                         int32_t event_id,
                         void *event_data)
{
    switch (event_id)
    {
    case WIFI_EVENT_STA_START:
        printf("WIFI CONNECTING....\n");
        break;
    case WIFI_EVENT_STA_CONNECTED:
        printf("WiFi CONNECTED\n");
        break;
```

```
    case WIFI_EVENT_STA_DISCONNECTED:
        printf("WiFi lost connection\n");
        if (retry_num < 5)
        {
            esp_wifi_connect();
            retry_num++;
            printf("Retrying to Connect...\n");
        }
        break;
    }
}
```

If you add this code to the previous example and run it you will now discover that the red warnings have vanished and you see the progress of the connection as the output of the printf functions.

You can see the complete program in folder WiFi2.

As well as simply choosing to ignore a WiFi event you can also set which events should be generated using an event mask. You can set or get the event mask using:

- esp_err_t esp_wifi_set_event_mask(uint32_t mask)
- esp_err_t esp_wifi_get_event_mask(uint32_t *mask)

The mask can be the logical OR of any of the WIFI_EVENT_MASK_ constants. The default is WIFI_EVENT_MASK_AP_PROBEREQRECVED which suppresses event generation when a probe request is received as happens with a high frequency.

Scan

While in station mode, the WiFi can perform a scan to find out what APs are available. You can scan while connected to an AP or not. If you are connected to an AP the scan is termed a "background" scan as opposed to a foreground scan that happens while the WiFi is not connected. The channel that the WiFi is connected to is called the "home channel".

The functions governing this provide more control than you generally need. The simplest scan involves a few new functions, the first being:

```
esp_err_t esp_wifi_scan_start(const wifi_scan_config_t *config,
                                                bool block)
```

which starts a scan after the WiFi has started in station mode. If the first parameter is NULL, a default scan is performed. If the second parameter is true then the function blocks until the scan is complete.

Once the scan returns you can find the number of APs detected using the second new function:

```
esp_err_t esp_wifi_scan_get_ap_num(uint16_t *number)
```

and you can return a struct for each one giving its details:

```
esp_err_t esp_wifi_scan_get_ap_record(wifi_ap_record_t *ap_record)
```

Getting a scan record removes it from storage and you can remove any unused records that remain using:

```
esp_err_t esp_wifi_clear_ap_list(void)
```

Thus the simplest scan program is, folder Scan:

```
#include <stdio.h>
#include "nvs_flash.h"
#include "esp_wifi.h"
void app_main(void)
{
    nvs_flash_init();
    esp_event_loop_create_default();
    wifi_init_config_t wificonfig = WIFI_INIT_CONFIG_DEFAULT();
    esp_wifi_init(&wificonfig);
    esp_wifi_set_mode(WIFI_MODE_STA);
    esp_wifi_start();
    esp_wifi_scan_start(NULL, true);
    uint16_t n;
    esp_wifi_scan_get_ap_num(&n);
    wifi_ap_record_t rec;
    for (int i = 0; i < n; i++)
    {
        esp_wifi_scan_get_ap_record(&rec);
        printf("%s\n", rec.ssid);
    }
}
```

This performs a default scan and then prints the SSID of each one found. Of course, you could display more information from the struct.

Alternatively you can use:

```
esp_err_t esp_wifi_scan_get_ap_records(uint16_t *number,
                       wifi_ap_record_t *ap_records)
```

to get an array of structs and clear the storage at the same time.

You can customize the scan by setting or getting the scan parameters:

- ```
  esp_err_t esp_wifi_set_scan_parameters(
            const wifi_scan_default_params_t *config)
  ```
- ```
  esp_err_t esp_wifi_get_scan_parameters(
              wifi_scan_default_params_t *config)
  ```

where the options are:

- ssid   ssid of AP to scan
- bssid M   AC address of AP to scan
- channel   scan specific channel
- show_hidden   If true shows hidden SSIDs
- scan_type   Active or passive scan
- scan_time   Scan time per channel min and max
- home_chan_dwell_time   Time spent on home channel
- channel_bitmap   Bitmask specifying channels to scan
- coex_background_scan   Performs scan in background

The defaults are:

```
show_hidden:false
scan_type:active
scan_time.active.min:0
scan_time.active.max:120 ms
scan_time.passive:360 ms
home_chan_dwell_time:30ms
```

You can run the scan in non-blocking mode and find out when the scan is complete using the WIFI_EVENT_SCAN_DONE event.

This example is in folder scan2:

```c
#include <stdio.h>
#include "nvs_flash.h"
#include "esp_wifi.h"

static void wifi_event_handler(void *event_handler_arg,
                               esp_event_base_t event_base,
                               int32_t event_id,
                               void *event_data)
{
    uint16_t n;
    esp_wifi_scan_get_ap_num(&n);
    wifi_ap_record_t rec;
    for (int i = 0; i < n; i++)
    {
        esp_wifi_scan_get_ap_record(&rec);
        printf("%s\n", rec.ssid);
    }
}
```

```
void app_main(void)
{
    esp_event_loop_create_default();
    esp_event_handler_register(WIFI_EVENT, WIFI_EVENT_SCAN_DONE,
                                        wifi_event_handler, NULL);

    nvs_flash_init();
    esp_event_loop_create_default();
    wifi_init_config_t wificonfig = WIFI_INIT_CONFIG_DEFAULT();
    esp_wifi_init(&wificonfig);
    esp_wifi_set_mode(WIFI_MODE_STA);
    esp_wifi_start();
    esp_wifi_scan_start(NULL, false);
}
```

It allows the task that started the scan to continue. Notice that as the event handler is registered only for a single event we don't need to test the event id in the handler.

Summary

- The WiFi is controlled by two components the esp_wifi library which sets up the WiFi connection and esp_netif which deals with the network connection.

- The WiFi system uses the esp_event library to handle events generated by the WiFi and netif system.

- You only have to handle the events that you want to respond to.

- Before you can make use of the WiFi for anything at all you have to initialize its driver and hardware.

- After this you can set up the appropriate mode station or access point or both.

- Setup a country code if you want to operate within the bands that are legal.

- Every device has a unique MAC address but you can get and set the one used by the WiFi.

- To setup station mode you need to supply the ssid of the AP you want to connect to, a password and the minimum security you will use.

- As well as station mode you can scan to discover what APs are available.

So far we have looked at how to use the WiFi in station mode but no application data has been sent or received. The WiFi driver and its associated functions serve to configure and connect the WiFi to an AP. Sending data needs another layer of software and the ESP32 has opted to use lwIP, an open source library that implements the Internet Protocol IP. While you can use lwIP directly, there is an ESP32-specific intermediate library, ESP-NETIF that handles TCP/IP communication. The functions in ESP-NETIF call functions in lwIP to get the job done, but it provides a uniform API that could be modified to use another TCP/IP library. It also makes lwIP thread-safe, which is an important simplification when using it with FreeRTOS.

Ethernet, IP, TCP and HTTP

It isn't entirely necessary to understand the details of how modern networking is implemented to make use of it, but a rough idea helps. At this point most accounts would introduce the OSI (Open Systems Interconnection) model, but this is more than the working programmer needs to know. In practice, there is just one common lower-level, Ethernet, and on top of that we have IP (Internet Protocol).

Most computers are physically connected together by Ethernet networks. This is a packet-switched network, which means that data is transmitted in chunks called packets and each packet has the address of the machine it is being sent to and the address of the machine that sent it.

For Ethernet the addresses are called MAC (Media Access Control) addresses. These are 48-bit unique identifiers. When anyone manufactures an Ethernet interface they apply for a unique MAC address for it. This means that, in principle, every machine on an Ethernet network has a unique MAC address. This can be useful if you need a unique identifier and a machine's MAC address is often used to create a 128-bit GUID (Globally Unique IDentifier) by incorporating the exact date and time. Some devices, such as routers, have software-definable MAC addresses and this does spoil the simple picture. In the main, however, you can regard a MAC address as being effectively unique.

Ethernet packets are sent from their source to their destination on the basis of the MAC address specified. The hardware that makes up the network, usually switches, learn which machines are connected on which ports by monitoring network traffic and sends the packets to the correct destination.

The problem with the MAC address is that it isn't routable. You cannot take a MAC address and work out that the destination is on some other network and send the packet there for further routing. All of the machines that are reachable by Ethernet packets are essentially on the same physical network. Ethernet is a local area networking protocol.

The IP address is, however, routable and it was designed to be so. An IP data packet uses IP addresses rather than MAC addresses, even though the packets are actually transported within Ethernet packets complete with MAC addresses. The network software resolves the IP address to a local MAC address and then the Ethernet takes care of delivery to the destination machine where the IP packet is removed from the Ethernet packet and passed to higher-level software. The matching up of IP addresses and MAC addresses is done by a protocol called the Address Resolution Protocol, ARP. As long as the IP address can be resolved to a local MAC address, delivery is simple and direct via the network switches.

When an IP address is used that doesn't correspond to a local address, i.e. one not on the specified sub-net, then the packet is sent to the designated router and it is expected to send the packet on to other routers which will see it safely delivered to the correct network. In principle, IP networking can sit on top of any hardware-implemented network and not just Ethernet.

Mostly you can ignore the Ethernet component of the network apart from the occasional need to know about or work with a MAC address. The IP component, however, is much more important and is what you work with most of the time. This is a raw packet switching protocol which simply sends packets to their destinations without needing to know anything about what is in them.

On top of IP you can create other protocols. The simplest is UDP (User Datagram Protocol) which basically allows you to send packets of data to one or more recipients without error correction or even any guarantees of delivery. UDP is a fast but unreliable data transfer protocol. Another protocol built on IP is TCP (Transmission Control Protocol)TCP is less efficient than UDP, but it provides a reliable connection with error correction and guarantees not only delivery of each packet but delivery in the correct order. TCP is the protocol used to transfer web pages between client and server and it is a completely general data transfer protocol.

When transferring web pages, yet another protocol is employed to control exactly what data is transferred. The HTTP (HyperText Transfer Protocol) is a set of requests that determine what data a client and a server will exchange. It is transported as the data within a TCP connection.

Now that we know how things work, the usual network layer diagram should make sense:

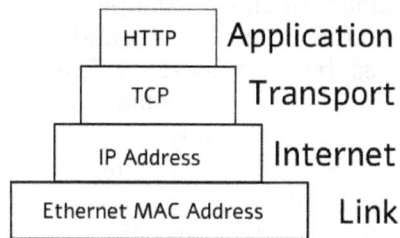

HTTP	Application
TCP	Transport
IP Address	Internet
Ethernet MAC Address	Link

To recap:

- IP packets are transferred on the local network within Ethernet packets which are sent from source to destination using MAC addresses.
- IP packets can be routed outside of the local network via a router. The source and destination are specified using an IP address and the IP address is mapped to a MAC address once the packet reaches the local network.
- UDP is a simple protocol that uses IP packets to send datagrams without error checking or assured delivery.
- TCP uses IP packets to transfer metadata that the software can use to ensure a reliable connection including error correction and tests for data integrity.
- HTTP uses a TCP connection to send requests for particular data or actions to be performed.

In principle each of these layers could be changed, but in practice only the Application and Transport layers vary significantly in practice.

Once the WiFi connection has been made, most of the details of the IP connection are handled by `esp_netif` and are implemented by lwIP.

IP, Netmask and Gateway

When connecting to a local network the network interface needs to be supplied with a number of parameters.

It has to have an IP address to use to identify it and this can either be a static, manually-assigned, IP address or one provided by the network via a Dynamic Host Configuration Protocol, DHCP server. If the network doesn't have a DHCP server, or if the ESP32 needs to use a special IP address, then it can be manually assigned and will work perfectly well as long as it is unique on the network.

The `netmask` parameter is a bit mask that specifies which portion of the IP address determines the local network. An IP address is just a 32-bit number, but it is usually reported as a "dotted decimal" with each decimal specifying a byte. That is `0xFF0423FF` would be written `255.04.35.255`. A netmask is usually written in the same format. For example, `255.255.0.0` would mean that the first eight bits are the network prefix and when used with the IP address `255.2.3.255` gives the prefix as `255.2`. Every IP address starting `255.2` is local and all others need to be routed to another network. Notice that the non-prefix bits govern how many machines can be on the local network and in this case it is 65,535. As the bits of the netmask have to be contiguous, an alternative notation is to write `ip/`*n* where *n* is the number of bits in the prefix. For example, the address `255.2.3.255/16` specifies that the top 16 bits are the prefix and the bottom 16 bits gives the host address.

Any IP address that is not local as determined by the netmask is routed to another network and to do this it has to be sent to the network's router. This is specified as the gateway address i.e. the gateway is the address on the local network of the router that connects it to other networks.

WiFi driver provides the connection but it is the `esp_netif` component that has to supply the IP setup, IP address, netmask, gateway, host name, etc, either by setting or using a DHCP server.

Using esp_netif

The main job of the `esp_netif` API is to create a net interface, `netif`, and connect it to the WiFi. It does this automatically if you set it up before connecting the WiFi.

The function:

`esp_netif_init()`

initializes the `lwIP` and the semaphore which is used to control access to it so as to make it thread-safe.

Once initialized you can create a `netif` using:

`esp_netif_t* netif = esp_netif_create_default_wifi_sta();`

Notice that this returns a pointer to the `netif` struct which can be used to get/set the configuration of the `netif`. This function has to be called after the event loop has been created as it registers default event handlers and before the WiFi connection is made. If you do this then, when the connection is made, the DHCP client that is part of the `netif` queries the DHCP server and obtains an IP address.

The `netif` has a set of events in the event base `IP_EVENT`:

- `IP_EVENT_STA_GOT_IP`   Station has IP address
- `IP_EVENT_STA_LOST_IP`   Station lost IP address
- `IP_EVENT_AP_STAIPASSIGNED`   AP has assigned IP to station
- `IP_EVENT_GOT_IP6`   Use station or AP as IP6 address
- `IP_EVENT_ETH_GOT_IP`   Ethernet got IP from connected AP
- `IP_EVENT_ETH_LOST_IP`   Ethernet lost IP and the IP is reset to 0
- `IP_EVENT_PPP_GOT_IP,`   PPP interface got IP
- `IP_EVENT_PPP_LOST_IP`   PPP interface lost IP
- `IP_EVENT_TX_RX`   Transmitting or receiving data packet

For example;

```
esp_event_handler_register(IP_EVENT, IP_EVENT_STA_GOT_IP,
                                     netif_event_handler, NULL);
```

and

```
void netif_event_handler(void *event_handler_arg,
                         esp_event_base_t event_base,
                         int32_t event_id,
                         void *event_data){
    printf("WiFi got IP...\n\n");
}
```

As we have only registered a single event handler to a single event, there is no need to test why the handler has been called. With this modification the client connects and displays its address when it acquires an IP address, folder `WiFi1`.

Working with the IP Address

We can do a little better in that the `event_data` is an `ip_event_got_ip_t` struct:

- `*esp_netif`   Pointer to esp-netif object
- `ip_info`   IP address, netmask, gateway IP address
- `bool ip_changed` Indicates whether assigned IP changed or not

and `ip_info` is:

- `ip`   IPV4 address
- `netmask` IPV4 netmask
- `gw`   IPV4 address of gateway

```
static void netif_event_handler(void *event_handler_arg,
                                esp_event_base_t event_base,
                                int32_t event_id,
                                void *event_data)
{
    ip_event_got_ip_t *info = ( ip_event_got_ip_t *)event_data;
    printf("Wifi got IP =%lX...\n\n", info->ip_info.ip.addr);
}
```

The `netif` struct that is returned by `esp_netif_create_default_wifi_sta` also stores the IP address and many other details, but these are only valid after the connection has been made.

When the WiFi connection is set up you can retrieve the default `netif` struct and a struct that gives the IP information:

```
esp_netif_t* netif = esp_netif_get_default_netif();
esp_netif_ip_info_t ip_info;
esp_netif_get_ip_info(netif, &ip_info);
```

This creates a struct, `esp_netif_ip_info_t` which contains the details of the default connection and which can be used to display the IP address.

The problem is that the IP address is a 32-bit integer and printing it as a hex or decimal value isn't the usual format. There are functions which convert the raw address into alternative formats. In particular, `ip4addr_ntoa` converts a 32-bit integer representation into the more usual dotted form.

For example:

```
char bufIP[20];
printf("IP:%s\n",esp_ip4addr_ntoa(&(ip_info.ip),bufIP, 20));
printf("Mask:%s\n",esp_ip4addr_ntoa(&(ip_info.netmask),bufIP, 20));
printf("Gateway:%s\n",esp_ip4addr_ntoa(&(ip_info.gw),bufIP, 20));
```

displays:

```
IP: 192.168.253.46
Mask: 255.255.255.0
Gateway: 192.168.253.1
```

You can also get the current host name, by default `espressif`, using:

```
const char *hostName;
esp_netif_get_hostname(netif,&hostName);
printf("Host Name: %s\n", hostName );
```

You can use `netif_set_hostname` to set the host name, but you have to be careful to do it after setting client mode and before the connect:

```
esp_netif_t *netif = esp_netif_create_default_wifi_sta();
esp_netif_set_hostname(netif, "MyESP32S3");
esp_wifi_start();
esp_wifi_connect();
```

If you set the hostname after the WiFi has connected then it only takes effect on a reconnect. You can see the entire program in folder `WiFi2`.

There are some useful conversion functions:

- `char * esp_ip4addr_ntoa(const esp_ip4_addr_t *addr,`
                          `char *buf, int buflen)`
  Converts IP4 address into a dotted string format
- `uint32_t esp_ip4addr_aton(const char *addr)`
  Converts a dotted string format to a numeric IP address as a 32 bit integer

- `esp_err_t esp_netif_str_to_ip4(const char *src,`
  `esp_ip4_addr_t *dst)`
  Converts a dotted string format to a `esp_ip4_addr_t` struct
- `esp_err_t esp_netif_str_to_ip6(const char *src,`
  `esp_ip6_addr_t *dst)`
  Converts a dotted string format to a `esp_ip6_addr_t` struct

DHCP

You can control the way the DHCP (Dynamic Host Configuration Protocol) client behaves. In particular, you can turn it off and assign a static IP. To enable the DHCP client you have to set the netif flags to `ESP_NETIF_DHCP_CLIENT` which is the default for a client. You can remove the DHCP client completely by resetting the flag bit:

`netif->flags = (netif->flags) & ~ESP_NETIF_DHCP_CLIENT;`

In general you should only do this with custom netif objects.

A better method is to use the functions:

- `esp_err_t esp_netif_dhcpc_start(esp_netif_t *esp_netif);`
- `esp_err_t esp_netif_dhcpc_stop(esp_netif_t *esp_netif);`

to start and stop the DHCP client respectively.

You can discover the status of the DHCP client using:

`esp_err_t esp_netif_dhcpc_get_status(esp_netif_t *esp_netif,`
`esp_netif_dhcp_status_t *status);`

where *status* is:

- `ESP_NETIF_DHCP_INIT`   Initalized
- `ESP_NETIF_DHCP_STARTED`   Started
- `ESP_NETIF_DHCP_STOPPED`   Stopped

For example:

```
esp_netif_dhcpc_get_status(netif, &status);
printf("status %d\n",status);
```

If you want to configure the client you can use:

`esp_err_t esp_netif_dhcpc_option(esp_netif_t *esp_netif,`
`esp_netif_dhcp_option_mode_t opt_op,`
`esp_netif_dhcp_option_id_t opt_id,`
`void *opt_val,`
`uint32_t opt_len);`

The *opt_op* controls whether the operation is a get or a set:

- `ESP_NETIF_OP_SET`
- `ESP_NETIF_OP_GET`

The *opt_id* can be any of:

- ESP_NETIF_SUBNET_MASK   Network mask
- ESP_NETIF_DOMAIN_NAME_SERVER   Domain name server
- ESP_NETIF_ROUTER_SOLICITATION_ADDRESS   IP6 solicitation address
- ESP_NETIF_REQUESTED_IP_ADDRESS   Request specific IP address
- ESP_NETIF_IP_ADDRESS_LEASE_TIME   Request IP address where *opt_val* is uint8_t
- ESP_NETIF_IP_REQUEST_RETRY_TIME   Request retry counter
- ESP_NETIF_VENDOR_CLASS_IDENTIFIER   Vendor Class Identifier
- ESP_NETIF_VENDOR_SPECIFIC_INFO   Vendor Specific Information
- ESP_NETIF_CAPTIVEPORTAL_URI   Captive Portal Identification

You can find out the meaning of these by looking up the DHCP protocol.

Each option may have an *opt_val* and *opt_len* associated with the data needed to set or get it.

The bad news is that at the time of writing the only option supported is retry time in both get and set modes:

```
case IP_EVENT_STA_GOT_IP:
    wifiStatus = 1010;
    ip_event_got_ip_t *info = (ip_event_got_ip_t *)event_data;
    printf("Wifi got IP =%lX...\n\n", info->ip_info.ip.addr);

    uint8_t t;
    esp_netif_dhcp_status_t status;
    esp_err_t err = esp_netif_dhcpc_option(info→esp_netif,
        ESP_NETIF_OP_GET, ESP_NETIF_IP_REQUEST_RETRY_TIME,
                                            &t, sizeof t);
    printf("retry time %d\n", t);
    printf("error %d\n", err);
    esp_netif_dhcpc_get_status(info->esp_netif, &status);
    printf("status %d\n", status);
    break;
}
```

The same mechanism can be used to configure a DHCP server in AP mode with many more options supported, see Chapter 16.

A Practical Connect Function

Connecting to WiFi is a standard operation and it makes sense to package it in a function that converts the event driven status into a shared static variable that can be used in a polling loop.

To make the following examples easier to work with, it is reasonable to put the connect functions into a header file, connectWiFi.h:

```
int retry_num = 0;
int wifiStatus = 1000;

static void wifi_event_handler(void *event_handler_arg,
  esp_event_base_t event_base, int32_t event_id, void *event_data)
{
    switch (event_id)
    {
    case WIFI_EVENT_STA_START:
        wifiStatus = 1001;
        break;
    case WIFI_EVENT_STA_CONNECTED:
        wifiStatus = 1002;
        break;
    case WIFI_EVENT_STA_DISCONNECTED:
        if (retry_num < 5)
        {
            esp_wifi_connect();
            retry_num++;
            wifiStatus = 1001;
        }
        break;
    case IP_EVENT_STA_GOT_IP:
        wifiStatus = 1010;
        break;
    }
}

void wifiConnect(char *country, char *ssid, char *password,
                     char *hostname, esp_netif_ip_info_t *ip_info)
{
    nvs_flash_init();
    esp_netif_init();

    esp_event_loop_create_default();
    esp_event_handler_register(WIFI_EVENT, ESP_EVENT_ANY_ID,
                                     wifi_event_handler, NULL);
    esp_event_handler_register(IP_EVENT, IP_EVENT_STA_GOT_IP,
                                     wifi_event_handler, NULL);

    wifi_init_config_t wificonfig = WIFI_INIT_CONFIG_DEFAULT();
    esp_wifi_init(&wificonfig);

    esp_netif_t *netif = esp_netif_create_default_wifi_sta();
    if (ip_info != NULL)
    {
        esp_netif_dhcpc_stop(netif);
        esp_netif_set_ip_info(netif, ip_info);
    }
```

```
    if (hostname != NULL)
        esp_netif_set_hostname(netif, hostname);

    wifi_config_t staconf = {
        .sta = {
            .threshold.authmode = WIFI_AUTH_WPA_PSK}};
    strcpy((char *)staconf.sta.ssid, ssid);
    strcpy((char *)staconf.sta.password, password);

    esp_wifi_set_mode(WIFI_MODE_STA);
    esp_wifi_set_config(WIFI_IF_STA, &staconf);
    esp_wifi_set_country_code(country, false);

    esp_wifi_start();
    esp_wifi_connect();
}
```

Using this connection becomes easy:

```
#include "esp_wifi.h"
#include "string.h"
#include "nvs_flash.h"

#include "connectWiFi.h"

void app_main(void)
{
    wifiConnect("CO", "ssid", "password",NULL,NULL);
        while (wifiStatus != 1010) {
        vTaskDelay(10 / portTICK_PERIOD_MS);
    };
//use WiFi connection
}
```

The function also allows you to set an optional hostname and IP setup. If you specify an IP setup the DHCP client is turned off and the hostname cannot be assigned.

For example:

```
#include <stdio.h>
#include "esp_wifi.h"
#include "esp_netif.h"
#include "string.h"
#include "nvs_flash.h"

#include "connectWiFi.h"

void app_main(void)
{
    esp_netif_ip_info_t ip_info;

    esp_netif_str_to_ip4("192.168.253.204", &ip_info.ip);
    esp_netif_str_to_ip4("192.168.253.1", &ip_info.gw);
    esp_netif_str_to_ip4("255.255.255.0", &ip_info.netmask);
    wifiConnect("Co", "ssid", "password", NULL, &ip_info); */
    while (wifiStatus != 1010)
    {
        vTaskDelay(10 / portTICK_PERIOD_MS);
    };
    // use WiFi connection
}
```

Also notice that the use of a status variable allows the wifiConnect function to return at once, but we can still wait in the main program for the connection to be made. The vTaskDelay in the while loop allows other tasks to run while waiting.

In the rest of this book it is assumed that the connection function is available as a header file connectWiFi.h .

Summary

- The ethernet that connects most devices into a network makes use of MAC addresses to identify each device.
- A MAC address isn't routable and it cannot send data to other networks. To do this you need to use an IP address which is routable.
- IP packets can be used to implement a range of higher level network protocols the most common being TCP and UDP.
- TCP is an error checked reliable connection between two machines.
- UDP is not error checked and not reliable. Packets are sent between machines without the need to make a connection.
- HTTP is the protocol used to transfer web pages and it is built on top of TCP.
- Working on the local network requires a machine to have an IP address, a netmask which determines which addresses are on the local network and the address of a gateway.
- Most of the work in dealing with IP and TCP is done using esp_netif to create a net interface netif.
- There are a large number of utility functions that convert IP addresses into different formats.
- DHCP is a protocol for automatically assigning an IP address and netmask to a device and optionally a gateway device which will pass packets to other networks.
- The tasks of initializing the WiFi and connecting to an AP is common and it is worth standardizing on a connection function that will do the job.

Chapter 7

Sockets and HTTP Clients

Sockets are a general-purpose way of communicating over networks and similar infrastructure. Essentially, they are a generalization of files to things other than storage devices. They aren't part of the C standard, but are available on all POSIX-compliant operating systems such as Linux. As a result there are lots of programs that implement network transactions using sockets.

The ESP32 SDK supports sockets as its official way of using a network interface. These sockets are provided by the lwIP library with some additions to ensure that they are thread-safe. The lwIP library does support alternative methods of implementing TCP/IP, but these are lightweight alternatives to sockets that do not rely on FreeRTOS. They are not officially supported and sockets with FreeRTOS is a much simpler way of working.

The only problem is that lwIP's sockets are not a 100% implementation of the POSIX standard and you are almost certain to require some changes to any existing program that uses them. However, the differences are small enough not to be a burden when creating a new program.

Sockets simply transport data from one point to another, so you can use them to communicate using almost any standard protocol, like HTTP, or a custom protocol of your own devising. Put simply, a socket is a stream of bytes that you can send over a communication channel.

Socket Basics

The basic steps in using a socket are fairly simple:

1. Create socket
2. Connect the socket to an address
3. Transfer data.

Sockets connect to other sockets by their addresses. The simplest case is where there are just two sockets, or two endpoints, communicating. Once the connection is made, the two sockets at each end of the connection operate in more or less the same way. In general, one of the sockets, the client, will have initiated the connection and the other, the server, will have accepted it.

There is a conceptual difference between a client socket and a server socket. A server socket is set up and then it waits for clients to connect to it. A client socket actively seeks a connection with a server. Once connected, data can flow in both directions and the difference between the two ends of the connection becomes less. That is, the difference between client and server is only about who initiates the connection.

Socket Functions

There are several basic socket functions that are needed for specific purposes and these are common to all sockets implementations including lwIP:

Create a socket

```
sockfd = socket(int socket_family, int socket_type, int protocol);
```

This returns a socket descriptor, an int which you use in other socket functions. The socket_family is where you specify the type of communications link to be use and this is where sockets are most general. There are lots of communications methods that sockets can use, including AF_UNIX or AF_LOCAL, which don't use a network, but allow inter-communication between processes on the same machine. In most cases, you are going to be using AF_INET for IPv4 or AF_INET6 for IPv6 networking. lwIP supports both but IPv6 is only available if you enable it.

The socket_type specifies the general protocol to be used. In most cases you will use SOCK_STREAM which specifies a reliable two-way connection - for IP communications this means TCP/IP is used. For some applications you might want to use SOCK_DGRAM, which specifies that the data should be sent without confirming that it has been received. This is a broadcast mechanism that corresponds to UDP for IP communications. LwIP supports both and also SOCK_RAW.

The protocol parameter selects a sub-protocol of the socket type. In most cases you can simply set it to 0 or IPPROTO_IP. LwIP supports IPPROTO_ICMP, IPPROTO_IP, IPPROTO_IP and IPPROTO_IP

As we are going to be working with sockets that basically work with the web, we will use AF_INET and SOCK_STREAM.

Connect a socket to an address

To connect a socket as a client of another use the connect function:

```
int connect(int sockfd,const struct sockaddr *addr,
                                        socklen_t addrlen);
```

The sockfd parameter is just the socket file descriptor returned from the socket function. The addr parameter points at a sockaddr struct which contains the address of the socket you want to connect to. Of course, `addrlen` just specifies the size of the struct. The socket address type depends on the underlying communications medium that the socket uses, but in most cases it is just an IP address.

Reading and Writing

As an open socket is just a file, you can use the standard `read` and `write` functions that you would use to work with a file. There are two additional functions, `send` and `recv`, which work in the same way as `write` and `read` but have an additional final parameter that can be used to control exactly how the transaction is performed. It is worth noting that Windows sockets do not support `read` and `write` but they do work with `recv` and `send` and if you are developing a cross-platform or porting a Windows socket program then it might be easier to use these alternatives.

Both `read` and `write` are blocking in the sense that they do not return until there is either data to process or the data has been sent. This makes writing programs easier but without the use of threads or events brings the rest of the program to a halt. You can convert `read` and `write` into non-blocking operations but this is less commonly used. Alternatively you can use send and `recv` both of which support a flag that makes them non-blocking. This is generally preferable to converting the entire socket to non-blocking.

There are some subtle points about using `read` and `write` with a socket. Both of them may fail to complete a data transfer in one call. That is, when you use

```
int n = write(sockfd, buffer, m);
```

by definition there is no guarantee that all of the m byes of data will be written to the socket when the function returns. The return value n gives the number of bytes actually written and in most cases for sockets n is equivalent to m and the data transfer will complete. The reason for it failing to do so is that the data is transferred to the TCP buffer and the call will block until all of the data is sent. If the call is non-blocking and there is insufficient TCP buffer then it returns an error `EWOULDBLOCK`. This makes working with non-blocking writes more complicated.

For a socket running under Linux or a POSIX-conforming operating system, a `write` can be interrupted by a signal which causes it to return without sending all of the data and this requires calling `write` again to finish the send. As FreeRTOS and the ESP32 don't implement signals, this cannot happen.

What all this means is that, if you call `write` or `send` in blocking mode, then you can be sure that all of the data will be sent – data is only not completely sent if there is an error such as the server disconnecting.

This said most code, example and production, does check that all of the bytes have been sent and even retries the write should this happens.

When it comes to reading data the situation is very different. The source of the data may not send the data as a single block and the data in the buffer may only be a part of the total. This means that rereading the socket is almost unavoidable. The problem is not repeatedly reading the socket, the problem is knowing when to stop. The simplest solution is to read data until the flow of data stops for a given amount of time – i.e. a repeated `read` with timeout. For an HTTP payload you can also check that you have all of the data by looking at the headers and decoding the content length header to give the number of bytes in the HTML page.

A function to perform a timeout-limited read is presented as part of the following example. Processing the HTML headers and the rest of the HTML page is left as an exercise for the reader.

Configuring TCP

The standard way to configure lwIP's implementation of TCP is to edit a configuration file `lwipopts.h` but ESP 32 IDF makes use of the `menuconfig` utility to create a local configuration file. The `lwipopts.h` file still exists, but now it is set by the project configuration. If you want to set the TCP parameters, open `menuconfig` and search for TCP:

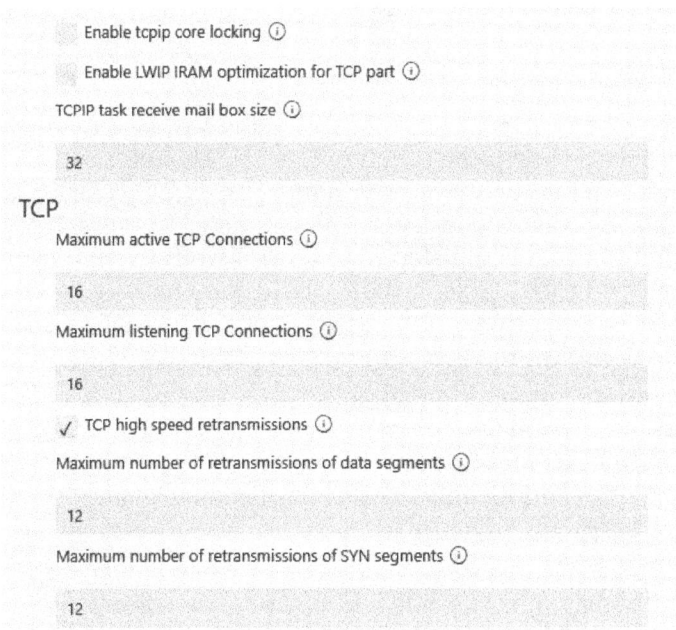

Enable tcpip core locking ⓘ

Enable LWIP IRAM optimization for TCP part ⓘ

TCPIP task receive mail box size ⓘ

32

TCP

Maximum active TCP Connections ⓘ

16

Maximum listening TCP Connections ⓘ

16

✓ TCP high speed retransmissions ⓘ

Maximum number of retransmissions of data segments ⓘ

12

Maximum number of retransmissions of SYN segments ⓘ

12

A Simple Web Client

Now that we have a WiFi connection we can start using it. The ESP32 makes use of the standard sockets interface to transfer data over an IP link. This works in terms of general IP packets, but usually we want to customize the packets to carry a particular protocol. In this case, a web client using HTTP is required. It has to be admitted that a web client isn't as common a requirement as a web server, but it is simpler and illustrates most of the points of using sockets to implement an HTTP packet using a TCP/IP transaction.

The first thing we have to do is create a socket and the TCP needed for an HTTP transaction:

```
int sockfd = socket(AF_INET, SOCK_STREAM, 0);
```

`AF_INET` defines the transaction as an internet connection and `SOCK_STREAM` means a two way communication – in this case TCP/IP.

To allow this to work you have to add:

```
#include "socket.h"
```

Next we need to get the address of the server we want to connect to. For the web this would usually be done using a DNS lookup on a domain name. To make things simple, we will skip the lookup and use a known IP address. `example.com` is a domain name provided for use by examples and you can find its address by pinging it. At the time of writing it was hosted at:

```
23.192.228.80
```

This could change so check before concluding that "nothing works".

There are three fields in the address structure. The first is:

```
struct sockaddr_in addr;
```

Then comes `sin_family`, which is set to:

```
addr.sin_family = AF_INET;
```

to indicate an IPv4 address.

The next field is the port number of the IP address, but you can't simply use:

```
addr.sin_port = 80;
```

because the bit order used on the Internet isn't the same as that used on most processors. Instead you have to use a utility function that will ensure the correct bit order:

```
addr.sin_port = htons(80);
```

The function name stands for "host to network short" and there are other similarly named functions.

The actual address is defined in the `in_addr` field. This is a struct with only one field, `s_addr`, a 32-bit representation of an IP address. The format is fairly simple. Regard the 32-bit value as four bytes with each byte coding one value of the "dotted" IP address. That is, if the IP address is `w.x.y.z` then `w`, `x`, `y` and `z` are the bytes of `s_addr`. For example, the IP address of `example.com` is `23.192.228.80` and converting each value into its byte equivalent in hex gives `17.C0.E4.50`, which would be the hex value we have to store in `s_addr` if it wasn't for the fact that the bytes are stored in reverse order. So, the hex equivalent of the IP address is `0x50E4C0` and this can be used to initialize the address struct:

```
addr.sin_addr.s_addr = 0x50E4C0;
```

Fortunately we don't have to do this as there is a conversion function:

```
addr.sin_addr.s_addr = inet_addr("23.192.228.80");
```

To make all this work you need to add:

```
#include "esp_netif.h"
```

With the address worked out and safely stored we can now make the connection:

```
connect(sockfd, &addr, sizeof (addr));
```

This will return 0 if it successfully connects and we do need to test for this condition. You will also get a type warning because the pointer to the `addr` structure isn't as defined in the function. In fact, there are many variations on the `addr` structure which you could pass and it is the standard idiom to cast them to the function's pointer type:

```
connect(sockfd, (struct sockaddr *) &addr, sizeof (addr)
```

Finally we need to check for an error:

```
if(connect(sockfd, (struct sockaddr *) &addr, sizeof(addr))<0)
                                        return;
```

As long as there is no error we can start to send and receive data.

But what data? The answer is that it all depends on the protocol you are using. There is nothing about a socket that tells you what to send. It is a completely general I/O mechanism. You can send anything, but if you don't send what the server is expecting, you won't get very far.

The web uses the HTTP protocol and this is essentially a set of text headers that tell the server what to do, and a set of headers that the server sends back to tell you what it has done.

The most basic transaction the client can have with the server is to send a `GET` request for the server to send a particular file.

Thus the simplest header is:

```
char header[] = "GET /index.html HTTP/1.1\r\n\r\n";
```

which is a request for the server to send `index.html`.

However, in most cases we need one more header, `HOST`, which gives the domain name of the server. Why do we need to do this? Simply because HTTP says you should and many websites are hosted by a single server at the same IP address. Which website the server retrieves the file from is governed by the domain name you specify in the HOST header.

This means that the simplest set of headers we can send the server is:

```
char header[] = "GET /index.html HTTP/1.1\r\n
                          HOST:example.com\r\n\r\n";
```

which corresponds to the headers:

```
GET /index.html HTTP/1.1
HOST:example.com
```

An HTTP request always ends with a blank line. If you don't send the blank line then you will get no response from most servers. In addition, the `HOST` header has to have the domain name with no additional syntax - no slashes and no http: or similar.

With the headers defined we can send our first HTTP request using `write` as if the socket was just another file to write data to:

```
int n = write(sockfd, header, strlen(header));
```

and, of course, to use the `strlen` function we need to add:

```
#include <string.h>
```

We don't need to check that all of the data has been sent as the call to write is blocking and will block until either all of the data has been sent or there is an error.

The server receives the HTTP request and should respond by sending the data corresponding to the file specified, i.e. `index.html`. We can read the response just as if the socket was a file:

```
char buffer[2048];
n = read(sockfd, buffer, 2048);
printf("%s", buffer);
```

This works but only if the server sends all of the data in one packet and it is received into the TCP buffer before read is called.

For a small page served by example.com this is the case most of the time, but for larger pages or busy servers pages are generally sent in multiple packets that need to be read as they come in.

```
int len = 1024 * 2;
char buffer[len];
int m = 0;
do
{
    int n = read(sockfd, buffer + m, len - m -1);
    if (n < 0)
        break;
    m = m + n;
    buffer[m] = 0;
    printf("\ndata received %d\n\n", n);
    printf("%s\n", buffer);
} while (true);
```

This is a simple loop that loads the data into the buffer as it arrives. Notice that we need to leave space in the buffer for the terminating zero hence the use of len-m-1. Notice also that the server will send zero-length packets to the client as part of its "keep alive" procedure. If the client doesn't respond then the server disconnects and this generates an error in the read which terminates the loop.

The data returned is more than the HTML as you get the entire HTTP response, including the response headers:

```
HTTP/1.1 200 OK
Accept-Ranges: bytes
Age: 483961
Cache-Control: max-age=604800
Content-Type: text/html; charset=UTF-8
Date: Wed, 14 Aug 2024 08:49:49 GMT
Etag: "3147526947+gzip"
Expires: Wed, 21 Aug 2024 08:49:49 GMT
Last-Modified: Thu, 17 Oct 2019 07:18:26 GMT
Server: ECAcc (nyd/D169)
Vary: Accept-Encoding
X-Cache: HIT
Content-Length: 1256

<!doctype html>
<html>
```

and so on...

Notice the blank line marking the end of the header and signaling that the data payload follows. Also notice that the Content-Length header tells you how many bytes of data follow the header.

The complete program is, folder HTTPClient1:

```c
#include <stdio.h>
#include "freertos/FreeRTOS.h"
#include "esp_wifi.h"
#include "nvs_flash.h"
#include "esp_event.h"
#include "esp_netif.h"
#include "string.h"
#include "socket.h"
#include "connectWiFi.h"

void app_main(void)
{
    wifiConnect("Co", "SSID", "password", NULL, NULL);
    while (wifiStatus != 1010)
    {
        vTaskDelay(10 / portTICK_PERIOD_MS);
    };

    int sockfd = socket(AF_INET, SOCK_STREAM, 0);
    struct sockaddr_in addr;
    addr.sin_family = AF_INET;
    addr.sin_port = htons(80);
    addr.sin_addr.s_addr = inet_addr("23.192.228.80");
    if (connect(sockfd, (struct sockaddr *)&addr,
                                        sizeof(addr)) < 0)
        return;

    char header[] = "GET /index.html HTTP/1.1\r\n"
                    "Host:example.com\r\n\r\n";
    int n = write(sockfd, header, strlen(header));

    int len = 1024 * 2;
    char buffer[len];
    int m = 0;
    do
    {
        n = read(sockfd, buffer + m, len - m -1);
        if (n < 0)
            break;
        m = m + n;
        buffer[m] = 0;
        printf("\ndata received %d\n\n", n);
        printf("%s\n", buffer);
    } while (true);
    printf("Final buffer\n\n%s\n", buffer);
}
```

To make this work you will have to increase the size of the main task stack to 6000 bytes using the configuration editor:

Main task stack size ⓘ

```
6000
```

If you run this program, folder HTTPClient1, you will see whatever fragments the server sends. There are usually one or two and then there will be a long wait, up to tens of seconds, while the server waits for its timeout before breaking the connection. What tends to happen is that the server sends a zero-length "keep alive" packet which the client does not respond to and so the server disconnects. In a more sophisticated interaction the client could respond and keep the connection alive, but in this simple situation we need a better way to instruct the data transfer to time out.

Of course, we can do much better than this simple example. For one thing, each socket operation needs to be checked for errors. Here we only check for the most likely error, that the server refused the connection.

Non-Blocking Sockets and recv

Blocking sockets are very easy to use, but they come with a very big problem – knowing when all of the data has been read. When you use connect or write any problems will result in the function returning and an error condition. When you use read it will block forever if the server doesn't send any data and there is no error condition. The solution to the problem is to set a timeout, but sockets are blocking and have no facility to set a timeout.

The most commonly suggested solution to this problem is to convert the blocking sockets to non-blocking sockets. This is easy, just add:

```
fcntl(sockfd, F_SETFL, O_NONBLOCK);
```

before the first operation you want to be non-blocking. In a fully POSIX system you could even switch back to blocking to make implementation easier, but lwIP does not implement the fcntl call in a way that makes it possible to undo the flag setting in a simple way.

If you do this, socket functions that would block will return with EAGAIN (operation should be retried later) but connect will return EINPROGRESS. The problem you now have is finding out when the operation is complete. You can poll and keep testing to see what the return value is or you can use select to wait for the operation to complete, see the next section.

Using non-blocking to implement a timeout is possible, but not easy and not particularly sensible. Non-blocking is just that – the functions return as soon as they have either set an operation going or checked that it is in progress. The idea is that the calling program can get on with some other task while the operation completes. Using it to implement a timeout isn't what it was introduced for.

For example you can perform a read with a timeout using:

```
fcntl(sockfd, F_SETFL, O_NONBLOCK);
int len = 1024 * 2;
char buffer[len];
int m = 0;
int tout = 1000;
int inc = 10;
for (int t = 0; t < tout; t += inc)
{
    n = read(sockfd, buffer + m, len - m - 1);
    if (n >= 0)
    {
        m = m + n;
        buffer[m] = 0;
        printf("\ndata received %d\n\n", n);
    }
    else if (errno != EAGAIN)
    {
        printf("error");
        break;
    }
    vTaskDelay(inc / portTICK_PERIOD_MS);
}

printf("Final buffer\n\n%s\n", buffer);
}
```

This times out after 1 second and checks for more data to read every 20ms. Notice the need to distinguish between an error and EAGAIN. You can try this out in folder HTTPClient2.

In practice, you would have to convert all of the socket functions to non-blocking and add timeouts.

A better solution is to not convert the socket into a non-blocking socket but to use the recv function.

This works like the read function but it allows you to specify a flag that controls the operation. One of the flag settings is MSG_DONTWAIT. This causes the read to be non-blocking and it behaves in the same way as a read to a non-blocking socket. This has the advantage that you don't have to use non-blocking operations all the time, but you do still have to write the timeout handling. For example, if you remove the line:

```
 fcntl(sockfd, F_SETFL, O_NONBLOCK);
```

and change the read to:

```
 n = recv(sockfd, buffer + m, len - m - 1, MSG_DONTWAIT);
```

Then the previous non-blocking socket works in exactly the same way, but now other socket functions can continue to be blocking. You can try this out in folder HTTPClient3.

Timeout and `select`

A better way of handling timeout on sockets is the `select` function. This isn't a socket function, it is part of Linux, but lwIP has its own implementation of it. It is very similar to the `QueueSet` function introduced in Chapter 4, but works with sockets rather than queues or semaphores. The basic idea is that `select` can be provided with lists of file descriptors and it will suspend the task until one of the file descriptors is ready for use:

`select(maxfdp1,readset,writeset,exceptset,timeout)`

where `readset`, `writeset` and `exceptset` are structs that contain a list of file descriptors to monitor for ready-to-read, ready-to-write and exceptional states and `maxfdp1` is one more than the highest file descriptor you are waiting on. That is, if you add a socket with a file descriptor of 3 into the `readset` you need to specify `maxfdp1` as 4. `Timeout` is the specified timeout.

The `select` will wait for a maximum of timeout seconds and return with a value of zero. If a file descriptor is ready before this time, it returns with the number of file descriptors that are ready. The `readset`, `writeset` and `exceptset` are modified so that they only contain file descriptors that are ready. The timeout value is specified as a struct `timeval` and is also usually changed by `select`.

The `readset`, `writeset` and `exceptset` are instances of the `fdset` structure. This can be manipulated using standard macros:

- `FD_ZERO(fd_set *set)`   Clears all file descriptors
- `FD_SET(int fd, fd_set *set)`   Adds fd to the set
- `FD_CLR(int fd, fd_set *set)`   Removes fd from the set
- `FD_ISSET(int fd, fd_set *set)`   Zero if fd isn't in the set

Using this we can now wait for there to be data to read:

```
char buffer[2048];
    fd_set rfds;
    struct timeval tv;
    do
    {
        FD_ZERO(&rfds);
        FD_SET(sockfd, &rfds);
        tv.tv_sec = 6;
        tv.tv_usec = 0;
        int s = select(sockfd + 1, &rfds, NULL, NULL, &tv);
```

If n is negative there is an error, if it is 0 the select has timed out and if it is positive that is the number of file descriptors that are ready to read, one in this case.

Of course, we want to read data from the server until it has sent everything we need to read. This can be accomplished by repeatedly reading until we get a timeout. This is worth implementing as a function:

```c
void socketReadTimeout(int sockfd, char buffer[], int len, int
timeoutsec)
{
    int m = 0;
    fd_set rfds;
    struct timeval tv;
    do
    {
        FD_ZERO(&rfds);
        FD_SET(sockfd, &rfds);
        tv.tv_sec = timeoutsec;
        tv.tv_usec = 0;
        int s = select(sockfd + 1, &rfds, NULL, NULL, &tv);
        if (s < 0)
        {
            printf("read error %X\n", errno);
            break;
        }
        if (s == 0)
        {
            printf("read timeout\n");
            break;
        }
        int n = read(sockfd, buffer + m, len - m - 1);
        if (n >= 0)
        {
            m = m + n;
            buffer[m] = 0;
            printf("\ndata received %d\n\n", n);
        }
        if (n < 0)
        {
            if (errno == ENOTCONN)
            {
                printf("socket closed by server\n");
                break;
            }
            printf("read error %X\n", errno);
            break;
        }
        vTaskDelay(2);
    } while (true);
}
```

You can use the function to download `example.com`:

```
    int len = 1024 * 2;
    char buffer[len];
    socketReadTimeout(sockfd, buffer, len,2);
    printf("Final buffer\n\n%s\n", buffer);
}
```

In this case the timeout of two seconds might not be long enough for some servers, but it works well enough with `example.com`. The timeout is set to determine when the data transfer is complete. You can try a full program out in the folder `HTMLClient4`. Notice that, in general, we would have to test to see which socket was ready to read, but as we have used only a single socket in the function this isn't necessary in this case.

DNS Lookup

There is also a utility function that will perform a DNS lookup for you or convert an IP address so you don't need to specify an IP address struct. Surprisingly, this is almost an easier way to do things and it has become the standard way to set up a socket. The `getaddrinfo` function not only looks up the URL using DNS, it also constructs all of the structs you need to open a socket and connect. It will also return as many address specifications as you request, IPv4 and IPv6 for example.

The function specification is:

```
int getaddrinfo(const char *node,
                const char *service,
                const struct addrinfo *hints,
                struct addrinfo **res);
```

and you need to add the header:

```
#include <netdb.h>
```

You pass the IP address or the DNS name to `getaddrinfo`, i.e. either `"93.184.216.34"` or `"www.example.com"`, as node. The service can be specified as a port address `"80"` or as a service name `"http"`. The `hints` struct is used to specify what sort of socket and address you are going to use. The result is a linked list of structs pointed at by `addrinfo`. The only slight complication in using `getaddrinfo` is that you might have more than one result, one for IPv4 and one for IPv6, say, and then you have to work out which one to actually use.

The `result` struct contains structs that you need to both open the socket and to connect. For example, setting up the hints as:

```
struct addrinfo hints;
memset(&hints, 0, sizeof hints);
hints.ai_family = AF_INET ;
hints.ai_socktype = SOCK_STREAM;
```

asks for structs to be made for a TCP IPv4 socket.

We can now get the address details we need:

```
struct addrinfo *servinfo;
int status = getaddrinfo("www.example.com", "80",&hints,
                            &servinfo);
```

Notice that you could use the IP address as a string. As long as this works, the result should be a linked list with a single entry. In this case `servinfo` points to the first and only `addrinfo` struct. If there are any additional structs they are pointed at by:

```
servinfo->next
```

which is `NULL` if there is no `next` struct.

The `addrinfo` struct is allocated by the `getaddrinfo` function and to avoid a memory leak you have to dispose of it when you have finished using it:

```
freeaddrinfo(servinfo);
```

Using the single result is easy. To create the socket we use:

```
int sockfd = socket(servinfo->ai_family,
                    servinfo->ai_socktype,
                    servinfo->ai_protocol);
```

and to connect to the server we use:

```
connect(sockfd,
        servinfo->ai_addr,
        servinfo->ai_addrlen);
```

This is so much simpler that, whenever you need a socket connected to a given URL or IP address and port, you tend to fall into the idiom of writing:

```
struct addrinfo hints;
memset(&hints, 0, sizeof hints);
hints.ai_family = AF_INET ;
hints.ai_socktype = SOCK_STREAM;
struct addrinfo *servinfo;
int status = getaddrinfo("www.example.com", "80",
                                    &hints, &servinfo);
int sockfd = socket(servinfo->ai_family,
                    servinfo->ai_socktype,
                    servinfo->ai_protocol);
connect(sockfd,
        servinfo->ai_addr,
        servinfo->ai_addrlen);
```

The only minor complication is that you need to remember to free the linked list once you are finished with it using:

```
freeaddrinfo(servinfo);
```

Of course, this all assumes that the netif has the address of a DNS server. If the WiFi connection has been made with the help of DHCP, then a DNS server is likely to have been assigned along with the IP address, but only if the DHCP server is configured to supply it. If it isn't, or if a static IP address is used, then you need to to set a DNS server using a set function:

```
esp_err_t esp_netif_set_dns_info(esp_netif_t *esp_netif,
            esp_netif_dns_type_t type, esp_netif_dns_info_t *dns)
```

To get the current setup, you can use:

```
esp_err_t esp_netif_get_dns_info(esp_netif_t *esp_netif,
            esp_netif_dns_type_t type, esp_netif_dns_info_t *dns)
```

The DNS type can be any of:
- ESP_NETIF_DNS_MAIN
- ESP_NETIF_DNS_BACKUP
- ESP_NETIF_DNS_FALLBACK

If the DNS servers have been set by DHCP, only the fallback DNS can be set.

For example, to add DNS to the HTTP client example we need to modify the initial address setup:

```
esp_netif_t *netif = esp_netif_get_default_netif();
esp_netif_dns_info_t dns;
esp_netif_get_dns_info(netif, ESP_NETIF_DNS_MAIN, &dns);
char bufIP[20];
printf("DNS:%s\n", esp_ip4addr_ntoa(&(dns.ip.u_addr.ip4),
                                        bufIP, 20));

int sockfd = socket(AF_INET, SOCK_STREAM, 0);
struct addrinfo hints;
memset(&hints, 0, sizeof hints);
hints.ai_family = AF_INET;
hints.ai_socktype = SOCK_STREAM;

struct addrinfo *servinfo;

int status = getaddrinfo("www.example.com", "80", &hints,
                                        &servinfo);

printf("IP address found:%s\n", esp_ip4addr_ntoa(
        (esp_ip4_addr_t *)&(servinfo→ai_addr→sa_data[2]),
                                        bufIP, 20));

if (connect(sockfd, servinfo→ai_addr,
                        servinfo->ai_addrlen) < 0)
    return;
freeaddrinfo(servinfo);
```

You can see the full program in folder HTMLClient5.

A Select Client Function

Now we have all of the parts needed to implement a web download function. This example is close to the sort of thing you might use in production. The function should be non-blocking and it should provide a data structure that allows the calling program to set what page is required, allow the calling program to test for "task complete" and provide the data. In other languages this data structure would take the form of a promise or a future, but a simple C struct can do the job almost as well:

```
typedef struct
{
    char *url;
    char *path;
    char *buffer;
    int len;
    bool done;
} Page;
```

the url is the server we want to connect to, path gives the page to load, buffer[len] is the character array that will store the result and done is true when the data is in buffer. While not necessary, an initialization function makes the struct easier to use:

```
Page initPage(char url[], char path[], char buffer[], int len)
{
    Page page;
    page.url = url;
    page.path = path;
    page.buffer = buffer;
    page.len = len;
    page.done = false;
    return page;
}
```

Recall that a struct is the only C data structure that is returned by value. This is important as we need the lifetime of struct to be long enough for the non-blocking function to deliver its result.

The non-blocking part of the function is very easy:

```
void getPage(Page *page)
{
    TaskHandle_t asyncgetpage;
    xTaskCreate(asyncgetPage, "asyncgetPage", 1024 * 4,
                                page, 0, &asyncgetpage);
    return;
}
```

All it has to do is pass on the page struct to the asyncgetPage function, which it starts as a new task. You can set a core affinity if you want to, but in this case we are leaving FreeRTOS to decide.

The `asyncgetPage` function is where all the work happens and for once it is worth filling in some of the details of the error handling as it is so important. The first thing to do is to get the page data structure and lookup the URL:

```c
void asyncgetPage(void *arg)
{
    Page *page = (Page *)arg;

    struct addrinfo hints;
    memset(&hints, 0, sizeof hints);
    hints.ai_family = AF_INET;
    hints.ai_socktype = SOCK_STREAM;
    struct addrinfo *servinfo;
    int status = getaddrinfo(page->url, "80", &hints, &servinfo);
    if (status < 0)
        printf("dns fail\n");
```

Once we have the IP address we can create the socket and connect it:

```c
    int sockfd = socket(AF_INET, SOCK_STREAM, IPPROTO_IP);

    if (connect(sockfd, servinfo->ai_addr,
                                servinfo->ai_addrlen) < 0)
    {
        printf("no connection %X\n", errno);
        printf("close socket %d\n", sockfd);
        close(sockfd);
        vTaskDelete(NULL);
    }
    freeaddrinfo(servinfo);
    printf("connect \n");
```

This is more or less as before, but now we at least check that a connection has been made. If the connection fails we simply close the socket and terminate the task. In a production version, we should also return an error code using the `Page` struct.

As long as we have a connection, we can send the headers to the server:

```c
    char header[100];
    sprintf(header, "GET %s HTTP/1.1\r\nHost:%s\r\n\r\n ",
                                page->path, page->url);
    int n = write(sockfd, header, strlen(header));
    if (n < 0)
    {
        printf("no write %X\n", errno);
        printf("close socket %d\n", sockfd);
        close(sockfd);
        vTaskDelete(NULL);
    }
    else
        printf("data sent socket %d %d\n", sockfd, n);
```

This is as before with the addition of simple error checking. In this case, if there is an error you could try again and finally give up if nothing works. We should also deal with the situation where the full set of headers cannot be sent in one go. Notice the way that the headers are constructed using sprintf, which is one of the most useful string manipulation functions.

The read loop follows and uses the socketReadTimeout function given earlier:

```
    socketReadTimeout(sockfd, page->buffer, page-> len, 4);
    printf("close socket %d\n", sockfd);
    close(sockfd);
    page->done = true;
    vTaskDelete(NULL);
}
```

We are using the select function to wait for there to be something to read with a timeout of 4 seconds. If s is less than zero then we have a read error which can only occur if the server goes down or the connection is broken. If s is 0 we have a timeout and the loop should end as there is assumed to be no more data to read. If s is 1 then we have data to read into the pages buffer.

The only way that the function can exit the loop is after a timeout or an error when it just has to set done to true, close the socket and kill the task.

A main task to make use of this would be something like:

```
void app_main(void)
{
    wifiConnect("Co", "SSID", "password", NULL, NULL);
    while (wifiStatus != 1010)
    {
        vTaskDelay(10 / portTICK_PERIOD_MS);
    };

    char buffer1[2000];
    char url[] = "example.com";
    char path[] = "/index.html";
    Page pagetemp1 = initPage(url, path, buffer1, 2000);
    getPage(&pagetemp1);

    char buffer2[8000];
    Page pagetemp2 = initPage("httpforever.com", "/",
                                        buffer2, 10000);
    getPage(&pagetemp2);
    while (true)
    {
        if (pagetemp1.done)
        {
            printf("\n******first request \n %s\n", buffer1);
            pagetemp1.done = false;
        }
```

```
        if (pagetemp2.done)
        {
            printf("\n******second request \n %s\n", buffer2);
            pagetemp2.done = false;
        }
        vTaskDelay(200);
    };
}
```

The main task has to set up a `Page` struct for each page it wants to download. The struct cannot be reused unless the page data is no longer needed and it isn't actively being used to download something. The final `while` loop simply waits for the `done` field to be `true` in each case and prints the contents of the appropriate buffer. Notice that you will have to increase the size of the `app_main` stack to 6,000 bytes to allow for the storage of the data. You can try the program out using the folder `HTTPClient6`.

One of the big problems in testing an HTML client is the lack of public HTML servers – most are HTTPS. Creating HTTPS clients is the subject of Chapter 10.

The HTTP Client Component

A web client and a server are available as components within the API and, for simple tasks, these are easy to use. The client supports both HTTP and HTTPS requests, but it is easier to get things working without the complications of security.

There are only two important HTTP client functions. The first is an initialization function:

```
esp_http_client_handle_t httphandle =
                    esp_http_client_init(phttpconfig);
```

which sets up the HTTP protocol to use as specified in the struct `esp_http_client_config_t` referenced by `phttpconfig`.

There are a lot of fields that you can set to control the way that the client behaves, but a minimal set for connecting to http://example.com is:

```
esp_http_client_config_t httpconfig = {
    .url = "http://example.com",
    .method = HTTP_METHOD_GET,
    .event_handler = http_event_handler,
    .buffer_size = DEFAULT_HTTP_BUF_SIZE,
    .buffer_size_tx = DEFAULT_HTTP_BUF_SIZE,
    .user_data = httpdata,
};
esp_http_client_handle_t httphandle =
                    esp_http_client_init(&httpconfig);
```

The HTTP method is GET and we need to set up an event handler to respond to the stages in the HTTP transaction. To get the transaction started we need to use:

```
esp_http_client_perform(httphandle);
```

By default this blocks until the transaction is complete. However, to get any results, we need to create an event handler. The key event to deal with is the reception of data, HTTP_EVENT_ON_DATA. The event struct passed to the handler includes the fields:

- event_id   Cause of the event
- client   HTTP client handle
- pdata   Pointer to the data
- data_len   Length of data
- puser_data   Pointer to user data
- pheader_key   Pointer to the header key
- pheader_value Pointer to the header value

Essentially, when the HTTP_EVENT_ON_DATA event occurs the data field has the data sent from the server. The only problem is that the complete HTML page may be sent in more than one chunk and we have to put it together into a single char array. To get the data back to the main program we can pass a pointer to a char array as user data:

```
case HTTP_EVENT_ON_DATA:
    printf("HTTP_EVENT_ON_DATA, len=%d\n", evt->data_len);
    if (!esp_http_client_is_chunked_response(evt->client)) {
        char *buf = (char*)(evt->user_data);
        memcpy(buf+pos, evt->data, evt->data_len);
        pos+ = evt->data_len;
        buf[pos] = NULL;
    }
    break
```

You can see that we are using the static variable pos to keep track of where the data should be stored in the buffer. Notice that we add NULL to the end of the buffer to make sure that we have a C string. You can try it out using the folder HTTPClient7.

The HTTP client component also has functions that let you open the connection and then read a stream of data from the server. If you want to reuse a connection, you don't have to use esp_http_client_init again. It is much more efficient to use the range of set and get functions for the parameters of the transaction such as the URL and reuse the http handle.

Summary

- The most commonly used method of establishing communication between two endpoints is the socket.
- FreeRTOS and lwIP support an implementation of sockets which you can use to create clients and servers.
- A socket-based web client is very easy.
- Sockets are blocking by default, but you can set them to be non-blocking.
- If you need to wait for a socket operation to complete, use the select function.
- There is also an HTTP client module which can be used to download web pages.

Servers are always slightly more difficult than clients because of the need to service requests from clients that arrive at a time determined by the client not the server. There is also the problem of having to handle more than one client at a time. However, FreeRTOS makes this much easier.

Bind a Socket to an Address

Servers follow the same initial setup as a client. However ,when it comes to activating the socket they use bind rather than connect.

To assign a server socket to the address it will respond to, use bind:

```
int bind(int sockfd, const struct sockaddr *addr,
                                  socklen_t addrlen);
```

Beginners often ask what the difference is between connect and bind. The answer is that connect makes a connection to the socket with the specified address whereas bind makes the socket respond to that address. Put another way, use connect with a client socket and bind with a server socket.

Listen and Accept

If you have opened a socket and bound it to an IP address then it is acting as a server socket and is waiting for a connection. How do you know when there is a connection, and how do you know when to read or write data? Notice this problem doesn't arise with a client socket because it initiates the complete connection and sends and receives data when it is ready.

The function:

```
int listen(int sockfd, int backlog);
```

sets the socket as an active server. From this point on it listens for the IP address it is bound to and accepts incoming connections. The backlog parameter sets how many pending connections will be queued for processing. The actual processing of a connection is specified by:

```
int accept(int sockfd, struct sockaddr *addr, socklen_t *addrlen);
```

The `accept` command provides the address of the client trying to make the connection in the `sockaddr` structure. It also returns a new socket file descriptor to use to talk to the client. The original socket carries on operating as before. Notice that this is slightly more complicated than you might expect in that it is not the socket that you created that is used to communicate with the client. The socket you created just listens out for clients and creates a queue of pending requests. The `accept` function processes these requests and creates new sockets used to communicate with the client.

This still doesn't solve the problem of how the server detects that there are clients pending. This is a complicated question with many different solutions. You can set up the listening socket to be either blocking or non-blocking. If it is blocking then a call to `accept` will not return until there is a client ready to be processed. If it is non-blocking then a call to `accept` returns at once with an error code equal to `EAGAIN` or `EWOULDBLOCK`. So you can either use a blocking call or you can poll for clients to be ready.

A more complex approach would be to use another thread to call the `select()` function which performs a `wait` with no CPU overhead while the file descriptor isn't ready.

A Simple Server

A server is more or less the same as a client from an implementation point of view. The only real difference is that it has to wait until a client connects before dealing with a transaction.

This first server example, in folder `Server1`, is intended to be as simple as it can be so as to make clear how it works.

The first step is to create the socket and this follows the same pattern as for the client. First we create a suitable socket for TCP/IP:

```
int sockfd = socket(AF_INET, SOCK_STREAM, IPPROTO_IP);
```

For a server, the address associated with the socket is the range of local IP addresses that the server will respond to. In many cases `INADDR_ANY` is appropriate as this simply means that the server will respond to any IP address that the machine supports:

```
struct sockaddr_in addr;
addr.sin_family = AF_INET;
addr.sin_port = htons(80);
addr.sin_addr.s_addr = INADDR_ANY;
```

Instead of connecting the socket to an endpoint we now bind the socket to the address and start listening for incoming connections:

```
bind(sockfd, (struct sockaddr *)&addr, sizeof(addr));
listen(sockfd, 3);
```

We can now use `accept` to wait for a client to connect:

```
struct sockaddr_storage client_addr;
socklen_t addr_size = sizeof client_addr;
int client_fd = accept(sockfd, (struct sockaddr *)&client_addr,
                                                &addr_size);
```

At this point our program is blocked waiting for a client to connect to the socket. If you want to keep processing things in this task then you need to use a socket in a way that doesn't block.

For the moment we can assume that when `accept` returns there is a new socket descriptor in `client_fd` and details of the client in `client_addr`. Again for simplicity, we are not going to check to see who the client is, just serve them a web page. The client will first send the server an HTTP `GET` packet, assuming they do want to `GET` a web page. We can read this in using:

```
char buffer[2048];
int n = read(client_fd, buffer, 2048);
buffer[n] = 0;
printf("%s", buffer);
```

The data in the `GET` headers tell the server which file is required and you can do some string handling to process it to get the name. In this case, we are going to send the same HTML file no matter what the client asks for. To do this we need some HTTP headers defining what we are sending and some HTML to define the page we are sending. The simplest set of headers that work is:

```
        char headers[] = "HTTP/1.1 200 OK\r\n"
                         "Content-Type:text/html;"
                         "charset=UTF-8\r\n"
                         "Server:ESP32\r\n"
                         "Content-Length:";
```

which corresponds to sending:

```
HTTP/1.1 200 OK
Content-Type:text/html;charset=UTF-8\r\n
Server:ESP32
Content-Length:
```

HTTP 1.1 needs the `Content-Length` header to supply the number of bytes that follow the header.

Some sample HTML:

```
        char html[] = "<html><head>"
                      "<title>Hello HTTP World</title>"
                      "</head><body>"
                      "<p>Hello HTTP World</p>"
                      "</body></html>\r\n";
```

The HTML could be anything you need to construct a page.

Now we can assemble the data and send it to the client:

```
    char data[2048] = {0};
    snprintf(data, sizeof data, "%s%d\r\n\r\n%s",
                              headers, strlen(html), html);
    n = write(client_fd, data, strlen(data));
    printf("data sent \n");

    while (true)
    {
       vTaskDelay(2000);
    };
}
```

If you put all of this together and run the program you will find that the server waits until a client, any web browser, connects. To connect use:

http://*IPAddress*/

The web page will then be displayed in the browser.

Of course, this only works once as the program simply waits for the first client to connect. To make the whole thing continue to work we have to put the entire client handling code into a loop:

```
    while (true)
    {
        int client_fd = accept(sockfd,
                (struct sockaddr *)&client_addr, &addr_size);
        char buffer[2048];
        int n = read(client_fd, buffer, 2048);
        buffer[n] = 0;
        printf("%s", buffer);

        char headers[] = "HTTP/1.1 200 OK\r\n"
                         "Content-Type:text/html;"
                         "charset=UTF-8\r\n"
                         "Server:ESP32\r\n"
                         "Content-Length:";

        char html[] = "<html><head>"
                      "<title>Hello HTTP World</title>"
                      "</head><body>"
                      "<p>Hello HTTP World</p>"
                      "</body></html>\r\n";
        char data[2048] = {0};
        snprintf(data, sizeof data, "%s%d\r\n\r\n%s",
                headers, strlen(html), html);
        n = write(client_fd, data, strlen(data));
        printf("data sent \n");
        close(client_fd);
    };
```

A problem with this loop is that `accept` is a blocking call which means you can't include any additional processing in the loop. This doesn't matter too much if you are using different tasks for processing that have to continue while the accept is blocked. Another problem is that while the page is being sent to the client another client cannot connect. That is, clients are processed in the order in which they arrive.

The complete program is in folder `Server1`.

Client Accept as a Task

Of course we have a multi-tasking operating system and the obvious thing to do is to take advantage of it and start a task to deal with each new client. To do this we simply need to change the `app_main` so that it starts a new task with each accept:

```
void app_main(void)
{
    wifiConnect("Co", "SSID", "password", NULL, NULL);
    while (wifiStatus != 1010)
    {
        vTaskDelay(10 / portTICK_PERIOD_MS);
    };

    int sockfd = socket(AF_INET, SOCK_STREAM, IPPROTO_IP);

    struct sockaddr_in addr;
    addr.sin_family = AF_INET;
    addr.sin_port = htons(80);
    addr.sin_addr.s_addr = INADDR_ANY;

    bind(sockfd, (struct sockaddr *)&addr, sizeof(addr));
    listen(sockfd, 3);
    struct sockaddr_storage client_addr;
    socklen_t addr_size = sizeof client_addr;
    while (true)
    {
        int client_fd = accept(sockfd,
                    (struct sockaddr *)&client_addr, &addr_size);
        xTaskCreate(asyncServePage, "asyncServePage",
                        1024 * 10, (void *)client_fd, 1, NULL);
    };
}
```

The only complication in this code is the need to send a pointer to the client's socket. The `asyncServerPage` is:

```c
void asyncServePage(void *arg)
{
    int client_fd = (int)arg;

    char buffer[2048];
    int n = read(client_fd, buffer, 2048);
    buffer[n] = 0;
    printf("%s", buffer);

    char headers[] = "HTTP/1.1 200 OK\r\n"
                     "Content-Type:text/html;"
                     "charset=UTF-8\r\n"
                     "Server:ESP32\r\n"
                     "Content-Length:";

    char html[] = "<html><head>"
                  "<title>Hello HTTP World</title>"
                  "</head><body>"
                  "<p>Hello HTTP World</p>"
                  "</body></html>\r\n";
    char data[2048] = {0};
    snprintf(data, sizeof data, "%s%d\r\n\r\n%s",
             headers, strlen(html), html);

    n = write(client_fd, data, strlen(data));
    printf("data sent \n");
    close(client_fd);
    vTaskDelete(NULL);
}
```

Apart from the need to delete the task, this is more-or-less the same as the first server. The complete program is in folder `Server2`.

The HTTP Server Component

As well as an HTTP client component, there is a server component which is very easy to use. All you have to do is specify handlers for each request method and the path to the resource.

For example, to handle basic GET requests all you need is:

```c
#include <stdio.h>
#include "freertos/FreeRTOS.h"
#include "esp_wifi.h"
#include "nvs_flash.h"
#include "esp_event.h"
#include "esp_netif.h"
#include "string.h"
#include "connectwifi.h"
#include "esp_http_server.h"
```

```c
esp_err_t get_handler(httpd_req_t* req)
{
    const char resp[] = "Temperature is 20.3";
    httpd_resp_send(req, resp, HTTPD_RESP_USE_STRLEN);
    return ESP_OK;
}

void app_main(void)
{
    wifiConnect("CO", "ssid", "password");
    while (wifiStatus != 1010) {
        vTaskDelay(10 / portTICK_PERIOD_MS);
    };

    httpd_config_t config = HTTPD_DEFAULT_CONFIG();
    httpd_handle_t server = NULL;
    httpd_uri_t uri_get = {
    .uri = "/temp",
    .method = HTTP_GET,
    .handler = get_handler,
    .user_ctx = NULL
    };
    if (httpd_start(&server, &config) == ESP_OK) {
        httpd_register_uri_handler(server, &uri_get);
    }
```

You can see that the GET handler is defined to respond to /temp and call
get_handler, which simply sends some text back in response to the request,
when the event occurs. You can register multiple handlers for each request
method with different URLs. For example:

```c
    httpd_config_t config = HTTPD_DEFAULT_CONFIG();
    httpd_handle_t server = NULL;
    httpd_uri_t uri_get = {
    .uri = "/temp",
    .method = HTTP_GET,
    .handler = get_handlertemp,
    .user_ctx = NULL
    };

    if (httpd_start(&server,&config) == ESP_OK) {
        httpd_register_uri_handler(server, &uri_get);
        uri_get.uri = "/hum";
        uri_get.handler = get_handlerhum;
        httpd_register_uri_handler(server, &uri_get);
    }
```

This registers two handlers one for /temp returning the temperature and one
for /hum returning the humidity.

The server takes care of listening for the client to connect, checking the request method and the URL and calling the handler. Notice that all of the headers are taken care of by the server.

When you have finished with the server use:

```
httpd_stop(handle)
```

The server runs as a separate task and runs even after the main program has ended. There are also functions that let you customize the response and access and modify the headers.

A full program using the HTTP server is in the folder `Server3`.

Alternatives to a Server

HTTP servers are by their very nature more complex than HTTP clients. In most cases it is possible to avoid using a server simply by making use of HTTP requests that transfer data from the client to a server rather than the other way round. Of course, to do this you need to set up a standalone server that the ESP32 can connect to, but even this is sometimes an advantage.

HTTP supports a number of request methods which transfer data. Usually these are described in terms of what they do to resources hosted by a web server, but from our point of view what matters is what happens to the data.

The HTTP request methods available are:

- GET   Transfers data from server to client
- HEAD   Transfers only the HTTP headers
- PUT   Transfers data from the client to the server
- POST   Transfers data from the client to the server
- PATCH   Transfers data from the client to the server
- DELETE   Specifies that the data on the server should be deleted
- OPTIONS   Transfers data from the client to the server

If you know about HTTP request methods you will find the above list disconcerting. If you don't know about HTTP requests then you will be wondering why there are so many requests that transfer data from the client to the server? The answer is that in the HTTP model the server stores the master copy of the resource – usually a file or a database entry. The client can request a copy of the resource using GET and then ask the server to modify the resource using the other requests. For example, the PUT request sends a new copy of the resource for the server to use, i.e. it replaces the old copy. POST does the same thing, but PUT should be idempotent, which means if you repeat it the result is as if you had done it just once. With POST you are allowed side effects. For example, PUT 1 might just store 1 but POST 1 might increment a count.

Another example is where you send some text to the server to save under a supplied file name. For this you should use a PUT as repeating the request with the same text changes nothing. If, on the other hand, you supply text to the server and allow it to assign a name and store it, then you should use a POST as you get a new file each time you send the data, even if it is the same.

Similarly the PATCH request should be used by the client to request that that server makes a change to part of an existing resource. Exactly how the change is specified depends on the server. Usually a key value scheme is used, but this isn't part of the specification.

Notice that all of these interpretations of the HTTP request methods are "optional" in the sense that it is up to you and the server you are using to interpret them and implement them. If you write your own server, or server application, then you can treat POST as if it was PUT and vice versa. Also notice that the only difference between client and server is which one initiates the transaction.

A client always contacts a server, but once the connection is made data can be transferred in either direction – a GET sends data to the client and a PUT sends data to the server and we can use this to implement a client that provides data.

The standard approach to implementing a sensor device that makes its readings available to other devices is to implement a web server or a custom protocol on the ESP32 that allows other devices to connect. A simpler solution is to implement an HTTP client and allow the sensor device to send data to a server, using PUT or POST, which other devices can then connect to as required.

A Socket PUT

As an example of using PUT to send data to a server, we can easily modify the previous HTTP clients. All we have to do is change the GET in the header to PUT and store the data to be sent to the server after the end of the headers, i.e. after the double linefeed carriage return:

```
char headerTemplate[] = "%s %s HTTP/1.1\r\n"
                        "HOST:%s:%s\r\n"
                        "Connection: close\r\n"
                        "Content-length: %d\r\n\r\n%s";
int len = snprintf(NULL, 0, headerTemplate,
          page->req, page->path, page->url, page->port,
                    strlen(page->senddata), page->senddata);
    char *requestData = malloc(len + 1);
    snprintf(requestData, len + 1, headerTemplate,
          page->req, page->path, page->url, page->port,
                    strlen(page->senddata), page->senddata);
    int n = write(sockfd, requestData, len + 1);
```

The first `snprintf` is used to discover the total size of the string to be sent to the server. The second constructs the data from the `headerTemplate` and the data. Notice that we now add `senddata` to the end of the string – this is the payload to be sent to the server. To make this work we need to update the page struct and its initialization function:

```
typedef struct
{
    char *req;
    char *port;
    char *url;
    char *path;
    char *buffer;
    char *senddata;
    int len;
    bool done;
} Page;

Page initPage(char req[], char port[], char url[], char path[],
                        char buffer[], int len, char *senddata)
{
    Page page;
    page.req = req;
    page.url = url;
    page.path = path;
    page.port = port;
    page.buffer = buffer;
    page.len = len;
    page.senddata = senddata;
    page.done = false;
    return page;
}
```

The `getPage` function is exactly the same as before but it makes sense to change its name to `doPage` now that we allow other requests than `GET`. The app_main is now:

```
void app_main(void)
{
    wifiConnect("Co", "SSID", "password", NULL, NULL);
    while (wifiStatus != 1010)
    {
        vTaskDelay(10 / portTICK_PERIOD_MS);
    };

    char buffer1[4000];
    char url[] = "192.168.253.75";
    char path[] = "/";
    Page pagetemp1 = initPage("PUT", "80", url, path,
                            buffer1, 4000, "20.34C");
    doPage(&pagetemp1);
```

```
    while (true)
    {
        if (pagetemp1.done)
        {
            printf("\nrequest \n %s\n", buffer1);
            pagetemp1.done = false;
            break;
        }
    };
    vTaskDelete(NULL);
}
```

You can see that the payload is "20.34C" and this could be used by the server to update a variable which is then used by other clients to discover what the temperature is using a GET. You can try the program out from folder ClientPUT.

The server simply has to respond to the PUT request and convert the bytes to a string and then a float.

A Python program that acts as a basic server is simple, server.py in folder ClientPUT:

```
from http.server import HTTPServer, BaseHTTPRequestHandler
from io import BytesIO
temp=100.1234
class SimpleHTTPRequestHandler(BaseHTTPRequestHandler):
    def do_GET(self):
        self.send_response(200)
        self.end_headers()
        global temp
        print(round(temp,2))
        self.wfile.write(str(round(temp,2)).encode("utf-8"))
    def do_PUT(self):
        global temp
        content_length = int(self.headers['Content-Length'])
        body = self.rfile.read(content_length)
        bodyString= body.decode(encoding="utf-8")
        temp=float(bodyString)
        print(round(temp,2))
        self.send_response(200)
        self.end_headers()
httpd = HTTPServer(('', 80), SimpleHTTPRequestHandler)
httpd.serve_forever()
```

This server will receive a temperature from the PUT client and send it to a GET client. Of course this could be made much more sophisticated. Also notice that POST works in the same way.

Binary PUT

It is often thought that HTTP is a text based protocol. This is true as far as the headers go, but the payload can be binary – or octets in the jargon of IP. Creating a PUT request client is fairly easy as all we really have to do is modify our existing program to send fixed length buffers rather than strings. This is a trivial modification. First we need to update the Page struct so that it records the length of the senddata:

```
typedef struct
{
    char *req;
    char *port;
    char *url;
    char *path;
    char *buffer;
    int len;
    char *senddata;
    int lensenddata;
    bool done;
} Page;
Page initPage(char req[], char port[], char url[], char path[],
char buffer[], int len, char *senddata, int lensenddata)
{
    Page page;
    page.req = req;
    page.url = url;
    page.path = path;
    page.port = port;
    page.buffer = buffer;
    page.len = len;
    page.senddata = senddata;
    page.lensenddata = lensenddata;
    page.done = false;
    return page;
}
```

Next we need to update the construction of the request array to use the length:

```
    char headerTemplate[] = "%s %s HTTP/1.1\r\n"
                            "HOST:%s:%s\r\n"
                            "Connection: close\r\n"
                            "Content-length: %d\r\n\r\n%s";
    int len = snprintf(NULL, 0, headerTemplate, page->req,
        page->path, page->url, page->port, page->lensenddata,
                                            page->senddata);
    char *requestData = malloc(len + 1);
    snprintf(requestData, len + 1, headerTemplate, page->req,
        page->path, page->url, page->port, page→lensenddata,
                                            page->senddata);
    int n = write(sockfd, requestData, len + 1);
```

The start of the main function can call the new doPage with binary data:

```
char buffer1[4000];
char url[] = "192.168.253.75";
char path[] = "/";
char senddata[] = {0xFF, 0x55, 0xF0, 0x0F, 0xFF};
Page pagetemp1 = initPage("PUT", "80", url, path,
                          buffer1, 4000, senddata, 5);
doPage(&pagetemp1);
```

The full program is in folder ClientPutBinary

If you change the PUT handler in the Python server given earlier to read, file server.py in folder ClientPutBinary:

```
def do_PUT(self):
    global temp
    content_length = int(self.headers['Content-Length'])
    body = self.rfile.read(content_length)
    print(body)
    self.send_response(200)
    self.end_headers()
```

Then you will see:

b'\xffU\xf0\x0f\xff'

Using PUT, or equivalently POST, you can send any data you want to a server and enable any number of clients to connect and collect the update. This is, of course exactly what protocols such as MQTT allow you to do, see Chapter 15. While there are many advantages of standardized protocols being able to implement an optimized custom protocol has its attractions.

Summary

- A server has to wait for a client to connect by listening on a socket.

- When a client connects, the server receives a new socket which it uses to communicate with the client.

- The server can process clients in a simple polling loop. This limits the server to handling one client at a time.

- An alternative is to start a new task each time a client connects. This is slightly more complicated, but it allows the server to deal with more than one client at a time.

- The IDF provides a server component that you can use to implement an event driven server.

- If you need to send data to another device, you can use PUT and POST to avoid having to implement a server.

Chapter 9

Details of Cryptography

Until quite recently the average programmer could easily avoid having to worry about cryptography but the insistence on web servers using HTTPS has changed all of this. Today almost every programmer needs to have a grasp of what cryptography is all about and how to make use of it. In this chapter we look at the basics of practical cryptography.

Cryptography is hard and you need to be an expert to implement almost any of its methods. However you also need to be something of an expert to understand what the choices are in making use of a library like mbedTLS. This chapter is a collection of theory and practice concerning the various things you have to get right to ensure that you are using the cryptography provided by the library in a secure way. This is by no means a complete or advanced treatment and at the end of the chapter there is still much to know but you should be able to appreciate some of the difficulties in achieving and maintaining security. It's a "get you started" practical guide.

The ESP32 IDF supports two different encryption packages, mbedTLS and wolfSSL. Only mbedTLS is included as standard and it is the one used in the rest of this chapter. The ESP32 IDF provides its own encryption functions to wrap the most commonly used functions in making a TLS connection, i.e. HTTPS, and these make using mbedTLS and wolfSSL very similar.

The Problem of Random Numbers

One of the requirements of IoT devices that are intended for anything other than personal or experimental use is that the device is secure. The best way to do this is to use a well-known and widely-used cryptographic library such as mbedTLS. If you do this you can claim "uses industry standard encryption". Unfortunately all of the security rests on the foundation of a good random number source.

The reason for this is not difficult to see. The random numbers are used to generate the key used in the symmetric key encryption used to transmit the bulk of the data between client and server. The public and private key encryption, which doesn't rely on a random number generation, is secure, as long as you keep the private key secret and as long as it has enough bits to make working it out from the public key, or guessing it, difficult.

Symmetric key encryption, on the other hand, is vulnerable to simply guessing the key. You can try to decrypt the data using trial keys until you get something intelligible as plain text. Again, this is difficult as long as the key has enough bits and has been chosen at random. However, if the random number generator has any statistical flaws then the search space of trial keys can be much reduced. For example, any random number generator that delivers more zeros than ones cuts the search space in half. If you can find enough statistical irregularities you can reduce the initial huge search space into something more reasonable.

In short, the security of symmetric key encryption depends on the quality of the random number generator.

The question is how much quality do you need in a random number generator? In practice, the chance of a device being hacked due to a not-quite-perfect random number generator is small because it generally isn't worth the effort and there are lots of easier ways to compromise a system, especially if you have physical access to it. However, there is also the matter of how things are presented. Some users are very security-conscious and the only reasonable way of satisfying them is to use industry standard encryption with industry standard best practices. If you have to state "we use a standard cryptographic library but use a homemade random number generator" then confidence will be dented.

To make use of TLS you have to provide a random number generator, `mbedtls_hardware_poll`, to ensure the key exchange works. A standard implementation of `mbedtls_hardware_poll` is made available with the hardware random number generator `esp_random`. However, this doesn't mean you can ignore the problem. Random numbers are important and understanding the problem is worth the investment.

Pseudo Randomness

The first distinction to be made is the difference between a pseudo-random number generator (PRNG) and a true random number generator. The former is just an algorithm that produces numbers that "look" random. Each number occurs with equal frequency and there is no connection between the numbers generated that would help you predict one from the other. For example, while a simple for loop generates numbers that are equally probable 0,1,2,3,4,5,6,7,8,9 and so on, it is a very poor pseudo-random number generator because as soon as I tell you the current value is 5 you can work out the that the next number is 6.

Clearly the difficulty here is in defining what method we can use to predict the values. If you know the algorithm in use you can always predict the next or any value that will be produced. In this sense no pseudo-random number generator is truly random.

The sequence that a PRNG produces depends on where it is started from. The starting value is usually called the "seed" and starting from a fixed seed always produces the same sequence. There are some situations where this is useful and others where it is definitely to be avoided. For example, if you are programming a card game using a PRNG and use the same seed to start it off each time the program is run, the players will be subjected to the same sequence of cards. In this case, you need some mechanism to select a different seed each time the program is run. On the other hand, if you are testing a set of alternatives to see how they perform then using the same sequence of pseudo-random numbers for each test is much more informative than using truly random numbers.

Even though pseudo-random numbers are generated by an algorithm, we can still perform statistical tests on them and look for statistical relationships that can help with guessing the next number. For example, if the PRNG tends to produce an odd number after an even number then we can use this to improve our guessing of the next number. However, if you know the type of PRNG being used then you might be able to use a small sample of random numbers to work out exactly what is being used and hence predict all of the subsequent numbers exactly. This defect is not shared by hardware random number generators.

There are many approaches to creating a PRNG, but two are particularly important for small machines and form the basis for most complicated algorithms – the Linear Congruential Generator (LCG) and the Linear-Feedback Shift Register (LFSR). In both cases, given samples of random numbers from the generator you can work out its exact setup and generate subsequent numbers accurately.

The standard C function rand is an LCG PRNG. The call:

```
r = rand();
```

returns the next integer in the sequence. If you want to set a seed then you use:

```
srand(seed);
```

If you don't specify seed then 1 is used and rand produces a sequence that is so well known it is listed and recognized by The On-Line Encyclopedia of Integer Sequences. It may have random properties, but it is still well known and anyone recognizing it can easily give you any values in the sequence in any order. In fact, the version of rand supplied with the IDF fails most of the tests of randomness.

There is also the POSIX pseudo-random number generator, random(). If you need high quality random numbers this should be avoided as it too fails most of the standard tests for randomness.

Hardware Random Generator

The obvious thing to do to obtain a cryptographic random number generator is to use hardware to produce real physical random numbers. Truly random numbers are not predictable, no matter how many samples you take and even if you know how they are generated. In this sense a perfect hardware random number generator (HRNG) is what we need. Of course, any physicist will tell you that the only source of truly random numbers is quantum mechanics. Some electronic devices can generate randomness based on quantum effects, but in practice you generally don't need to be so esoteric. We regularly treat complex physical systems as if they were truly random. When you toss a coin you regard the outcome as random, but in principle if you could measure the initial position of the coin, the force used to propel it into the air and the disposition of the ground, you could work out which side it would land on. In practice, of course, you can't and there are physical systems that are so sensitive to the initial conditions that, even if you knew them, accurate prediction would be difficult. In this sense even physical sources or randomness only produce pseudo-random numbers – if you knew the generating algorithm you could predict them. In practice of course you don't and you can't and so hardware-generated random numbers are what we need.

In practice, physical sources of noise or entropy can be very simple. For example, you can take readings from an analog to digital converter that isn't connected to anything or measure the voltage on a reverse-biased diode. The problem with all such ideas is that they are easily spoiled by interactions with the outside world. For example, reading data from an unconnected A-to-D is vulnerable to whatever coherent signal the input picks up, as it acts as an aerial. Similarly timers, often used as sources of random bits, no matter how erratic they tend to be, show short range correlations in output.

In short, actually designing a good physical source of entropy that provides good random numbers is much more difficult than theory suggests. A hardware source of random numbers that has statistical regularities can be predicted in the same way that imperfect pseudo-random numbers can.

Cryptographic Random Generator

Now that we have considered the two major types of random number generators and their strengths and failings we can consider what would make a good generator. A cryptographic random number generator (CRNG) is usually defined as one where it has been proved that any algorithm that can predict the $n+1$ value with a better than 50% chance of being right, given n values, has to take more than polynomial time. The idea is that even if there is a prediction method, it will be so slow as to be impractical.

A second condition requires that, even if part of its internal state has been revealed or guessed, it should be impossible to reconstruct the sequence. This means that a congruential generator (LCG) is ruled out on both counts, as is an LFSR. Just appearing to be random isn't enough to be a CRNG. You have to have a cast iron guarantee that no matter how many samples are gathered you cannot deduce the algorithm used to generate them in anything like a reasonable time.

A CRNG not only has to pass the first test of appearing to be random, it also has to not reveal details of how the values are generated. It might seem that any algorithmic method of generating random numbers cannot be a CRNG as there is an algorithm to be discovered. However, there are provably secure CRNGs based on mathematical problems known to be hard to solve. For example, the Blum Blum Shub algorithm produces a sequence based on the quadratic residue problem, which is not solvable in polynomial time. In this case, having a sample from the sequence is provably difficult to reverse-engineer, in the sense that it would take an attacker too long to go from values in the sequence to the parameters of the mechanism that created it.

In short, algorithmic CRNGs do exist. However, while it is good to know that such things exist, they are mostly not practical for IoT use due to their computational demands.

An additional consideration, not normally discussed in the literature, is that in many cases an IoT device is in the hands of the end user. That is, IoT devices are generally not physically secure. What this means is that, if you program a cryptographically sound random number generator, it is only a matter of time before someone reverse-engineers your device, and the details of the generator are accurately known, including the configuration parameters. Consequently, any pseudo-random number generator, cryptographically secure or not, is insecure when installed in an IoT device.

The only practical approach is to make use of an algorithm to improve the statistical qualities of a hardware-based random number generator. In this case you can make the argument that the good statistical qualities makes it difficult for an attacker to guess the next number and even if they had a set of numbers from the sequence the hardware generated component makes this knowledge useless in predicting future values.

What all this means is that, contrary to what you will often read, for an IoT device the task is not to install a CRNG that is provably secure, but to improve any HRNG sufficiently to make it pass a battery of statistical tests of randomness.

There are three general approaches to enhancing a hardware source of randomness:

1. You can use a randomness extractor – an algorithm that makes the HRNG even more random. For example, you could XOR the output of the HRNG with the output of a good PRNG. Even if you know the details of the PRNG, you still can't reliably predict subsequent numbers.

2. Hash functions and encryption methods are designed to break up patterns in the source text and these can be applied to the output of a HRNG to improve its statistical properties. This is the reason you will often encounter the strange idea of encrypting, or hashing, hardware generated random numbers. You can use multiple HRNGs and combine them together to produce numbers with better statistical properties. This is often called using an entropy pool and it is an approach that has become very popular – Linux uses it, for example, to implement dev/random and dev/urandom.

Testing Random Numbers

Before you decide to use any random number generator you need to either test it yourself or rely on tests already performed to confirm that it is indeed generating random numbers. While there are a number of libraries of testing software, they are poorly supported. The best known are diehard, dieharder and the NIST. None of them are particularly easy to use, but at least if your random numbers pass enough of the NIST suite you can claim that you are using something that conforms to the National Institute of Standards and Technology.

To test random numbers you need to generate a large sample – 100,000 or more - and consider the potential weaknesses of the generator according to the tests that they fail.

Harnessing Entropy

The ESP32 makes use of a number of hardware sources of entropy to make its random number generator close to truly random. Unfortunately, the documentation of how it all works, and how to make use of it, is very confusing. However, the good news is that most of the time, and without even trying too hard, the quality of the random numbers is very good and they pass all relevant NIST tests.

The hardware of the generator is very simple and it merges three entropy sources with a software random number generator:

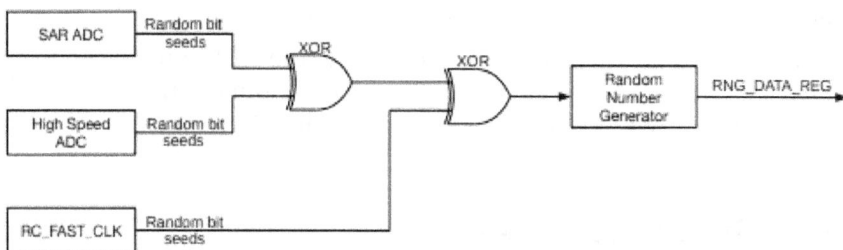

As long as one of the entropy sources is available, then the random numbers are high quality and pass the NIST tests. If there are no sources then the random number generator fails most of the tests.

The High Speed ADC, or ADC2, is automatically enabled if you use the ESP32's WiFi or Bluetooth, but the SAR ADC or ADC1 has to be explicitly enabled. According to the documentation, the RC_FAST_CLK, the Internal 8MHz RC Oscillator, is always connected.

You can enable/disable the ADC entropy sources using:

```
#include "bootloader_random.h"
bootloader_random_enable();
bootloader_random_disable();
```

If you disable the ADC then the "secondary source" is still active:

> "ESP32-S3 RNG contains a secondary entropy source, based on sampling an asynchronous 8 MHz internal oscillator (see the Technical Reference Manual for details). This entropy source is always enabled in ESP-IDF and is continuously mixed into the RNG state by hardware."

The documentation then goes on to say:

> *"However, it is currently only guaranteed that true random numbers are produced when the main entropy source is also enabled as described above."*

The documentation goes on to claim that just using secondary entropy the random numbers passed the Dieharder tests. They also pass all of the relevant NIST tests.

There also seems to be no way of turning off the secondary source of entropy, despite instructions being given to do just this in the documentation.

In short, no matter how you configure the random number hardware it produces random numbers that pass the NIST tests.

If you want to be extra cautious you can enable the ADC entropy sources, but this poses additional problems if you are also going to use WiFi/Bluetooth or ADC1 when you have to disable these entropy sources.

ESP32 IDF Randomness

There are two functions that get random numbers from the ESP32 hardware random number generator:

- ◆ `uint32_t esp_random(void)`
- ◆ `void esp_fill_random(void *buf, size_t len)`

which return 32 bit random numbers

The random number function that mbedTLS uses, as defined in `components\mbedtls\port\esp_hardware.c`, is:

```
int mbedtls_hardware_poll( void *data,
            unsigned char *output, size_t len, size_t *olen )
{
    esp_fill_random(output, len);
    *olen = len;
    return 0;
}
```

Random numbers are the foundation of good security, but what you do with them also matters.

Symmetric Encryption

The most basic form of encryption is symmetric key encryption. This is where a single key is used to encrypt and decrypt data. Symmetric encryption is fast and efficient, but it suffers from one very big drawback – you have to get the private key from the originator of the message to the receiver of the message. This is the key exchange problem and it is mostly solved by asymmetric key encryption also known as public key cryptography, which is the subject of the next chapter in its application to HTTPS.

We can use a symmetric encryption algorithm and assume that the problem of key exchange has been solved in some way or other. For an IoT device, using symmetric encryption has the advantage that you are only using a cheap-to-produce random key and not a public/private key pair. In this way each device can have its own encryption key rather than a single key being used by all devices. Of course, we still have the standard problem that if the IoT device is physically in the hands of an attacker then any key is easy enough to discover. If you're using a system where each device generates a fixed random key, at least its discovery would not compromise other devices. More importantly, using your own symmetric encryption allows you to send the data over any type of connection, not just HTTPS, and store it safely on unsecured devices. As long as the key is kept private, then so is the data. Of course, the flip side of this is that if you lose the key you have also lost the data.

In this example, the encryption method used is AES, which is still considered to be strong and effectively uncrackable, as long as you use a large key size. At the time of writing, 128-bit and 256-bit keys are considered secure when used in conjunction with best practices. The keys cannot be broken from a sample of the encrypted text, but you can weaken them by accidentally providing information about them.

AES encryption is a block cipher which means that it encrypts a fixed size buffer of plain text. Any plain text has to be broken into blocks of the correct size and any that are too small have to be padded to make a complete block. There are a number of standard ways of padding a block, but usually mbedTLS will do the job for you.

There are a number of small variations or modes of AES that modify how blocks are processed. The simplest is ECB or Electronic Codebook Block. This is simple, but it is no longer used as it is insecure in a very obvious way. It simply makes use of the key to encrypt each block in turn. The problem with this is that if you encrypt two identical blocks then the cipher text will also be identical and this can be noticed by an attacker and used to infer information. Even so, it is worth implementing AES using ECB as an example because it is so simple.

Configuring Symmetric Encryption

If you are using mbedTLS directly, configuring it using its configuration file is very difficult with a range of interlocking options. The ESP32 IDF has done a lot of work to make it much easier to use. To configure each mbedTLS component you can use the relevant section in the SDK Configuration Editor (menuconfig). The Symmetric Ciphers section, as its name suggests, lets you select which ciphers and modifications to ciphers the software supports:

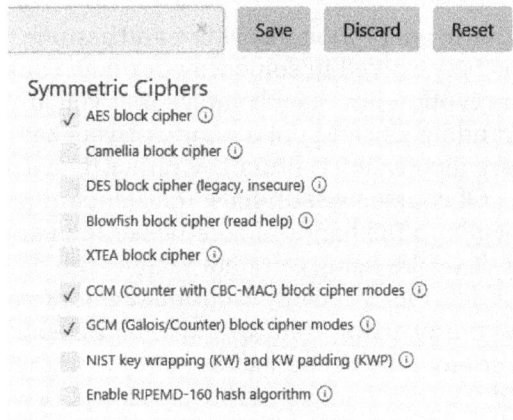

For the rest of this chapter we need AES, CCM and GCM selected. You can try out any of the other ciphers using slight modifications.

AES ECB Encryption Decryption

Using any of the encryption methods supported by mbedtls follows similar lines.

Encryption is controlled by a cipher_context struct which needs to be set to appropriate values for the encryption being used:

```
mbedtls_cipher_context_t cipher_ctx;
mbedtls_cipher_init(&cipher_ctx);
```

The latest version of mbedTLS has made structs like this private and there are access functions to read its fields:

- mbedtls_cipher_get_block_size
- mbedtls_cipher_get_cipher_mode
- mbedtls_cipher_get_iv_size
- mbedtls_cipher_get_type
- mbedtls_cipher_get_name
- mbedtls_cipher_get_key_bitlen
- mbedtls_cipher_get_operation

The most important field in the context is a `cipher_info` struct that defines the operation of a particular encryption method. To use a particular method you have to first retrieve its `cipher_info` struct and use this to set the `cipher_context` struct. There are a set of access functions that work with `cipher_info`:

- `mbedtls_cipher_info_get_block_size`
- `mbedtls_cipher_info_get_cipher_mode`
- `mbedtls_cipher_info_get_iv_size`
- `mbedtls_cipher_info_get_type`
- `mbedtls_cipher_info_get_name`
- `mbedtls_cipher_info_get_key_bitlen`

There are a number of functions which return an `info` struct specified in different ways:

Setting `info` from `type` involves using one of the predefined macros like:

`mbedtls_cipher_info_from_type(MBEDTLS_CIPHER_AES_128_ECB)`

which you can see a list of in `cipher.h`.

Setting it from `string` involves using strings like

`mbedtls_cipher_info_from_string("AES-128-ECB")`

The option to set the encryption from `values` lets you specify what you want in three parts:

`mbedtls_cipher_info_from_values(MBEDTLS_CIPHER_ID_AES,128, MBEDTLS_MODE_ECB)`

Use whichever is most convenient.

To connect the `info` to the `context` use `mbedtls_cipher_setup`. Putting this together gives:

```
mbedtls_cipher_context_t cipher_ctx;
const mbedtls_cipher_info_t *cipher_info;
cipher_info = mbedtls_cipher_info_from_string("AES-128-ECB");
ret = mbedtls_cipher_setup(&cipher_ctx, cipher_info);
```

Notice that setup only stores a pointer to info and so you have to keep the struct alive while using context.

You can see that for this example we have selected `AES-128-ECB`. This means that we need to create a 16-byte 128-bit key and we can use the `fill_random` function introduced earlier:

```
unsigned char key[16];
esp_fill_random(key, 16);
```

To use the key we have to store it in the `cipher_context` struct:

```
ret = mbedtls_cipher_setkey(&cipher_ctx, key,
    mbedtls_cipher_get_key_bitlen(&cipher_ctx), MBEDTLS_ENCRYPT);
```

We could have specified the key length as 128, but retrieving it from the `cipher_ctx` struct makes this more general. Also notice that we set the encryption direction at this point with `MBEDTLS_ENCRYPT`, i.e. plain text to cipher text.

Notice that the key size is set in bits.

Now we are all set to start encoding some data, but as this is a block cipher we have to initialize the `cipher_context` struct to be ready to process the first block as it keeps track of the number of bytes encoded:

```
ret = mbedtls_cipher_reset(&cipher_ctx);
```

You can now start encrypting blocks of bytes but, as this is a block cipher, you have to supply 16-byte blocks of data. The function to use is:

```
ret = mbedtls_cipher_update(&cipher_ctx, buffer,
                                     ilen, output, &olen);
```

where `buffer` has the plain text block and is `ilen` long and `output` is the computed cipher text and is `olen` long. For AES ECB both `ilen` and `olen` are 16, but this isn't generally true. If you pass a block smaller than the block size then the function returns an error. It is perfectly acceptable to pad the block with zeros, which is what happens if you use a C string in a fixed size `char` array.

As an example, we can encode a single 16-byte block:

```
char buffer[16] = "Hello World";
char output[16];
int olen;
ret = mbedtls_cipher_update(&cipher_ctx, buffer, 16,
                                     output, &olen);
```

You can add additional blocks to the buffer by calling `update` as often as you need to.

We can decrypt the cipher text just as easily:

```
 u_char plaintext[16];
 ret = mbedtls_cipher_setkey(&cipher_ctx, key,
 mbedtls_cipher_get_key_bitlen(&cipher_ctx), MBEDTLS_DECRYPT);
 ret = mbedtls_cipher_reset(&cipher_ctx);
 mbedtls_cipher_update(&cipher_ctx, output, 16,
                                     plaintext, &olen);
```

You can see that this follows the same steps and the only difference is that it is set to `MBEDTLS_DECRYPT`. Also notice that we don't really need to set the key again but you do have to use the function to set the `DECRYPT` option.

Putting all this together, in folder AES, with some instructions to display the cipher text and the reconstructed plain text, gives:

```
#include <stdio.h>
#include "freertos/FreeRTOS.h"
#include "esp_random.h"
#include "esp_tls.h"
#include "mbedtls\cipher.h"

void app_main(void)
{
    int ret;
    mbedtls_cipher_context_t cipher_ctx;
    const mbedtls_cipher_info_t *cipher_info;
    cipher_info = mbedtls_cipher_info_from_string("AES-128-ECB");
    ret = mbedtls_cipher_setup(&cipher_ctx, cipher_info);

    unsigned char key[16];
    esp_fill_random(key, 16);
    ret = mbedtls_cipher_setkey(&cipher_ctx, key,
            mbedtls_cipher_get_key_bitlen(&cipher_ctx),
                MBEDTLS_ENCRYPT);

    ret = mbedtls_cipher_reset(&cipher_ctx);

    u_char buffer[16] = "Hello World";
    u_char output[16];
    size_t olen;
    ret = mbedtls_cipher_update(&cipher_ctx, buffer,
                                        16, output, &olen);
    printf("cipher text ");
    for (int i = 0; i < olen; i++)
    {
        printf("%02X", output[i]);
    }
    printf("\n");

    u_char plaintext[16];
    ret = mbedtls_cipher_setkey(&cipher_ctx, key,
            mbedtls_cipher_get_key_bitlen(&cipher_ctx),
                    MBEDTLS_DECRYPT);
    ret = mbedtls_cipher_reset(&cipher_ctx);
    mbedtls_cipher_update(&cipher_ctx, output,
                                16, plaintext, &olen);
    printf("plain text %.16s\n", plaintext);
}
```

If you try it out you will see the plain text and cipher text displayed. You can extend the program to process multiple blocks, but notice that they all have to be 16 bytes. To send or save the encrypted data, all you have to do is concatenate them into a larger block. As long as the decryption client can split them into blocks and has the key, everything works. Also notice that in this mode you can encrypt and decrypt blocks in any order as they are independent of one another and this means you can use parallel operations to speed things up.

AES CBC Mode

The previous program generates cipher text that is difficult to decrypt unless you have the key, but it doesn't do a good job of hiding the information. The problem is that if you encrypt two identical blocks you generate identical cipher text. In some situations this isn't a big security problem. In others it can invalidate the attempt at encryption. The best known example is using the ECB mode to encrypt an image:

Despite this image being encrypted using AES ECB you can see that it is the Linux mascot, Tux. The problem is that for an image the encryption has only managed to change the color of each of the encrypted blocks.

There are a number of block-encryption modes that solve the problem by adding known, but variable, data to each block before it is encrypted. The simplest is CBC, Cipher Block Chaining. This XORs the previous cipher text with the plain text before encrypting it. This means that even if you encrypt the same plain text you get a different result. Decryption is still possible as you simply decrypt the block and then XOR it with the plain text of the previous block to recover the plain text. The only problem is what do you do about getting the process started, i.e. what do you XOR with the first block? The answer is that you have to provide an Initialization Vector (IV) which acts as a block zero and is XORed with the plain text of the first block. This also has to be made available to anyone wanting to decrypt a set of blocks.

Changing our previous program to use CBC is fairly simple. First we need to select an CBC encryption:

```
mbedtls_cipher_context_t cipher_ctx;
const mbedtls_cipher_info_t *cipher_info;
cipher_info = mbedtls_cipher_info_from_string("AES-128-CBC");
ret = mbedtls_cipher_setup(&cipher_ctx, cipher_info);
```

We have to create an IV and this can be just 16 bytes of random data:

```
unsigned char IV[16];
esp_fill_random(IV, 16);
ret = mbedtls_cipher_set_iv(&cipher_ctx, IV,
                    mbedtls_cipher_get_iv_size(&cipher_ctx));
```

Notice that now we have to store the IV in the `cipher_context` struct.

After this the rest of the program is identical. The IV is used to encrypt the first block and then after that `mbedtls` automatically uses the cipher text block to XOR with the current plain text. You can start the process over using the IV again by calling the `mbedtls_cipher_reset` function which you can think of as starting the chain of blocks.

To decrypt the blocks you have to process them in the order that they were created and you need the IV used to start the chain off:

```
u_char plaintext[16];
ret = mbedtls_cipher_setkey(&cipher_ctx, key,
     mbedtls_cipher_get_key_bitlen(&cipher_ctx), MBEDTLS_DECRYPT);
ret = mbedtls_cipher_set_iv(&cipher_ctx, IV,
                            mbedtls_cipher_get_iv_size(&cipher_ctx));
ret = mbedtls_cipher_reset(&cipher_ctx);
mbedtls_cipher_update(&cipher_ctx, output, 16, plaintext, &olen);
printf("plain text %.16s\n", plaintext);
```

There is no need to worry about padding when using CBC mode as `mbedtls` will add bytes to make the block up to full size.

The full modified program is in folder `AESCBC`. If you try it you will see the plain text and cipher text displayed as before. If you use the program to encrypt Tux then the result would look like random noise and you will have successfully hidden the patterns in the blocks.

Notice that as each block depends on the previous block you cannot parallelize the encryption. However, as each block is XORed with the cipher text of the previous block you can parallelize decryption and to decrypt a block all you need is the previous encrypted block and the key.

CTR, CCM, and GCM Modes

There are a great many variations on how block ciphers are applied to data, their so-called "modes". As well as CBC, it is worth knowing about CTR, CCM, and GCM modes as these are commonly encountered.

CTR, CounTeR, mode seems to turn the encryption on its head. It takes a reproducible sequence of numbers and encrypts these rather than the plain text. The final cipher text is generated by XORing the plain text with the encrypted sequence. This is a form of "one-time pad" and it is provably secure as long as the sequence is kept secure. Of course, in this case the sequence is usually generated by a simple algorithm and hence it is possible for it to be discovered. To make this less likely, an IV is used to make the encryption more secure. The IV is appended to the counter, encrypted and XORed with the plain text. To decrypt the cipher text all you need is the IV and the key and, of course, knowledge of how the counter sequence was generated. Surprisingly most CTR modes use a sequential block count, i.e. 0, 1, 2, 3 and so on. The argument is that any weakness that this might create is a problem with the encryption algorithm, not the regular sequence used, as the encryption is supposed to mask any regularities in the plain text.

There are two other modes in common use and they improve over CBC and CTR by making it possible to authenticate the data. Using AES in ECB or CBC provides security, but it does nothing to authenticate the data. If any transmission errors occur, or if an attacker changes the data, the blocks will still decrypt without any indication of a problem, but the recovered plain text will be incorrect.

The obvious solution is to include a hash of the plain text in the cipher text and use this to detect any modifications to the data. There are many possible ways of doing this, but one of the most commonly encountered is CCM, (Counter with cipher block Chaining Message) mode, a modification of CTR mode. First a Message Authentication Code (MAC) is computed, specifically a CBC-MAC. This works by starting with an IV of zero and performing the usual CBC algorithm, i.e. XOR the IV with the plain text and then encrypt, using the resulting cipher text as the IV for the next block. The MAC is the final block. You can see that this is usable as a MAC as it depends in a complex way on all of the plain text. After this the plain text and the MAC are encrypted using CTR mode. The cipher text can be decrypted using CTR mode with the key and IV and the plain text can be checked by computing the MAC and comparing it to the original. CCM is used in IEEE 802.11 as part of WPA2, IPSec VPN, TLS 1.2 and BLE. It is also used in the Zigbee standard with extensions.

A widely used alternative GCM, Galois Counter Mode, is based on similar ideas. It uses CTR mode for encryption, but the MAC is computed using a sophisticated hash function based on a polynomial field which is beyond the scope of this book. However, you can make use of GCM with mbedTLS without needing to understand the mathematics as AES GCM is one of the available options. GCM is used in IEEE 802.1, IPSec VPN, SSH, TLS 1.2 and 1.3.

Encryption Methods

There are lots of other functions to explore, but using them to implement any cryptographic task follows the same general lines as the AES encryption example given earlier. For example, computing a hash value is very similar to implementing AES encryption but calling functions which are specific to hashing.

One useful technique is to find out what encryption types are supported, folder encryptlist:

```
#include <stdio.h>
#include "freertos/FreeRTOS.h"
#include "esp_random.h"
#include "esp_tls.h"
#include "mbedtls\cipher.h"

void app_main(void)
{

    const mbedtls_cipher_info_t *cipher_info;
    const int *list;
    printf("Available ciphers:\n");
    list = mbedtls_cipher_list();
    while (*list)
    {
        cipher_info = mbedtls_cipher_info_from_type(*list);
        printf("  %s\n",
                mbedtls_cipher_info_get_name(cipher_info));
        list++;
    }
}
```

A typical output from this is:

```
Available ciphers:
 AES-128-ECB
 AES-192-ECB
 AES-256-ECB
 AES-128-CBC
 AES-192-CBC
 AES-256-CBC
 AES-128-CCM
 AES-192-CCM
 AES-256-CCM
```

and so on.

The Password Problem

The simplest method of ensuring that a user has the authority to make a change to the way a program works is to ask them to set a password during initialization and then to supply the password to get permission to make a change. The problem is that, to validate the password, you have to store it as part of the program and this means that the password is essentially public knowledge. Anyone with access to the device would find it comparatively easy to reverse-engineer the code and find the password.

The solution to the problem is to not store the password at all. The usual approach is to compute a hash of the password. A hash function is a function that accepts data as its input and outputs a fixed size value that summarizes the data:

`h = hash(data)`

As the data is generally much larger than the hash, the value cannot be unique and it has to be possible that different data give the same hash – this is called a collision. A good hash function can be used to detect if changes have been made to the data without a detailed examination. If the data has changed the hash value will be different.

A good hash function has the smallest number of collisions and collisions should show no patterns that allow a user to work out a collision given a hash. That is, if:

`h1 = hash(data1)`

then a good hash function will make it very difficult to find a `data2` that has the same hash:

`h1 = hash(data2)`

Given a suitable hash function, we can now implement password protection without storing a password. What we do is compute a hash when the password is set and save that instead. When the user presents the password we again compute the hash and compare it to the stored hash. If the password is correct then the hash values will match. Of course, the hash value can now be found by an attacker, but this doesn't matter as much as the attacker now has to present not the hash but the password that produces the hash. As long as it is very difficult to find a collision with the given hash value, the system is secure against the hash value becoming public.

This is the case for hash functions such as SHA-256 and they can be used to implement password protection. To make it very secure you have to implement it with care. In particular, to avoid brute force attacks, you have to use a "salt" value, a random string which is concatenated with the password before the hash is computed:

h = hash(password+salt)

The salt is randomly generated for each password and stored along with the hash:

h,salt

That is, with salt the same password produces different hash values each time it is used. This prevents the construction of hash lookup tables for common passwords.

When it comes to password protection the details matter.

Implementing SH256

MbedTLS supports a range of hashing methods including the very common SH256. You can select which hashing methods it supports using the SDK Configuration Editor, menuconfig:

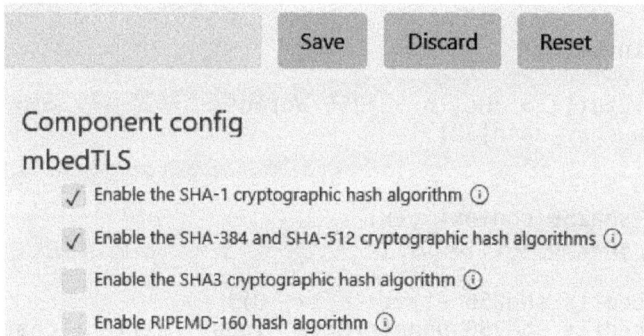

Using mbedTLS for hashing is very similar to using it to encrypt/decrypt data.

You first have to create and initialize a hash context:

```
mbedtls_sha256_context ctx;
mbedtls_sha256_init(&ctx);
```

Once you have done this you can use the context to hash a stream of bytes. Before you can begin you need to start the hash hardware:

```
ret = mbedtls_sha256_starts(&ctx, 0);
```

The final parameter specifies SHA256 or SHA224, by being set to 0 or 1 respectively. Only one hash context can be started at any given time.

Now you can start to hash bytes:

```
ret = mbedtls_sha256_update(&ctx, input, strlen(input));
```

where *input* is a string of byte characters. You can carry on updating the hash with more data by calling the update as many times as you want. When you have added all of the data to the hash you can ask for the final value:

```
ret = mbedtls_sha256_finish(&ctx, hash);
```

where *hash* is a 32-byte array.

If you have finished with the hash context you can free it with:

```
 mbedtls_sha256_free(&ctx);
```

The ESP 32 has an SHA256 hardware accelerator which mbedTLS makes use of unless you explicitly tell it not to.

A complete demonstration program in folder Hash which hashes a single string is:

```
#include <stdio.h>
#include "freertos/FreeRTOS.h"
#include "esp_random.h"
#include "esp_tls.h"
#include <string.h>
#include "mbedtls/sha256.h"

void app_main(void)
{
    u_char input[] = "Hello SHA256 World";
    unsigned char hash[32];
    int ret;

    mbedtls_sha256_context ctx;
    mbedtls_sha256_init(&ctx);

    ret = mbedtls_sha256_starts(&ctx, 0);
    ret = mbedtls_sha256_update(&ctx, input, strlen((char*)input));
    ret = mbedtls_sha256_finish(&ctx, hash);

    printf("Input string: \"%s\"\n", input);
    printf("SHA256 Hash: ");
    for (int i = 0; i < 32; i++)
    {
        printf("%02X", hash[i]);
    }
    printf("\n");
    mbedtls_sha256_free(&ctx);
}
```

There is also a utility function which starts the hardware, hashes a buffer and frees the context:

```
ret = mbedtls_sha256(input, strlen(input), hash, 0);
```

Summary

- Having a good source of random numbers is a key component of practical cryptography.

- Pseudo-random number generators create numbers that "look" random in the sense that it is difficult to predict the next number without knowledge of the way they are generated.

- Hardware random number generators make use of apparent physical randomness to produce numbers that are difficult to predict.

- Cryptographic generators are essentially pseudo-random number generators with a proof that the sequence cannot be predicted in a reasonable time, even if you know the details of the generator.

- Hardware generators, the best choice for small machines, suffer from not being perfectly random, but can be improved using randomness extractors.

- The ESP32's random function is a good potential source of randomness and passes the NIST tests.

- Public key cryptography works with two keys, a private key and a public key, and hence is called asymmetric key cryptography. The public key is not secret and can be used by anyone to encrypt a text. The encrypted text can only be decrypted using the private key, which is kept secret.

- Symmetric key cryptography uses a single key, which has to be kept private to the sender and receiver, to encrypt and decrypt text.

- Symmetric key cryptography is much faster than asymmetric and so what happens is that asymmetric keys are used to establish a single secret symmetric key that both the client and server use.

- As well as implementing TLS, you can also use mbedTLS for a range of different cryptographic tasks such as symmetric key encryption without the need to implement key exchange.

- AES encryption is a block-encryption method and there are range of sub-methods concerning how the blocks are chained together to make the entire text secure.

- Passwords should never be stored. Instead a password hash with a random salt value should be used. Creating an SHA256 hash is very easy using mbedTLS.

Chapter 10

SSL/TLS and HTTPS

HTTP using TCP/IP is a simple and relatively efficient way to transport data, but it isn't secure. Today many web servers will only deliver data if it is protected by encryption and identity confirmation using HTTPS. This, and the general concern for security, causes problems for IoT programmers. Security, and encryption in particular, are not cheap in terms of the resources needed to implement them, but if you are planning to make your code available to the wider world you really don't have a choice but to implement security. There are many ways of doing this but the best advice is, if possible, don't do it from scratch. If you are not a security expert you are likely to get it wrong and make all of the effort you put into building something "secure" a waste of time. Users also like to know that your application is secure by recognizing well known standards. In short, there is a lot of pressure to use security standards even if they might be more than is actually required for an IoT device.

What this means in practice is that you most likely need to support HTTPS for web-based interactions and SSL/TLS (Secure Sockets Layer/Transport Layer Security), which is the basis of HTTPS, for other interactions. Fortunately, lwIP has a degree of integration with mbedTLS, the standard SSL/TLS library we are already familiar with.

In this chapter we look at how to use mbedTLS to create an HTTPS client, but this is just a step in using mbedTLS to implement a range of secure data transfers.

Public Key Certificates

The basis of modern security is Public Key Infrastructure, PKI. This in turn is based on the use of public key, or asymmetrical, cryptography. As discussed in the previous chapter, the simplest approach to cryptography is to use the same key for encryption as decryption. In this case, the key is private and has to be known to both the sender and the receiver and has to be kept secret from everyone else. This creates the problem of "key exchange". How can you get a key securely from the sender to the receiver of the data. In transit the key is vulnerable.

Public key cryptography is amazing because it works with two keys – a public key that anyone can know and use to encrypt a message and a private key that only the receiver knows and can be used to decrypt the message. This is asymmetrical cryptography because different keys are used for encryption and decryption. Its big advantage is that it removes the need to exchange keys. Its big disadvantage is that it is very slow. Because it is so slow and inefficient public key cryptography is used to exchange symmetric keys. That is, most of the time you are using symmetric key cryptography with keys provided by public key cryptography. Keys are generally stored in a special format that associates the keys with an identity – a certificate.

What happens is that, when a client connects to a server, the private and public keys are used to create a shared encryption key which is then used for all further communication. There are two general situations. If the server has a certificate but the client doesn't then the client generates a random number and uses the server's public key to securely send this to the server. Of course, as only the server has the private key only the server can decrypt the message and so the client and the server now have a shared secret that they can use to generate a symmetric key. The second situation is where both parties have a certificate and in this case the private and public keys available at each end of the connection are used to transport a random number to act as a shared secret.

What this means in practice is that a client doesn't need a certificate to establish secure communication. A client only needs a certificate if it needs to prove its identity. What is more, a client IoT device is less secure with a certificate that contains a private key as this has to be stored in the device and most don't have the necessary hardware to stop someone from connecting to the device and reading the key. Servers can keep their private keys secure because they are physically secure and protecting the key is a matter of software security. For most IoT devices no amount of software security can keep the key safe from a physical attack.

It is also important to know that key exchange can occur more than once in the lifetime of a connection to ensure the maximum security. The actual symmetric key encryption algorithm that is used can also be negotiated between the client and server. This all makes the connection more complicated.

Identity and Root Certificates

Encryption solves the privacy issue, but it doesn't solve the identity problem. How does the client know that the server it is connecting to is the real server and not an impostor? This is where digital certificates come into the picture as a way of proving identity. At the simplest level, a certificate is simply a container for a pair of public and private keys. More commonly, the certificate only contains the public key as having the private key stored in a separate key file allows the certificate to be shared. Certificates also contain other information about the entity that the certificate is issued to, such as name, address, domain name and so on. Obtaining a certificate is one way for a client to gain information about a server, including its public key, which allows key exchange to take place.

Certificates are also digitally signed to indicate their validity. Of course, how much trust you can put in the certificate depends on who signed it. You can easily create a certificate that you also sign – a self-signed certificate - and while this is useful as a way to supply a public key, it does nothing to prove that you are who you claim to be. To be convincing evidence of identity, a certificate has to be digitally signed by one of a number of well-known certificate-issuing authorities. The CertificateAuthority (CA) will make checks and ask for documentation that proves who you are and it makes a charge for this service.

How can you know that a CA is authentic? It is usually the case that the certificate-issuing authority has a certificate that proves its authenticity, signed by another, higher, authority. This leads to the idea of a chain of certificates which ultimately end in a signature from a trusted final authority with a certificate that is installed in most browsers and used to give the final verdict on the validity of a certificate. Following a certificate chain and validating an identity is time-consuming and resource heavy, but often necessary.

Encrypted communication doesn't require a client certificate. However, for the client to validate the server's identity, it must possess a set of trusted root certificates that verify the server's own certificate. The challenge lies in acquiring a trusted certificate from a CA. This sounds easy, but there are hundreds of root certificates. You can collect your own if you want to, but the ESP32 IDF has a certificate bundle derived from those used by the Firefox browser. This currently has 130 root certificates. As it is used by Firefox, this is likely to be enough to allow you to validate most servers. However, if you need to conserve memory, you can opt for a reduced set of just 42 which is claimed to work for 93% or all certificates and 99% of those you are likely to encounter in practice. If this is still too much memory usage, you can opt not to validate the server, i.e. not to load any root certificates, and just use encryption.

You can configure the certificate bundle using the SDK Configuration Editor, `menuconfig`:

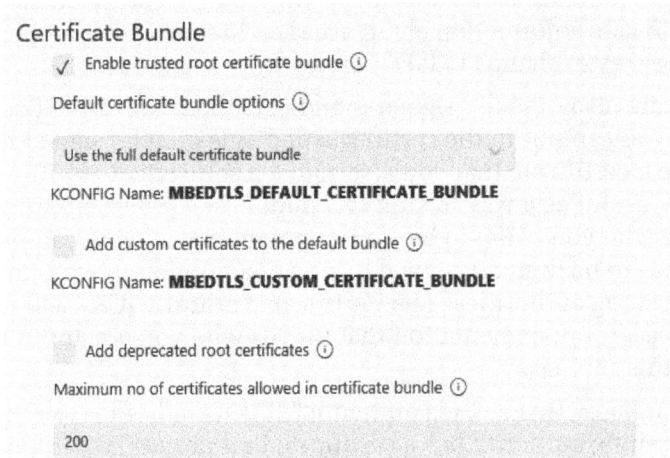

Certificate Bundle

☑ Enable trusted root certificate bundle ⓘ

Default certificate bundle options ⓘ

Use the full default certificate bundle ⌄

KCONFIG Name: **MBEDTLS_DEFAULT_CERTIFICATE_BUNDLE**

☐ Add custom certificates to the default bundle ⓘ

KCONFIG Name: **MBEDTLS_CUSTOM_CERTIFICATE_BUNDLE**

☐ Add deprecated root certificates ⓘ

Maximum no of certificates allowed in certificate bundle ⓘ

200

You can customize the certificate bundle by adding or removing certificates. For IoT applications you often only want to connect to a single server and then all you need is a set of certificates that validates that particular server. Alternatively, you could connect without using root certificates and validate the identity of the server in some other way.

SSL and TLS

A very common use of certificates is in the TLS, Transport Security Layer. This is used in HTTPS to transport data between client and server, but it is also used in email and other types of server. TLS evolved out of SSL, Secure Sockets Layer, which is still used to refer to it. SSL was designed to be used to convert a standard non-encrypted socket-based connection to an encrypted socket-based connection with minimal change to the program. That is:

- TLS/SSL is a way to add encryption and authentication to existing protocols.
- While SSL is now obsolete, you will still find that TLS facilities, such as the OPENSSL library, have SSL in their names, even though they support TLS.
- TLS is generally added to a socket-based implementation of a protocol.

There have been a number of revisions of the TLS/SSL protocol over time. The first three versions, SSL 1 to 3, and are all deprecated. TLS 1.0 was issued in 1999 and deprecated in 2021. TLS 1.1 was also deprecated in 2021. Currently, the two supported versions are TLS 1.2, introduced in 2008, and TLS 1.3, introduced in 2018, which is the latest version.

At the time of writing, TLS 1.2 is supported by 99% of all servers and TLS 1.3 by 95%. A server can support multiple versions of TLS and roughly 95% still support TLS 1.1 although TLS 1.0 was removed from major browsers.

All the latest web browsers support TLS 1.1 and 1.2 by default. TLS 1.3, which is supported by almost all current browsers, is thought to be secure in all its possible configurations, but TLS 1.2 has vulnerabilities if you select a weak configuration. Currently the mbedTLS library that the ESP32 uses supports TLS 1.2 and 1.3.

Every TLS connection starts out unencrypted. The client then requests that the server sets up a TLS connection. Usually this happens if the client attempts to connect using port 443, but it can also use a protocol-specific STARTTLS request to the server; this is often used with email servers – see Chapter 14.

The next step is that a handshaking procedure starts using public keys. The handshake establishes what encryption and hash methods the client and server support. The server picks a method that they both support. Then, the server sends the client its certificate and the client checks it for validity. The client can also provide a certificate to the server for it to check. Finally, a shared secret is constructed by the client and passed to the server.

From this point on, everything is encrypted using the agreed method and key. The higher-level protocol, HTTPS in this case, submits its data packets to be transferred and they are automatically encrypted on transmission and decrypted on reception. In this way the program can work as if encryption wasn't being used.

In practice, the server and client often have to have more than one attempt at making the connection work and this can result in empty packets being transmitted and received. HTTPS can be messy.

HTTPS and ESP IDF

A great deal of work has been done to make the ESP IDF work with HTTPS, or TLS, in general easier. The TCP/IP part of the transaction is provided by lwIP and its sockets. The encryption part of the connection i.e. the TLS, is provided by mbedTLS. The problem is that using mbedTLS is complicated as it provides functions to "wrap" sockets so that they work with encrypted data. While this is conceptually simple, in practice it involves setting up a socket connection, wrapping it with functions that perform the encryption and then making use of the socket to perform the communication. This can be simplified by wrapping the TLS with the socket creation function into a single function that creates an encrypted connection using functions from lwIP and mbedTLS. There is also a programmable HTTP/S client which can be used almost without knowing anything about TLS.

In the remainder of this chapter we start at the highest level with the HTTPS client module, then use the ESP-TLS simplified functions and finally come to the lowest level with a TLS wrapping of the lwIP sockets.

Unless you are doing something that is highly customized and as long as you have plenty of memory to spare then the HTTPS module is a good choice for its simplicity. If you need to customize things a little then the ESP-TLS functions are easy to use, but are specific to the EPS32. The full TLS wrapping of sockets is useful if you need portability to other platforms.

HTTPS Client

The HTTP client (folder `HTTPClient7`) introduced in Chapter 7 is easy to extend to handle HTTPS. All we need to do is modify the `esp_http_client_config_t` struct to specify an HTTPS connection.

You need to specify the URL as `https` and the transport type as `HTTP_TRANSPORT_OVER_SSL`:

```
esp_http_client_config_t httpconfig = {
    .url = "https://example.com",
    .method = HTTP_METHOD_GET,
    .event_handler = http_event_handler,
    .buffer_size = DEFAULT_HTTP_BUF_SIZE,
    .buffer_size_tx = DEFAULT_HTTP_BUF_SIZE,
    .user_data = httpdata,
    .transport_type = HTTP_TRANSPORT_OVER_SSL,
    .crt_bundle_attach = esp_crt_bundle_attach,
};
```

This won't work unless you set the SDK to allow the client not to have a certificate:

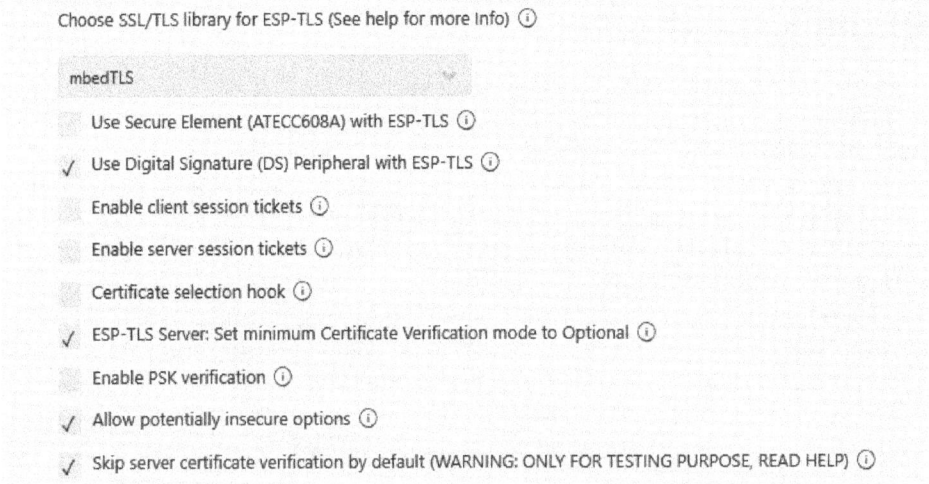

As well as choosing mbedTLS you need to opt to use potentially insecure options and Skip server certificate verification by default. As you understand what is happening, you can ignore the warning about this mode being only for testing purposes. As long as you are happy about not checking the server's identity via a certificate, it is perfectly acceptable. For a general web browser it would be quite unacceptable, but for an IoT application, perhaps connecting to a single server, it should be perfectly OK.

The complete program, in folder HTTPSclient1, is:

```c
#include <stdio.h>
#include "freertos/FreeRTOS.h"
#include "esp_wifi.h"
#include "nvs_flash.h"
#include "esp_event.h"
#include "esp_netif.h"
#include "string.h"
#include "esp_http_client.h"
#include "connectwifi.h"
esp_err_t http_event_handler(esp_http_client_event_t* evt)
{
    static int pos = 0;
    switch (evt->event_id) {
    case HTTP_EVENT_ERROR:
        printf("HTTP_EVENT_ERROR\n");
        break;
    case HTTP_EVENT_ON_CONNECTED:
        printf("HTTP_EVENT_ON_CONNECTED\n");
        break;
    case HTTP_EVENT_HEADER_SENT:
        printf("HTTP_EVENT_HEADER_SENT\n");
        break;
    case HTTP_EVENT_ON_HEADER:
        printf("HTTP_EVENT_ON_HEADER\n");
        printf("header = %s , %s\n", evt->header_key,
                                         evt->header_value);
        break;
    case HTTP_EVENT_ON_DATA:
        printf("HTTP_EVENT_ON_DATA, len=%d\n", evt->data_len);
        if (!esp_http_client_is_chunked_response(evt->client)) {
            printf("%.*s", evt->data_len, (char*)evt->data);
            char* buf = (char*)(evt->user_data);
            memcpy(buf + pos, evt->data, evt->data_len);
            pos += evt->data_len;
            buf[pos] = 0;
        }
        break;
    case HTTP_EVENT_ON_FINISH:
        printf("HTTP_EVENT_ON_FINISH\n");
        pos = 0;
        break;
```

```
    case HTTP_EVENT_DISCONNECTED:
        printf("HTTP_EVENT_DISCONNECTED\n");
        break;
    default:
    }
    return ESP_OK;
}

char httpdata[2000];

void app_main(void)
{
    wifiConnect("Co", "SSID", "password", NULL, NULL);
    while (wifiStatus != 1010)
    {
        vTaskDelay(10 / portTICK_PERIOD_MS);
    };
    esp_http_client_config_t httpconfig = {
        .url = "https://example.com",
        .method = HTTP_METHOD_GET,
        .event_handler = http_event_handler,
        .buffer_size = DEFAULT_HTTP_BUF_SIZE,
        .buffer_size_tx = DEFAULT_HTTP_BUF_SIZE,
        .user_data = httpdata,
       .transport_type = HTTP_TRANSPORT_OVER_SSL,
    };

    esp_http_client_handle_t httphandle =
                        esp_http_client_init(&httpconfig);
    esp_http_client_perform(httphandle);
    printf("len data= %d\n", strlen(httpdata));
    printf("html \n %s\n ", httpdata);
}
```

The event handler also prints the headers that the server returns. If you run the program you should see all of the HTML from the website.

If you want to check the identity of the server then you need to make two small changes. To use the certificate bundle you need to add

```
#include "esp_crt_bundle.h"
```

and you need to add a single additional field to the configuration:

```
    esp_http_client_config_t httpconfig = {
        .url = "https://example.com",
        .method = HTTP_METHOD_GET,
        .event_handler = http_event_handler,
        .buffer_size = DEFAULT_HTTP_BUF_SIZE,
        .buffer_size_tx = DEFAULT_HTTP_BUF_SIZE,
        .user_data = httpdata,
        .transport_type = HTTP_TRANSPORT_OVER_SSL,
        .crt_bundle_attach = esp_crt_bundle_attach,
    };
```

You also have to untick "Allow potentially insecure options" and "Skip server certificate verification".

With this change the connection is a reasonably secure HTTPS connection in that it is using encryption and it has verified the server's certificate. You can try the program out in folder `HTTPSclient2`.

ESP TLS

The ESP TLS module provides a set of functions that let you set up a client HTTPS connection and read and write data in a completely general way. It does this by combining the encryption facilities provided by mbedTLS and the socket facilities provided by lwIP.

To make a TLS connection you have to make use of an `esp_tls` struct which stores details of the connection as it progresses:

`esp_tls_t *tls = esp_tls_init();`

To set the initial configuration you need to create `esp_tls_cfg_t`, specifying details of how the connection should be made and what certificates should be used. The simplest configuration is to use the root certificate bundle:

```
esp_tls_cfg_t cfg = {
    .crt_bundle_attach = esp_crt_bundle_attach,
};
```

If you don't want to use the bundle and are happy not validating the identity of the server then you can leave the field as NULL and set the SDK to Skip server certificate verification.

Once you have a configuration set up you can try to make a connection with the server using one of:

- `esp_tls_conn_new_sync(const char *hostname, int hostlen, int port, const esp_tls_cfg_t *cfg, esp_tls_t *tls)`

- `esp_tls_conn_http_new_sync(const char *url, const esp_tls_cfg_t *cfg, esp_tls_t *tls)`

- `esp_tls_conn_new_async(const char *hostname, int hostlen, int port, const esp_tls_cfg_t *cfg, esp_tls_t *tls)`

- `esp_tls_conn_http_new_async(const char *url, const esp_tls_cfg_t *cfg, esp_tls_t *tls)`

The difference between them is that the sync functions block and the async functions don't. The http functions allow you to use a full HTTP URL and the non-http functions need the URL of the server.

There is also a function that allows you to make a plain unencrypted TCP connection:

- ```
  esp_err_t esp_tls_plain_tcp_connect(const char *host,
          int hostlen, int port, const esp_tls_cfg_t *cfg,
              esp_tls_error_handle_t error_handle, int *sockfd)
  ```

which returns a socket file descriptor.

You can close the connection using:

```
esp_tls_conn_destroy(esp_tls_t *tls)
```

Once you have a connection you can use:

- ```
  ssize_t esp_tls_conn_read(esp_tls_t *tls, void *data,
                                      size_t datalen)
  ```

to read data and:

- ```
  ssize_t esp_tls_conn_write(esp_tls_t *tls, const void *data,
                                      size_t datalen)
  ```

to write it.

Both can return before they have processed all of the data and you need to test the return value to see if you have to read again – this is exactly the same as a raw socket read/write.

There is also a function:

- ```
  ssize_t esp_tls_get_bytes_avail(esp_tls_t *tls)
  ```

that will tell you how many bytes are remaining in the buffer.

As ESP TLS is built on top of sockets, you can use:

- ```
  esp_tls_get_conn_sockfd(esp_tls_t *tls, int *sockfd)
  ```

which returns the socket file descriptor so that you can work with it directly. This isn't usually necessary. There is also a put function that allows you to specify the socket to use. As it is also built on top of mbedTLS, you can get the TLS context with:

- ```
  void *esp_tls_get_ssl_context(esp_tls_t *tls)
  ```

ESP TLS also provides its own error handling:

- ```
  esp_tls_get_and_clear_last_error(esp_tls_error_handle_t h,
                      int *esp_tls_code, int *esp_tls_flags)
  ```
- ```
  esp_err_t esp_tls_get_and_clear_error_type(
      esp_tls_error_handle_t h, esp_tls_error_type_t err_type,
                                      int *error_code)
  ```
- ```
  esp_err_t esp_tls_get_error_handle(esp_tls_t *tls,
                      esp_tls_error_handle_t *error_handle)
  ```
  ```

ESP TLS Client

The only complication in writing an ESP TLS client is to make sure that we have read or written all of the data. In this respect it is much like writing a simple HTTP client.

Making the connection is easy:

```
esp_tls_t *tls = esp_tls_init();
esp_tls_cfg_t cfg = {
    .crt_bundle_attach = esp_crt_bundle_attach,
};
esp_tls_conn_http_new_sync("https://example.com", &cfg, tls);
```

The tls struct now contains all of the information about the connection that the other functions need to send and receive data.

Next we have to send the request:

```
char header[] = "GET /index.html HTTP/1.1\r\n"
                "Host:example.com\r\n\r\n";
int m = 0;
int n = 0;
do
{
    n = esp_tls_conn_write(tls, header + m, strlen(header) - m);
    if (n >= 0)
    {
        m += n;
    }
    else if (n != ESP_TLS_ERR_SSL_WANT_READ &&
                        n != ESP_TLS_ERR_SSL_WANT_WRITE)
    {
        esp_tls_conn_destroy(tls);
    }
} while (m < strlen(header));
```

This works in the usual way, n is the number of bytes written by the last write and m is the cumulative number of bytes written. If n is greater than or equal to 0 then data has been received correctly, if n is negative then we have an error condition, two of which are acceptable, and we continue the loop. If we get a real error then we close the connection.

The receive loop is very similar:

```
char buffer[2000];
int len = sizeof(buffer) - 1;
do
{
    n = esp_tls_conn_read(tls, buffer, len);
    if (n == ESP_TLS_ERR_SSL_WANT_WRITE ||
                        n == ESP_TLS_ERR_SSL_WANT_READ)
    {
        continue;
    }
```

```
    else if (n < 0)
    {
        break;
    }
    else if (n == 0)
    {
        break;
    }
    buffer[n] = 0;
    printf("%s", buffer);
} while (true);
```

In this case we regard a zero size packet as an end of communication marker. Notice that we have to allow for the NULL to be added to the end of the string in the size of the receive buffer. You can try the complete program in folder HTTPSClient3.

Wrapping Sockets Using MbedTLS

The main principle of using sockets for a secure connection is simple enough. The socket establishes a basic connection between two endpoints and data can be transferred between them. Instead of inventing a new type of socket, we simply make use of what we have and upgrade it to work with encrypted data. The SSL/TLS code is used to convert the plain text data into encrypted data and this is sent to the server or client via the existing socket. This is slightly more complicated than it sounds because the initial socket is used to negotiate the type of encryption used in the transaction.

What happens first is that a socket connection is established, then there is a handshake phase where the two ends of the connection negotiate a key exchange and symmetric encryption protocol. As long as a cryptographic suite supported by both ends can be found, the handshake phase moves on to transferring only encrypted data.

This whole process is often referred to as "wrapping" the socket to create a secure socket. However, notice that you can use the same idea to wrap any point-to-point communication method and indeed this is possible using mbedTLS and it is fairly easy.

To wrap a socket using mbedTLS you first configure the SSL/TLS system so that it can perform a handshake and encrypt and decrypt data. Next you create a standard socket and tell mbedTLS to use its native read/write methods as its basic I/O.

The functions:

- mbedtls_ssl_write
- mbedtls_ssl_read

receive and send plain text data via the socket respectively.

For example, when you use:

```
 int n = mbedtls_ssl_write(&ssl, buffer, strlen(buffer));
```

the plain text data in buffer is encrypted and then sent over the socket using its write method.

One confusing issue in using mbedTLS to wrap a socket is that there is a module that performs the wrapping for Linux systems and this comes with pre-configured I/O functions that you will encounter in examples and the documentation, but they don't work on the ESP32. In this case we essentially have to port the ssl/tls functions to FreeRTOS.

A Simple HTTPS Client

As a first example, an HTTPS client is an obvious choice. This is based on the code of the simple socket client given in Chapter 7, folder HTTPClient1, and its code is mostly unchanged in this new example

The app_main starts in the same way:

```
void app_main(void)
{
    int err = 0;
    wifiConnect("Co", "SSID", "password", NULL, NULL);
    while (wifiStatus != 1010)
    {
        vTaskDelay(10 / portTICK_PERIOD_MS);
    };
    int sockfd = socket(AF_INET, SOCK_STREAM, 0);
    struct sockaddr_in addr;
    addr.sin_family = AF_INET;
    addr.sin_port = htons(443);
    addr.sin_addr.s_addr = inet_addr("23.192.228.80");
    err = connect(sockfd, (struct sockaddr *)&addr, sizeof(addr));
    if (err < 0)
    {
        printf("Socket error %X\n", errno);
    }
```

Now we have the socket connected to the server, but notice it is on port 433 which is the usual port for HTTPS. At the moment, however, the connection is not encrypted and the only data the server will respond to is a SSL/TLS handshake. If this doesn't happen or if it fails, then the connection is dropped.

Configuring SSL/TLS

Our next task is to construct an `mbedtls_ssl_config` struct. This is used to setup the SSL context which implements the handshake and the data encryption. The reason this is a two-step process is that you can use the `ssl_config` struct to create multiple related SSL `context` structs which can be used for multiple SSL connections.

It is easier to use the `config_init` function to initialize it and the `config_defaults` function to provide a starting point:

```
mbedtls_ssl_config conf;
mbedtls_ssl_config_init(&conf);
err = mbedtls_ssl_config_defaults(&conf,
        MBEDTLS_SSL_IS_CLIENT,
                MBEDTLS_SSL_TRANSPORT_STREAM,
                        MBEDTLS_SSL_PRESET_DEFAULT);
```

The second parameter can be either `CLIENT` or `SERVER`. The third can either be `STREAM` for TCP or `DATAGRAM` for encrypted UDP. The final parameter can either be `DEFAULT`, which `sets` a cryptographic suite that tends to work or `SUITEB`, which sets a more restrictive one defined by the NSA for use when creating USA national security applications.

You need to set up a random data generator for mbedTLS to use. For any given platform this is usually routine, but you still need to include the boilerplate code:

```
mbedtls_entropy_context entropy;
mbedtls_entropy_init(&entropy);
mbedtls_ctr_drbg_context ctr_drbg;
mbedtls_ctr_drbg_init(&ctr_drbg);
const char *pers = "https_client";
err = mbedtls_ctr_drbg_seed(&ctr_drbg,
                mbedtls_entropy_func, &entropy,
                        (const unsigned char *)pers, strlen(pers));
mbedtls_ssl_conf_rng(&conf, mbedtls_ctr_drbg_random, &ctr_drbg);
```

mbedTLS employs CTR-DRBG, a Deterministic Random Bit Generator that relies on AES in CounTeR mode. This needs to be supplied with an entropy source which varies according to the hardware it is running on. The ESP32 `esp_random` function is used as an entropy source.

You have to create and initialize the entropy structure and the DRGB structure and then use them to initialize the random number generator with a seed, "`https_client`" in this case. The seed should be different for each application to provide additional security. There are a number of alternative ways of providing a seed and of protecting the randomness of the generator, but a simple string is enough for most situations. The final line of code adds the DRBG random generator to the configuration.

You can use the CTR-DRB as source of random numbers using:

```
uint32_t r;
mbedtls_ctr_drbg_random(&ctr_drbg, (unsigned char *)&r, 4);
```

This can only be used after `ctr_drbg` has been setup. In practice, there is little point in doing this as `esp_random` provides random numbers that are as good and it is faster.

The final thing we need to setup before moving on to creating the SSL context is to specify how we want to verify the server's certificate. As this is a first example, we can avoid specifying a root certificate chain by not verifying the server's certificate:

```
mbedtls_ssl_conf_authmode(&conf, MBEDTLS_SSL_VERIFY_NONE);
```

Now everything is set up we can create the SSL context:

```
mbedtls_ssl_context ssl;
mbedtls_ssl_init(&ssl);
err = mbedtls_ssl_setup(&ssl, &conf);
```

This creates the SSL/TLS system ready to perform a handshake and encrypt and decrypt data. After that, all we have left to do is connect it to the socket that it will use.

Wrapping the Socket

To connect the socket to the SSL/TLS context we have to define some standard functions:

- ```
  int mbedtls_ssl_send_t(void *ctx,const unsigned char *buf,
                                                  size_t len);
  ```
- ```
  int mbedtls_ssl_recv_t(void *ctx,unsigned char *buf,
                                                  size_t len);
  ```
- ```
  int mbedtls_ssl_recv_timeout_t(void *ctx,
                 unsigned char *buf, size_t len, uint32_t timeout);
  ```

The first is used to send plain text data as encrypted data. The second receives encrypted data and passes it to the SSL context for decryption and the third implements a read with timeout. In most cases you won't need to define `recv_timeout`. The `ctx` parameter is simply the socket file descriptor, but it is implemented in this general way to allow you to work with connections other than sockets. In general, it has to specify the connection so that data can be transferred using it.
  ```

As already mentioned, these are predefined for Linux-based systems, but for FreeRTOS we generally have to define them. The simplest way of doing this is:

```
int mbedtls_net_send(void *ctx, const unsigned char *buf,
                                          size_t len)
{
    return write(*(int *)ctx, buf, len);
}
int mbedtls_net_recv(void *ctx, unsigned char *buf, size_t len)
{
    return (int)read(*(int *)ctx, buf, len);
}
```

The connection can be this simple or you can implement error checking within each function.

Once you have defined the functions you can make SSL/TLS use them:

```
mbedtls_ssl_set_bio(&ssl, &sockfd, mbedtls_net_send,
                                mbedtls_net_recv, NULL)
```

Notice that the receive timeout function has not been defined.

With everything set up we can now download a webpage:

```
    char header[] = "GET /index.html HTTP/1.1\r\n
                              Host: example.com\r\n\r\n ";

    int n = mbedtls_ssl_write(&ssl, header, strlen(header));
    char buffer[2048];
    do
    {
        n = mbedtls_ssl_read(&ssl, buffer, 2048);
        buffer[n] = 0;
        printf("data received %d\n", n);
        printf("%s\n", buffer);
    } while (n > 0);
```

This is exactly the same as the HTTP client, but we are now using mbedtls_ssl read and write functions which in turn use our read and write functions . We don't need to explicitly perform a handshake as the server usually does that during the initial connection.

The final complication is that when you close the socket you also have to clean up the SSL/TLS:

```
    mbedtls_ssl_free(&ssl);
    mbedtls_ssl_config_free(&conf);
    mbedtls_ctr_drbg_free(&ctr_drbg);
    mbedtls_entropy_free(&entropy);
```

Putting all this together and ensuring that header files are loaded, the complete program in folder HTTPSClient4. is:

```c
#include <stdio.h>
#include "freertos/FreeRTOS.h"
#include "esp_wifi.h"
#include "nvs_flash.h"
#include "esp_event.h"
#include "esp_netif.h"
#include "string.h"
#include "socket.h"
#include "connectWiFi.h"

#include "esp_tls.h"

#include "mbedtls/entropy.h"
#include "mbedtls/ctr_drbg.h"
int mbedtls_net_send(void *ctx, const unsigned char *buf,
                                              size_t len)
{
    return write(*(int *)ctx, buf, len);
}
int mbedtls_net_recv(void *ctx, unsigned char *buf, size_t len)
{
    return (int)read(*(int *)ctx, buf, len);
}

void app_main(void)
{
    int err = 0;
    wifiConnect("Co", "SSID", "password", NULL, NULL);
    while (wifiStatus != 1010)
    {
        vTaskDelay(10 / portTICK_PERIOD_MS);
    };
    int sockfd = socket(AF_INET, SOCK_STREAM, 0);
    struct sockaddr_in addr;
    addr.sin_family = AF_INET;
    addr.sin_port = htons(443);
    addr.sin_addr.s_addr = inet_addr("23.192.228.80");
    err = connect(sockfd, (struct sockaddr *)&addr, sizeof(addr));
    if (err < 0)
    {
        printf("Socket error %X\n", errno);
    }

    mbedtls_ssl_config conf;
    mbedtls_ssl_config_init(&conf);
    err = mbedtls_ssl_config_defaults(&conf,
                                      MBEDTLS_SSL_IS_CLIENT,
                                      MBEDTLS_SSL_TRANSPORT_STREAM,
                                      MBEDTLS_SSL_PRESET_DEFAULT);
```

```
        mbedtls_entropy_context entropy;
        mbedtls_entropy_init(&entropy);
        mbedtls_ctr_drbg_context ctr_drbg;
        mbedtls_ctr_drbg_init(&ctr_drbg);
        const char *pers = "https_client";
        err = mbedtls_ctr_drbg_seed(&ctr_drbg, mbedtls_entropy_func,
                &entropy, (const unsigned char *)pers, strlen(pers));
        mbedtls_ssl_conf_rng(&conf, mbedtls_ctr_drbg_random,&ctr_drbg);

        mbedtls_ssl_conf_authmode(&conf, MBEDTLS_SSL_VERIFY_NONE);
        mbedtls_ssl_context ssl;
        mbedtls_ssl_init(&ssl);
        err = mbedtls_ssl_setup(&ssl, &conf);
        mbedtls_ssl_set_bio(&ssl, &sockfd, mbedtls_net_send,
                                        mbedtls_net_recv, NULL);

        char header[] = "GET /index.html HTTP/1.1\r\n
                                Host:example.com\r\n\r\n";
        int n = mbedtls_ssl_write(&ssl,(u_char*) header,
                                        strlen(header));

        char buffer[2000];
        int len = sizeof(buffer) - 1;
        do
        {
            n = mbedtls_ssl_read(&ssl, (u_char*)buffer, len);

            if (n == ESP_TLS_ERR_SSL_WANT_WRITE || n ==
                                ESP_TLS_ERR_SSL_WANT_READ)
            {
                continue;
            }
            else if (n < 0)
            {
                break;
            }
            else if (n == 0)
            {
                break;
            }
            buffer[n] = 0;
            printf("%s", buffer);
        } while (true);
        close(sockfd);
        mbedtls_ssl_free(&ssl);
        mbedtls_ssl_config_free(&conf);
        mbedtls_ctr_drbg_free(&ctr_drbg);
        mbedtls_entropy_free(&entropy);

        printf("Final buffer\n\n%s\n", buffer);
}
```

One useful addition is to provide a debug function as finding out why an HTTPS connection isn't working is often difficult. A debug function can be defined something like:

```
#include "mbedtls/debug.h"
static void my_debug(void *ctx, int level,
                     const char *file, int line, const char *str)
{
    ((void)level);
    fprintf((FILE *)ctx, "%s", str);
    fflush((FILE *)ctx);
}
```

and you can add it to the ssl context using:

```
    mbedtls_debug_set_threshold(3);
    mbedtls_ssl_conf_dbg( &conf, my_debug, stdout );
```

The threshold level, 0 to 4, controls how much information you get and you can send the data to a file by changing stdout to a file descriptor. To make use of this you have to configure the SDK:

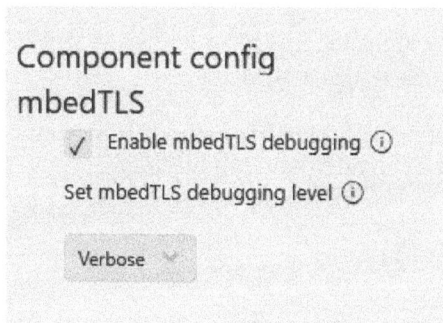

Component config
mbedTLS
✓ Enable mbedTLS debugging ⓘ

Set mbedTLS debugging level ⓘ

Verbose ⌄

You can find this modification to the client program in folder HTTPSClient5.

Encryption Suites

With luck the clients listed in this chapter should just connect correctly to almost any website. However, if you enable the debugging option given in the previous section you will notice that making a TLS connection is far from simple. The client and the server have to negotiate which encryption and key exchange methods to use, an encryption suite – and there are a lot to choose from. The ESP-TLS module is set up to handle most of the server configurations you are likely to encounter and this is the reason we can ignore the problem. However, supporting so many encryption suites is costly in time and memory and for an IoT device communicating with a single server it is usually a good idea to limit the possible suites to just those supported by the server.

Summary

- A certificate contains identity information and keys.

- A client and a server can establish encrypted communication in two ways. If both have a certificate then the keys are used to exchange a single symmetric key. If only the server has a certificate then this is used by both parties to construct a shared secret key.

- SSL, which has since evolved into TLS, is used to add encryption to sockets.

- To implement TLS you need to use ESP TLS or the mbedTLS library. The ESP TLS library uses mbedTLS and attempts to make it easier to use.

- The most commonly encountered methods are ECDHE key exchange followed by AES symmetric encryption.

- Putting all this together it is easy to create an HTTPS client without the need to work with certificates.

- There is also a complete HTTPS module which can be used to implement an event-driven web client.

We now have most of the components that we need to create an SSL or HTTPS server. We know how to use mbedTLS to handle encryption and we know the main difference between a server and a client. A client initiates a connection but a server has to wait for a client to connect. The only thing that is really different between an HTTP server and an HTTPS server is the need to specify a certificate for the server. So we first need to look at the problem of creating a certificate and incorporating it into our code.

Certificates

If you want to implement an SSL server then things are slightly more complicated because you need to provide a certificate. Getting a certificate can be an involved process. Even popular, free, certificate-issuing sites like Let's Encrypt require proof that you own the domain that the certificate applies to. To do this you have to write code which generates a new key pair and then either create a specific DNS record or store a file on the website. This is easy enough for production purposes, but not so easy when you are in the process of creating a program.

The usual solution is to create a self-signed certificate. If the operating system has OpenSSL installed, most versions of Linux do, then you have a command line way of creating a self-signed certificate. You can install OpenSSL on Windows but it is easier to get OpenSSL on Windows by installing Git desktop via VS Code:

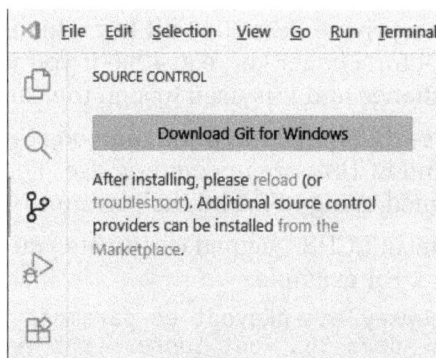

The primary use of Git for Windows is for project management with VS Code, but it also installs OpenSSL:

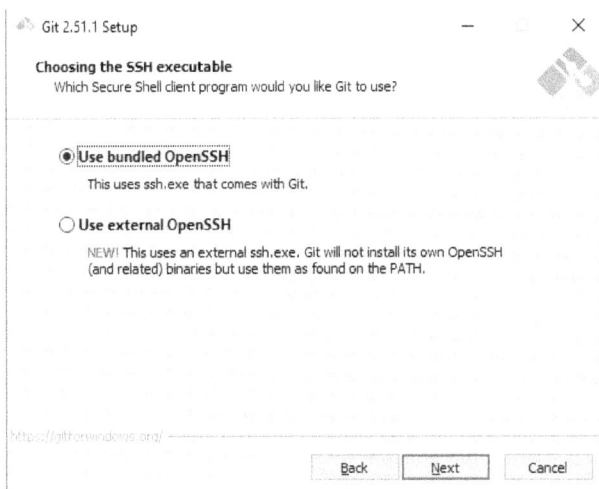

You will find OpenSSL at:

```
C:\"Program Files"\Git\usr\bin\openssl.exe
```

Once you have OpenSSL you can create a key and certificate pair using:

```
openssl req -newkey rsa:2048 -nodes -keyout iopress.key -x509
                                    -days 365 -out iopress.crt
```

changing *iopress* to the name of your server. You will be asked a set of questions for information required by the certificate. How you answer these questions only modifies what the user sees if they ask to inspect the certificate, so you can simply accept the defaults. The only exception to this is the common name prompt. This needs to match the name of the server that the certificate is intended for. It has to correspond to the server name returned in the server header.

The command creates a private RSA 2048-bit key which is used to sign the certificate. You can opt for a larger key, e.g. 4096 if you want to. The private key is used in key exchange and it is used to sign the certificate.

Notice that you can use different encryption methods to sign, but at the time of writing only RSA and ECDSA are in common use. The certificate generated above is signed using RSA and the private key.

If you want to generate an ECDSA-signed certificate you also have to choose an elliptic curve to use. For example:

```
openssl req -new -newkey ec -pkeyopt ec_paramgen_curve:prime256v1
        -x509 -nodes -days 365 -out iopress.crt -keyout iopress.key
```

In this case we have selected the curve `prime256v1`.

The openssl command creates two files, a .key file and a .crt file, which need to be processed to create strings that can be used in C programs. Both files are by default in PEM format and are often created with the .pem extension. Normally the files would be loaded into the server, but in this case there is no standard filing system and so the binary in the files needs to be loaded into a pair of strings.

There are two common certificate formats, PEM, standing for Privacy-Enhanced Mail and DER, Distinguished Encoding Rules, referring to a set of rules for encoding data structures, and we can use either format in mbedTLS. In the PEM format the certificate and key are saved on disk using an encoding called Base64 with a line of unencoded ASCII text at the start and end of each key and certificate:

```
-----BEGIN PRIVATE KEY-----
MIGHAgEAMBMGByqGSM49AgEGCCqGSM49AwEHBG0wawIBAQQgNgzd8KrRZldyzSSA
aeoQz6fseiJV4aflT2JzJDgFBZ+hRANCAARO0C3CI4jpsdWL/05GBCPivy9SlMGl
F8RqlGATf9Agz8nxmWGbWlyJ+/hV1AUjuOUvOeCUxaBoRc2zvqC0pdme
-----END PRIVATE KEY-----


-----BEGIN CERTIFICATE-----
MIIB3zCCAYWgAwIBAgIUfuveYhwTmXHCRI0buiTT/NGg/VUwCgYIKoZIzj0EAwIw
RTELMAkGA1UEBhMCVVMxEzARBgNVBAgMClNvbWUtU3RhdGUxITAfBgNVBAoMGElu
dGVybmV0IFdpZGdpdHMgUHR5IEx0ZDAeFw0yNTEwMjUxMDM2NTFaFw0yNjEwMjUx
MDM2NTFaMEUxCzAJBgNVBAYTAlVTMRMwEQYDVQQIDApTb21lLVN0YXRlMSEwHwYD
VQQKDBhJbnRlcm5ldCBXaWRnaXRzIFB0eSBMdGQwWTATBgcqhkjOPQIBBggqhkjO
PQMBBwNCAARO0C3CI4jpsdWL/05GBCPivy9SlMGlF8RqlGATf9Agz8nxmWGbWlyJ
+/hV1AUjuOUvOeCUxaBoRc2zvqC0pdmeo1MwUTAdBgNVHQ4EFgQUpWAfLSO3TxuE
wZQZwg8bKAT8IKMwHwYDVR0jBBgwFoAUpWAfLSO3TxuEwZQZwg8bKAT8IKMwDwYD
VR0TAQH/BAUwAwEB/zAKBggqhkjOPQQDAgNIADBFAiBruNYUmtPg0eWQGxFiA7U5
aVWQjidRBf67JQLQXa2dOAIhAPcreSEwtF7Pch12IWMJeGyCf+kKqRO82SbwWpyh
MdbX
-----END CERTIFICATE-----
```

A PEM file can contain multiple certificates and keys and each line has to end in a single \n. The file we have generated has only a single certificate and its key file is separate. Notice that the separators have to be -----BEGIN CERTIFICATE----- and -----END CERTIFICATE----- as these are used to parse the file.

We can convert the files into suitable C strings using a Python program:

```python
with open("iopress.key", 'rb') as f:
    lines = f.readlines()
for i, line in enumerate(lines):

lines[i]=line.decode().replace('\n','\n"'.encode("unicode_escape").
decode()+"\n")
command="u_char key[]="
command = command +'"'+ '"'.join(lines)
command=command+";"
print(command)
```

```
with open("iopress.crt", 'rb') as f:
    lines = f.readlines()
for i, line in enumerate(lines):
lines[i]=line.decode().replace('\n','\n"'.encode("unicode_escape").
decode()+"\n")
command="u_char cert[]="
command = command +'"'+ '"'.join(lines)
command=command+ ";"
print(command)
```

The program pem.py can be found in folder HTTPSServer1. It converts the pem files into two C instructions by adding \n at end of each line and quotes:

```
u_char key[]="-----BEGIN PRIVATE KEY-----\n"
"MIGHAgEAMBMGByqGSM49AgEGCCqGSM49AwEHBG0wawIBAQQgNgzd8KrRZldyzSSA\n"
"aeoQz6fseiJV4aflT2JzJDgFBZ+hRANCAARO0C3CI4jpsdWL/05GBCPivy9SlMGl\n"
"F8RqlGATf9Agz8nxmWGbWlyJ+/hV1AUjuOUvOeCUxaBoRc2zvqC0pdme\n"
"-----END PRIVATE KEY-----\n"
```

You can simply copy and paste the lines into a program.

The easiest way of creating a DER format file is to process the PEM file into a form that can be used by a C program. To do this, we have to remove the first and last line of the file and unencode the Base64 to a standard byte or ASCII string. This can be done using standard operating system command line programs, but it is also very easy to write a standard Python program, decode.py, in folder HTTPSServer, to do the job:

```
import binascii
with open("iopress.key", 'rb') as f:
    lines = f.readlines()
lines = b"".join(lines[1:-1])
key = binascii.a2b_base64(lines)
res = ""
for b in key:
    res += "0x%02x," % b
res="u_char key[]={"+res[:-1]+"};"
print(res)
with open("iopress.crt", 'rb') as f:
    lines = f.readlines()
lines = b"".join(lines[1:-1])
cert = binascii.a2b_base64(lines)
res = ""
for b in cert:
    res += "0x%02x," % b
res="u_char cert[]={"+res[:-1]+"};"
print()
print(res)
```

If you run this program, with the names of the .key and .crt files corrected to apply to the certificate you have generated, then it will read in each file, remove the first and last line, remove the Base64 encoding and print the C line needed to load the file's contents into an array.

```
u_char key[] = {0x30, 0x82, 0x04, 0xbd, 0x02, … };
u_char cert[] = {0x30, 0x82, 0x03, 0x9b, 0x30, … };
```

where the long list of hex codes has been truncated to save space. If you want to keep your code clean and make it easy to change certificates, then place the definitions into a cert.h file and include it.

You can simply copy and paste these two lines or the two lines from the PEM files to get the certificate you have generated into the program. Once we have the certificates in the program the rest is fairly straightforward.

If you look at the examples in the documentation, you will discover that this is not the way that certificates are generally installed. Instead, installation uses a specific feature of the GCC compiler and linker to include binary data in a program. To make it work you first have to use the GNU tool objcopy to convert the binary certificate file into a binary object file:

```
objcopy --input binary --output elf64-x86-64
    -binary-architecture i386:x86-64 \servercert.pem servercert.o
```

The object file looks like compiled code and contains three symbols that can be used by other programs:

- _binary_servercert_pem_start   Starting address of the data
- _binary_servercert_pem_end   Ending address of the data
- _binary_servercert_pem_size   Size of the data in bytes

These can be used in a program to create an array which uses the data as its contents:

```
extern const unsigned char servercert_start[]
                    asm("_binary_servercert_pem_start");
extern const unsigned char servercert_end[]
                    asm("_binary_servercert_pem_end");
```

This is relatively simple when you know how it works but it still needs an external tool to process the certificate and key files and you might as well use the Python code given earlier and an assignment to a character array.

It is useful to have a code snippet that will check that a certificate is valid before you try to use it in a full program.

```
    mbedtls_x509_crt srvcert;
    mbedtls_x509_crt_init(&srvcert);
    int err = mbedtls_x509_crt_parse(&srvcert, cert, sizeof(cert));
    printf("certificate error %X\n", -err);
    fflush(stdout);
    mbedtls_pk_context srvkey;
    mbedtls_pk_init(&srvkey);
    err = mbedtls_pk_parse_key(&srvkey, key, sizeof(key),
                                    NULL, 0,NULL,0);
    printf("key error %X\n", err);
```

These tests only prove that the certificate and key are correctly formatted, not that they will work with a particular client or server.

HTTPS Server Component

If you need secure HTTPS transactions the simplest way to get things working is to use the ESP HTTPS server component. This adds SSL encryption on top of the existing HTTP server component. So, what you know about the HTTP server is still useful and all you really have to do is supply and configure a certificate.

The HTTPS server component is not included by default and the first thing you have to do is to use Menu Config to enable it:

ESP HTTPS server

✓ Enable ESP_HTTPS_SERVER component ⓘ

Enable ESP HTTPS server component

You also need to increase the maximum header size to 1024:

Component config

HTTP Server

Max HTTP Request Header Length ⓘ

1024

Once we have the certificates in the program, the rest is fairly straightforward in that we simply have to set up the server. The event handlers are unchanged, the full program is in folder `HTTPSServer1`:

```
void app_main(void)
{
    wifiConnect("Co", "SSID", "password", NULL, NULL);
    while (wifiStatus != 1010)
    {
        vTaskDelay(10 / portTICK_PERIOD_MS);
    };
```

```
    u_char key[] = "-----BEGIN PRIVATE KEY-----\n"
"MIGHAgEAMBMGByqGSM49AgEGCCqGSM49AwEHBG0wawIBAQQgCb3W8d9cGuHL+s+b\n"
"ZIqjNac1GYI8Y48x9zqEQj+1eiihRANCAATEBr895ERVG8DHAvc8DRovkz0xYNKd\n"
"4WJKB23x4OBXXOAvdVRzKrmXYYMsZWZwehkTpTwEd3rHrDZaR54SzbZo\n"
                "-----END PRIVATE KEY-----\n";
```

```
    u_char cert[] = "-----BEGIN CERTIFICATE-----\n"
"MIIB3jCCAYWgAwIBAgIUFw6Y69PWFes18KM4d0k3yNTa3X0wCgYIKoZIzj0EAwIw\n"
"RTELMAkGA1UEBhMCVVMxEzARBgNVBAgMClNvbWUtU3RhdGUxITAfBgNVBAoMGElu\n"
"dGVybmV0IFdpZGdpdHMgUHR5IEx0ZDAeFw0yNTEwMjYwNjQ4MjBaFw0yNjEwMjYw\n"
"NjQ4MjBaMEUxCzAJBgNVBAYTAlVTMRMwEQYDVQQIDApTb211LVN0YXRlMSEwHwYD\n"
"VQQKDBhJbnRlcm5ldCBXaWRnaXRzIFB0eSBMdGQwWTATBgcqhkjOPQIBBggqhkjO\n"
"PQMBBwNCAATEBr895ERVG8DHAvc8DRovkz0xYNKd4WJKB23x4OBXXOAvdVRzKrmX\n"
"YYMsZWZwehkTpTwEd3rHrDZaR54SzbZoo1MwUTAdBgNVHQ4EFgQUonOHUDw/aPWK\n"
"mD/Gw8DTfEtiXdIwHwYDVR0jBBgwFoAUonOHUDw/aPWKmD/Gw8DTfEtiXdIwDwYD\n"
"VR0TAQH/BAUwAwEB/zAKBggqhkjOPQQDAgNHADBEAiBhcyxGHH9zbzYkMD6hkZHG\n"
"Qr+tES5jcYYPr0Xccw4iGAIgHL859AAriuORNw/yhjkczngIziwBZ3/aWOPUVkaH\n"
"k/o=\n"
"-----END CERTIFICATE-----\n";
```

```
httpd_ssl_config_t config = HTTPD_SSL_CONFIG_DEFAULT();
config.servercert = cert;
config.servercert_len = sizeof(cert);
config.prvtkey_pem = key;
config.prvtkey_len = sizeof(key);

httpd_handle_t server = NULL;
httpd_uri_t uri_get = {
    .uri = "/temp",
    .method = HTTP_GET,
    .handler = get_handlertemp,
    .user_ctx = NULL};

if (httpd_ssl_start(&server, &config) == ESP_OK)
{
    httpd_register_uri_handler(server, &uri_get);
    uri_get.uri = "/hum";
    uri_get.handler = get_handlerhum;
    httpd_register_uri_handler(server, &uri_get);
}
while (true)
{
    vTaskDelay(1000);
};
}
```

The only difference between this and the non-SSL version is that we now use an SSL configuration struct and set the additional fields to reference the new certificate and its key. The server is set up to serve two pages /temp and /hum and these are unchanged from the previous HTTP server.

The certificate strings have been truncated to save space. If you want to see what the full program looks like, it is in folder HTTPSServer1.

If you try this program, you will find that connecting with a browser using https:// *ip of server* causes a security warning to pop-up due to the use of a self-signed certificate. This is what you will see using Chrome.

Your connection is not private

Attackers might be trying to steal your information from **192.168.1.32**for example,
passwords, messages, or credit cards). Learn more

NET=ERR_CERT_AUTHORITY_INVALID

♀   To get Chrome's highest level of security, turn on enhanced protection

Advanced   Back to safety

Messages like this are displayed because browsers don't trust self-signed certificates. However, if you allow the page to download it will use SSL encryption. To do this, click on Advanced and then confirm that you want to proceed. You can force a browser to accept the certificate by adding it to its trusted root certification authorities tab. However, for most testing purposes this isn't necessary. If you have a valid certificate and key for a particular web server you can substitute it for the self-signed certificate.

It is worth saying that making an SSL connection is not fast. The ESP32 is being asked to do significant computation to implement the cryptography and the handshake process is involved and hence time-consuming. You will also see a number of exceptions caused by the client aborting the connection due to the self-signed certificate, which is perfectly normal. Firefox is a much more friendly browser to use when testing SSL connections. Chrome tends to want to lock things down as soon as it detects a problem with the certificate.

Also notice that a browser will generally attempt to negotiate the cryptographic protocol to exchange keys. If the server or the client don't support the proposed method then an error is reported at the server and a different protocol is tried. As a result it can take some time to make a SSL connection and you will see errors similar to:

```
W (68737) httpd: httpd_server: error accepting new connection
I (68737) esp_https_server: performing session handshake
E (69467) esp-tls-mbedtls: mbedtls_ssl_handshake returned -0x7780
E (69467) esp_https_server: esp_tls_create_server_session failed
E (69467) httpd: httpd_accept_conn: session creation failed
```

As long as everything works out and a connection is finally made, you can ignore these errors.

ESP-TLS Server

The ESP-TLS module that we used to create an HTTPS client can also be used to create an HTTPS server. The differences are that the server has to wait for a client to make a connection and a server-side certificate is essential. The first part of the interaction is conducted using unencrypted HTTPS and for this it is easy enough to use a standard socket. Once the socket is set up and listening, we only need to use encryption when the client connects and there are some additional functions in ESP-TLS that make this relatively easy.

The socket that is being used to connect the client is provided by the accept function and we can initiate a TLS session using:

```
int esp_tls_server_session_create(esp_tls_cfg_server_t *cfg,
                                  int sockfd, esp_tls_t *tls)
```

The socket specified by sockfd is wrapped using the information provided in cfg, which specifies things like the certificate and key to use. The final parameter, tls, is used by the system to keep track of the connection and it is set up by the create function. The create function is blocking and only returns when the handshake is complete or there is an error.

The function:

- ```
  esp_err_t esp_tls_server_session_init
          (esp_tls_cfg_server *cfg, int sockfd, esp_tls_t *tls)
  ```

works in the same way, but returns before the handshake is completed.

You need to loop until:

```
int esp_tls_server_session_continue_async(esp_tls_t *tls)
```

returns 0 to indicate that the handshake is complete. When the connection is ready you can read and write it in the usual way. When you have finished with it you can close the connection using:

```
void esp_tls_server_session_delete(esp_tls_t *tls)
```

To create an HTTPS server using ESP-TLS we first need to set up a socket and listen on it just as for an HTTP server:

```
void app_main(void)
{
    wifiConnect("Co", "SSID", "password", NULL, NULL);
    while (wifiStatus != 1010)
    {
        vTaskDelay(10 / portTICK_PERIOD_MS);
    };

    int sockfd = socket(AF_INET, SOCK_STREAM, IPPROTO_IP);
    struct sockaddr_in addr;
    addr.sin_family = AF_INET;
    addr.sin_port = htons(443);
    addr.sin_addr.s_addr = INADDR_ANY;
    bind(sockfd, (struct sockaddr *)&addr, sizeof(addr));
    listen(sockfd, 3);
```

Now we are ready to accept an incoming connection, but to make that connection we need to configure TLS with certificate etc:

```
    esp_tls_cfg_server_t cfg = {
        .servercert_buf = cert,
        .servercert_bytes = sizeof(cert),
        .serverkey_buf = key,
        .serverkey_bytes = sizeof(key),
    };
```
```

The certificate and key are specified as before using arrays. Now we are ready to start an accept loop:

```
int len = 1024 * 2;
 char buffer[len];
 struct sockaddr_storage client_addr;
 socklen_t addr_size = sizeof client_addr;
 while (true)
 {
     int client_fd = accept(sockfd,
                 (struct sockaddr *)&client_addr, &addr_size);

     esp_tls_t *tls = esp_tls_init();
     esp_err_t ret = esp_tls_server_session_create(&cfg,
                                         client_fd, tls);
     if (ret < 0)
     {
         esp_tls_conn_destroy(tls);
         continue;
     }
     printf("error session created %X\n", -ret);
```

When the accept returns, client_fd has the socket number of the client and then we can use esp_tls_server_session_create to wrap the socket with encryption, using the certificate and key stored in cfg. You cannot assume that the first handshake will work. Some browsers, Chrome for example, break the connection and start over with a new attempt at a handshake, others, Firefox for example, try another handshake without breaking the connection. You have to loop until you get a good handshake or an error.

Now we can read the data from the client in the usual way:

```
        int n = esp_tls_conn_read(tls, buffer, len - 1);
        buffer[n] = 0;
        printf("\ndata received %d\n\n", n);
        printf("Final buffer\n\n%s\n", buffer);
```

If you want to make sure that the client has finished sending data, the best way is to parse the headers and check that everything has been sent. Alternatively you can use:

```
ssize_t esp_tls_get_bytes_avail(esp_tls_t *tls)
```

in the loop with a timeout to check for more data. Notice that the read function is blocking and only returns when there is some data or an error.

You can now send a response to the request. Usually you would process it to discover what the client wanted, but for simplicity we will just send a hello world page:

```
char headers[] = "HTTP/1.1 200 OK\r\n"
                    "Content-Type:text/html;"
                    "charset=UTF-8\r\n"
                    "Server:ESP32\r\n"
                    "Content-Length:";
    char html[] = "<html><head><title>Hello HTTP
                                World</title></head>"
                "<body><p>Hello HTTP World</p></body>"
                "</html>\r\n";
    char data[2048] = {0};
    snprintf(data, sizeof data, "%s%d\r\n\r\n%s",
                    headers, strlen(html), html);

    n = esp_tls_conn_write(tls, data, strlen(data));

    printf("data sent \n");
    esp_tls_conn_destroy(tls);
}
```

You can see the complete listing of the server in folder HTTPSServer2. Notice that it can only handle one client at a time, but extending it to a more sophisticated approach works in the same way as for the HTTP server. Only the use of the certificate and starting a TLS session is different.

HTTPS Socket Server

The ESP-TLS module makes creating an HTTPS server very easy, but it is only a small step to implementing a completely socket-based server and this has the advantage of being portable and customizable.

The process of creating an HTTPS server is exactly the same as for the client. We are going to wrap a socket with SSL/TLS. The only difference is that it is the socket of the client that connects via an accept that we wrap and we have to provide a certificate, or better a certificate chain, to prove the identity of the server. The ESP-TLS module takes care of setting up the TLS session for us, but after this things proceed in much the same way.

Our main task in configuring the TLS/SSL session is setting up an SSL context and to do this we first need to set up the DRBG. This is exactly the same set of steps as in the client, but for this longer server example the setup code has been refactored to functions:

- mbedtls_ssl_config conf;
- mbedtls_entropy_context entropy;
- mbedtls_ctr_drbg_context ctr_drbg;
- setupSSLconfig(&conf, &entropy, &ctr_drbg);

Notice that the structs are declared at the `app_main` level so that they have the same lifetime. This is important as the `config` struct references them and we might have to free them at the end of the `app_main`.

The initialization function is:

```
void setupSSLconfig(mbedtls_ssl_config *conf,
                    mbedtls_entropy_context *entropy,
                        mbedtls_ctr_drbg_context *ctr_drbg)
{
  int err = 0;
  mbedtls_ssl_config_init(conf);
  err = mbedtls_ssl_config_defaults(conf, MBEDTLS_SSL_IS_SERVER,
          MBEDTLS_SSL_TRANSPORT_STREAM, MBEDTLS_SSL_PRESET_DEFAULT);
  if (err < 0)
      printf("%d", err);
  mbedtls_entropy_init(entropy);
  mbedtls_ctr_drbg_init(ctr_drbg);
  const char *pers = "https_server";
  err = mbedtls_ctr_drbg_seed(ctr_drbg, mbedtls_entropy_func,
              entropy, (const unsigned char *)pers, strlen(pers));
  mbedtls_ssl_conf_rng(conf, mbedtls_ctr_drbg_random, ctr_drbg);
}
```

When this function returns, the `config` struct is mostly initialized, but as this is a server we also need to add certificates:

```
mbedtls_x509_crt srvcert;
mbedtls_pk_context pkey;
setupCert(&srvcert, &pkey);
```

Again the work has been moved into a setup function. In this case, the code is initializing a self-signed certificate, which is an x509 certificate, with the public key used to sign it.

The `setupCert` function is:

```
void setupCert(mbedtls_x509_crt *srvcert,
                  mbedtls_pk_context *srvkey)
{

    mbedtls_x509_crt_init(srvcert);
    int err = mbedtls_x509_crt_parse(srvcert, cert, sizeof(cert));
    if (err < 0)
        printf("%d", err);

    mbedtls_pk_init(srvkey);
    err = mbedtls_pk_parse_key(srvkey, key, sizeof(key), NULL, 0);
    if (err < 0)
        printf("%d", err);
}
```

The key and certificate strings are created as described earlier and are identical to the certificates used in the previous server examples.

If you are working with a certificate chain associated with a properly signed certificate, then you can present all of the certificates in one long string in PEM format and they will be added to srvcert as a chain.

Now that you have the certificate you can install it into the SSL configuration by including:

```
err = mbedtls_ssl_conf_own_cert(&conf, &srvcert, &srvkey);
```

in void app_main(void).

SSL Context and Connection

The accept loop is as before:

```
int len = 1024 * 2;
    char buffer[len];
    struct sockaddr_storage client_addr;
    socklen_t addr_size = sizeof client_addr;
    while (true)
    {
        int client_fd = accept(sockfd,
              (struct sockaddr *)&client_addr, &addr_size);
```

Now we have to wrap the client_fd socket in an SSL context, but first we have to create it from the configuration struct we created earlier.

```
    mbedtls_ssl_context ssl;
    mbedtls_ssl_init(&ssl);
    err = mbedtls_ssl_setup(&ssl, &conf);
    if (err < 0)
        printf("%d", err);
```

The SSL context is all we need to wrap a client socket. If you want to wrap more than one socket at the same time, you need another SSL context. However, you can reset an SSL context so that it can be used to wrap another socket at a later time.

```
mbedtls_ssl_set_bio(&ssl, &client_fd,
                    mbedtls_net_send, mbedtls_net_recv, NULL);
```

Unlike the client situation, we now need to explicitly start a handshake. The actual handshake is implemented as a function and it is more complicated than you might expect:

```
int doHandshake(mbedtls_ssl_context *ssl)
{
    int err;
    while ((err = mbedtls_ssl_handshake(ssl)) != 0)
    {
        if (err != MBEDTLS_ERR_SSL_WANT_READ &&
                    err != MBEDTLS_ERR_SSL_WANT_WRITE)
            break;
    }
    return err;
}
```

We can no longer assume that the handshake will complete in one step and hence we keep trying to set up encryption until we get an error that isn't recoverable. The handshake establishes the cryptographic suite to use, it sends the certificate to the client and it sets up symmetric encryption after a key exchange. This is a lot of work and it takes some time. Some browsers, Firefox for example, will keep the connection and retry the handshake without aborting the connection. Others, in particular Chrome, will break the connection and retry with a new client socket. If the handshake fails, we need to clean up a little so that the accept loop can start over:

```
if (doHandshake(&ssl) < 0)
{
    mbedtls_ssl_session_reset(&ssl);
    close(client_fd);
    continue;
};
```

The SSL context is reset, which allows it to be reused, and the client socket is closed. The rest of the accept loop is then skipped and we start over afresh.

Now we have the secure connection we can read the client's request:

```
char buffer[2048] = {0};
if(readData(&ssl, buffer, sizeof(buffer))<0){
    mbedtls_ssl_session_reset(&ssl);
    close(client_fd);
    continue;
};
```

We cannot simply use the mbedtls_ssl_read function as the SSL connection is slow enough not to be ready to supply the data the client has sent. We need to poll until it is ready:

```
int readData(mbedtls_ssl_context *ssl, char buffer[], int len)
{
    int n;
    do
    {
        n = mbedtls_ssl_read(ssl, buffer, len);
    } while (n == MBEDTLS_ERR_SSL_WANT_READ || n ==
                            MBEDTLS_ERR_SSL_WANT_WRITE);
    if (n > 0)
        buffer[n] = 0;
    return n;
}
```

For simplicity we also assume that the client supplies the data in one chunk. This usually the case for simple requests but you may have to modify it to read additional data.

In a more complete server we would now process the headers that form the request and work out what to send back to the client.

For simplicity, we will send a fixed HTTP response created by a suitable function:

```
void getPage(char data[], int len)
{
    char headers[200] = "HTTP/1.1 200 OK\r\n"
                        "Content-Type:text/html;"
                        "charset=UTF-8\r\n"
                        "Server:ESP32\r\n";
    char html[] = "<html><head><title>Hello HTTP"
                  "World</title></head>"
                  "<body><p>Hello HTTP World</p></body>"
                  "</html>\r\n";
    char ContLen[100] = {0};
    snprintf(ContLen, sizeof ContLen,
             "Content-Length:%d \r\n\r\n", strlen(html));
    strcat(headers, ContLen);
    snprintf(data, len, "%s%s%c", headers, html, '\0');
}
```

There is nothing new in this function and it puts together an HTML page with minimal headers.

To send the data we need to use another custom write function:

```
        char data[2048] = {0};
        getPage(data, sizeof(data));
        if (writeData(&ssl, data, strlen(data)) < 0){
            mbedtls_ssl_session_reset(&ssl);
            close(client_fd);
            continue;
        };
        printf("page sent\n");
```

The writeData function has to poll the connection until the client is ready to receive the data and take into account that it might have to be sent in small chunks:

```
int writeData(mbedtls_ssl_context *ssl, char buffer[], int len)
{
    int n = 0;
    while (true)
    {
        n = mbedtls_ssl_write(ssl, (u_char *)buffer - n, len);
        if (n > 0)
            return n;
        if (n != MBEDTLS_ERR_SSL_WANT_WRITE ||
                        n != MBEDTLS_ERR_SSL_WANT_READ){
            printf(" failed\n
                    ! mbedtls_ssl_write returned %d\n\n", n);
            return n;
        }
    }
}
```

Finally, we close the connection:

```
        mbedtls_ssl_session_reset(&ssl);
        close(client_fd);
    }
}
```

The reset function is:

```
void notifyClose(mbedtls_ssl_context *ssl)
{
    int err;
    while ((err = mbedtls_ssl_close_notify(ssl)) < 0)
    {
        if (err != MBEDTLS_ERR_SSL_WANT_READ &&
                        err != MBEDTLS_ERR_SSL_WANT_WRITE)
            break;
    }
}
```

Closing the connection is the simplest thing to do, even if the client requests that the connection is kept open. Keeping the connection open means that we don't have to perform a time-consuming handshake to transfer more data. If you want to keep the connection open, you need to add code that tracks the interaction and this is much more complicated.

The complete listing can be seen in folder HTTPSServer3.

Encryption Suites

So far we haven't considered what types of encryption either the client or the server supports. Most servers support as wide a range of encryption standards as possible, but encryption methods that are considered insecure are usually left out of the mix. Some servers restrict the encryption methods a client can use to only the most secure in an attempt to improve their overall security. For example, you will find websites that only support the latest version of TLS. When a client connects to a server, it attempts to find the most secure encryption method that they both support. This is what happens during a handshake and as already mentioned different browsers do this in different ways.

This raises the question of what encryption methods we should support?

The usual solution of implementing a client is to include as many cryptographic methods as possible hoping that they support one of the methods that the server can work with, no matter how rarely encountered. If you are programming an IoT device then this approach is possible, but wasteful. Each crypto method you support increases the size and complexity of your program. In most cases, it is better to restrict the methods to just those used by the servers you are trying to connect to. In particular, if the server is one that is under your control, then you can select a single encryption method that works on both the client and the server.

An encryption suite is a combined set of cryptographic methods.

The big problem is that there are lots of alternative methods and they are identified using acronyms that are cryptic if you don't know what they mean. Here is a brief and incomplete guide:

RSA	Rivest-Shamir-Adleman public key encryption
CAMELLIA	Public key cipher alternative to RSA
AES	Advanced Encryption Standard
ECB	Electronic CodeBook block cipher mode
CBC	Cipher Block Chaining block cipher mode
CCM	Counter with Cipher Block Chaining Message authentication code
GCM	Galois Counter Mode for message authentication
DH or DHE	Diffie-Hellman key exchange
ECDH or ECDHE	Elliptic Curve Diffie-Hellman key exchange
PSK	PreShared Key used as a prefix/suffix as in PSK-RSA
SRP	Secure Remote Password
DSA	Digital Signature Algorithm
SHAn	Secure Hash Algorithm n-bit as a set of hash functions

A particular suite is generally written as a list in the order:

`Key exchange — Authentication - Encryption method - Hash`

So, for example, the TLS suite:

`TLS_ECDHE_ECDSA_WITH_AES_128_GCM_SHA256`

uses Elliptic Curve Diffie-Hellman key exchange, Elliptic Curve Digital Signature Algorithm (ECDSA) authentication, AES with a 128-bit key and GCM mode as the encryption method and SHA256 for a hash. Notice that this means that a connection is made by first using the key exchange method to exchange keys to be used with the encryption method. That is, Diffie-Hellman key exchange is used to establish the keys to be used with the AES encryption.

All of this raises the question of how to find out what encryption method or encryption suite a particular server supports. The only way to do this is to write a program that attempts to connect to the server using each possible suite in turn. You could do this using mbedtls, but it is much easier to use an off-the-shelf script or application. There are many to choose between but nmap is generally useful, easy to install and has a testing script included.

You can install nmap on Windows from https://nmap.org/.

Installation on the Raspberry Pi is also easy:

```
sudo apt update
sudo apt install nmap
```

Once you have nmap installed you can check that encryption suites offered by any website using:

```
nmap -sV --script ssl-enum-ciphers -p 443 host
```

where *host* is an IP address or a URL.

If you run the command on example.com you will see something like:

```
PORT    STATE SERVICE  VERSION
443/tcp open  ssl/http AkamaiGHost (Akamai's HTTP Acceleration/Mirror service)
| ssl-enum-ciphers:
|   TLSv1.2:
|     ciphers:
|       TLS_ECDHE_ECDSA_WITH_AES_256_GCM_SHA384 (secp256r1) - A
|       TLS_ECDHE_ECDSA_WITH_AES_128_GCM_SHA256 (secp256r1) - A
|       TLS_ECDHE_ECDSA_WITH_CHACHA20_POLY1305_SHA256 (secp256r1) - A
|     compressors:
|       NULL
|     cipher preference: server
|   TLSv1.3:
|     ciphers:
|       TLS_AKE_WITH_AES_128_GCM_SHA256 (secp256r1) - A
|       TLS_AKE_WITH_AES_256_GCM_SHA384 (secp256r1) - A
|       TLS_AKE_WITH_CHACHA20_POLY1305_SHA256 (secp256r1) - A
|     cipher preference: client
|_  least strength: A
```

You can see that it lists all of the methods and gives them a strength rating, reporting the least strong. In this case all of the supported methods rate an A and we might as well use any of them. The one we have opted to support in the client is TLS_ECDHE_ECDSA_WITH_AES_256_GCM_SHA384 (secp256r1). If you go back and look at the mbedtls_config.h file you will see that these are the key exchange, encryption and hash methods specified. Also notice that nmap includes secp256r1, the elliptic curve used in the key exchange.

Controlling Encryption Suites

In most cases, there are enough resources to support a good range of encryption suites. If you are using mbedTLS directly then you can control what suites are available by editing `mbedtls_config.h`, but this can be very complicated. The IDF SDK Configuration editor doesn't work in terms of encryption suites, but it lets you set the key exchange method and the symmetric encryption to be used:

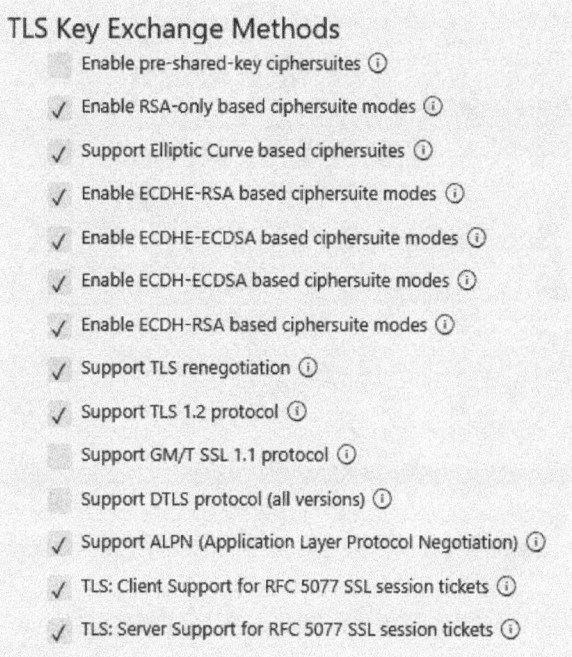

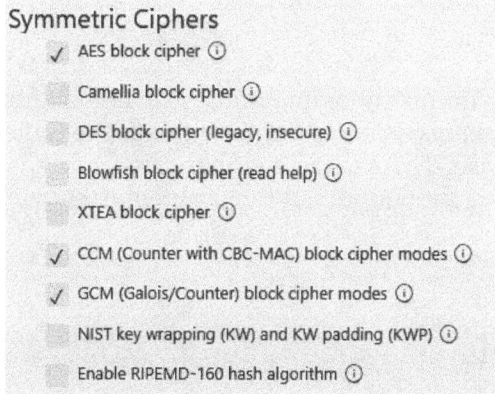

TLS Key Exchange Methods

- Enable pre-shared-key ciphersuites ⓘ
- ✓ Enable RSA-only based ciphersuite modes ⓘ
- ✓ Support Elliptic Curve based ciphersuites ⓘ
- ✓ Enable ECDHE-RSA based ciphersuite modes ⓘ
- ✓ Enable ECDHE-ECDSA based ciphersuite modes ⓘ
- ✓ Enable ECDH-ECDSA based ciphersuite modes ⓘ
- ✓ Enable ECDH-RSA based ciphersuite modes ⓘ
- ✓ Support TLS renegotiation ⓘ
- ✓ Support TLS 1.2 protocol ⓘ
- Support GM/T SSL 1.1 protocol ⓘ
- Support DTLS protocol (all versions) ⓘ
- ✓ Support ALPN (Application Layer Protocol Negotiation) ⓘ
- ✓ TLS: Client Support for RFC 5077 SSL session tickets ⓘ
- ✓ TLS: Server Support for RFC 5077 SSL session tickets ⓘ

Symmetric Ciphers

- ✓ AES block cipher ⓘ
- Camellia block cipher ⓘ
- DES block cipher (legacy, insecure) ⓘ
- Blowfish block cipher (read help) ⓘ
- XTEA block cipher ⓘ
- ✓ CCM (Counter with CBC-MAC) block cipher modes ⓘ
- ✓ GCM (Galois/Counter) block cipher modes ⓘ
- NIST key wrapping (KW) and KW padding (KWP) ⓘ
- Enable RIPEMD-160 hash algorithm ⓘ

It also lets you select the elliptic curves used in public key encryption:

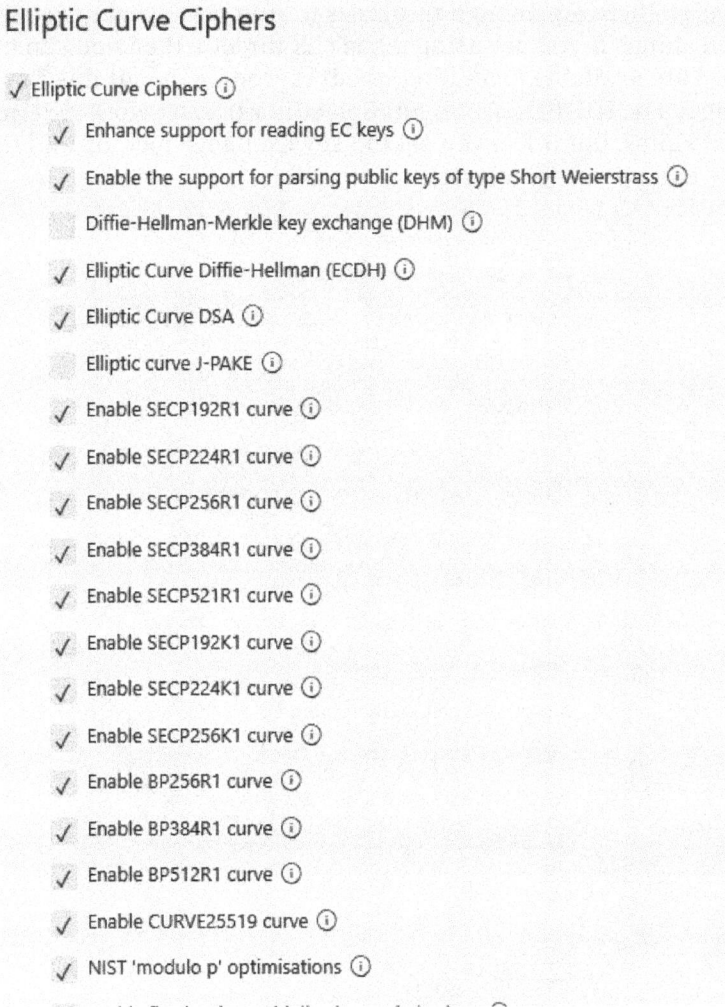

Elliptic Curve Ciphers

✓ Elliptic Curve Ciphers ⓘ

    ✓ Enhance support for reading EC keys ⓘ

    ✓ Enable the support for parsing public keys of type Short Weierstrass ⓘ

       Diffie-Hellman-Merkle key exchange (DHM) ⓘ

    ✓ Elliptic Curve Diffie-Hellman (ECDH) ⓘ

    ✓ Elliptic Curve DSA ⓘ

       Elliptic curve J-PAKE ⓘ

    ✓ Enable SECP192R1 curve ⓘ

    ✓ Enable SECP224R1 curve ⓘ

    ✓ Enable SECP256R1 curve ⓘ

    ✓ Enable SECP384R1 curve ⓘ

    ✓ Enable SECP521R1 curve ⓘ

    ✓ Enable SECP192K1 curve ⓘ

    ✓ Enable SECP224K1 curve ⓘ

    ✓ Enable SECP256K1 curve ⓘ

    ✓ Enable BP256R1 curve ⓘ

    ✓ Enable BP384R1 curve ⓘ

    ✓ Enable BP512R1 curve ⓘ

    ✓ Enable CURVE25519 curve ⓘ

    ✓ NIST 'modulo p' optimisations ⓘ

There is certainly a simplicity in including as many methods and curves as possible but each one uses memory and increases the time it takes to complete a handshake. This means that there are some advantages in reducing the number supported, but the problem is knowing which ones you need.

Summary

- An HTTPS server needs a certificate for encryption and authentication unless you use a self-signed certificate and set the browser to accept it.

- The ESP32 IDF provides an HTTPS server component which can be used to implement a web server with the addition of suitable certificates.

- The ESP-TLS library provides an easier way to create a socket based HTTPS server.

- You can also directly wrap a socket to setup a secure socket which can be used for encrypted communication.

- Any TLS connection involves a negotiation about which set of cryptographic methods, a cryptographic suite, to use.

- A particular suite is generally written as a list in the order Key exchange, Authentication, Encryption method, Hash.

Chapter 12

UDP For Speed

The UDP, User Datagram. protocol is very different from the more usual TCP, Transmission Control Protocol. UDP is very basic. There is no error correction and no guarantee that datagrams, i.e. packets, will arrive in the order they were sent. All you get is a checksum error detection mechanism that lets you detect any corruption in the data the datagram is carrying. Using IPv4 the data in a datagram is limited to 65,507 bytes, but this limit can be exceeded using IPv6. UDP can also broadcast datagrams simultaneously to as many clients as care to receive them.

After this description you may be wondering why anyone would consider using UDP in preference to TCP. The simple answer is speed. There are few overheads to UDP and it is ideal for sending fast packets of data, as long as packet loss and order don't matter or can be engineered to not matter. It is the basis for a number of other fast simple protocols such as DHCP (Dynamic Host Configuration Protocol), DNS (Domain Name System) and NTP (Network Time Protocol) and is used in audio and video applications to implement streams of data.

Basic UDP

A UDP packet is very simple. The usual IP header is used and its payload is a UDP datagram. This has a 32-bit header which has the format:

bytes	
0, 1	Source port number
2, 3	Destination port number
4, 5	Length of data payload including header
6, 7	Checksum

The source port number and checksum are optional and often set to zero and ignored. The length gives the total length of the payload including the header and hence has to be 8 or larger. The largest packet that can be sent is set by the use of a 16-bit value, but it is actually smaller than you might expect due to the need to accommodate the IP header.

For IPv4 the largest UDP packet is 65,507 bytes. The checksum field holds a checksum for all of the data, the header and the IP header and it is used for optional error checking.

There are a range of standard port numbers that are used for particular tasks, as is the case for TCP. For example, port 123 is used for SNTP and should be avoided for other purposes. Ports above 49152 are not standardized and can be used for anything. Of course, you still have to avoid collisions between different applications. One approach is to use a random assignment of port numbers with the server informing the client of the port in use by some other standard protocol.

UDP Server

A UDP Server waits for datagrams to be sent from other machines and can optionally send data back to the clients.

The basic operation of raw UDP is the same as for TCP sockets with some small differences. The first difference is that the socket has to be created to be a datagram socket:

```
 int sockfd = socket(AF_INET, SOCK_DGRAM, 0);
```

Once we have a socket we can bind it to an address and port so that it accepts UDP packets:

```
    struct sockaddr_in srvaddr;
    srvaddr.sin_family = AF_INET;
    srvaddr.sin_port = htons(8080);
    srvaddr.sin_addr.s_addr = htonl(INADDR_ANY);
    int err = bind(sockfd, (struct sockaddr *)&srvaddr,
                                    sizeof(srvaddr));
```

This binds the socket to the current internet address. The port used, 8080, isn't typically used for UDP, but it has a higher probability of working through firewalls. If this program doesn't work on a particular machine then it is almost certain that it is a firewall rule that is blocking it or the lack of a rule to allow it. If you specify a 0 for port it will automatically bind to a random port between UDP_LOCAL_PORT_RANGE_START and UDP_LOCAL_PORT_RANGE_END.

Once the socket is bound we can try to read any incoming packet using:

```
ssize_t recvfrom(int sockfd, void *buf, size_t len, int flags,
                struct sockaddr *src_addr, socklen_t *addrlen);
```

The packet's data is read into buf and the address of the client is stored in src_addr. Notice that addrlen has to be passed as a reference and the recvfrom will modify it according to the type of address actually received. The recvfrom is blocking and only returns when there is data. When recvfrom returns we have some edata in buf that we can work with.

The complete program, in folder Udpserver, is:

```c
#include <stdio.h>
#include "freertos/FreeRTOS.h"
#include "esp_wifi.h"
#include "nvs_flash.h"
#include "esp_event.h"
#include "esp_netif.h"
#include "string.h"

#include "socket.h"
#include "connectWiFi.h"

void app_main(void)
{
    wifiConnect("Co", "SSID", "password", NULL, NULL);
    while (wifiStatus != 1010)
    {
        vTaskDelay(10 / portTICK_PERIOD_MS);
    };

    int sockfd = socket(AF_INET, SOCK_DGRAM, 0);

    struct sockaddr_in srvaddr;
    srvaddr.sin_family = AF_INET;
    srvaddr.sin_port = htons(8080);
    srvaddr.sin_addr.s_addr = htonl(INADDR_ANY);
    int err = bind(sockfd, (struct sockaddr *)&srvaddr,
                                        sizeof(srvaddr));

    int len = 1024 * 2;
    char buffer[len];
    struct sockaddr_in clientaddr;
    int addrLen = sizeof clientaddr;
    int n = recvfrom(sockfd, buffer, len-1, 0,
        (struct sockaddr *)&clientaddr, (socklen_t *)&addrLen);
    buffer[n]=0;

    printf("Received message from IP: %s and port: %i\n",
                inet_ntoa(clientaddr.sin_addr),
                            ntohs(clientaddr.sin_port));
    printf("Msg from client: %s\n", buffer);
}
```

If you want a non-blocking recvfrom you can either change the socket to a non-blocking socket or you can use the flags parameter in recvfrom to set MSF_DONTWAIT. In this case the recvfrom returns immediately either with a positive n and some data in buf or a negative n and either an error or EAGAIN or EWOULDBLOCK which aren't errors but an indicattion that there is currently no data to return. If you want to try this out change the recvfrom into a while loop in the server to read:

```
while (true)
{
    n = recvfrom(sockfd, buffer, len - 1, MSG_DONTWAIT,
            (struct sockaddr *)&clientaddr, (socklen_t *)&addrLen);
    printf("%d\n", n);
    if (n > 0)
        break;
    if(errno != EAGAIN || errno!= EWOULDBLOCK)
        break;
    vTaskDelay(200);
}
```

Notice that if you want to send data back to the client you can simply use sendto after the recv.

A Python UDP Client

It can be difficult to test UDP programs without a suitable client or server to connect to. Using Python it is very easy to create a UDP client, udpclient.py, in folder Udpserverwhich can be used to test UDP servers:

```
import asyncio

async def main():
    loop = asyncio.get_running_loop()
    transport, protocol = await loop.create_datagram_endpoint(
                            lambda: asyncio.DatagramProtocol(),
                            local_addr=('0.0.0.0',8080))

    data=b"Hello UDP World"
    for i in range(20):
        transport.sendto(data,addr=("192.168.11.168",8080))
        await asyncio.sleep(1)
    transport.close()

asyncio.run(main())
```

This sends twenty packets at one-second intervals to the specified IP address. Again, it is from *Programmer's Python: Async*.

A UDP Client

The obvious thing to do is to write a client that can send the datagram received by the previous example or by the Python server given below. Many examples of using UDP do so on a single machine, passing the datagram between two programs via the local loopback connection. This usually works, but it doesn't make clear the distinction between client and server. In this case, it is assumed that the client is running on a different machine that is reachable by the server running on yet another machine.

The main difference is that now we have to set the address of the server waiting to receive the UDP packet:

```
struct sockaddr_in srvaddr;
srvaddr.sin_family = AF_INET;
srvaddr.sin_port = htons(8080);
srvaddr.sin_addr.s_addr = inet_addr("192.168.253.73");
```

To send data you have to specify the address of the destination each time as UDP isn't a connection-oriented protocol:

```
ssize_t sendto(int sockfd, const void *buf, size_t len, int flags,
               const struct sockaddr *dest_addr, socklen_t addrlen);
```

The complete program is:

```
#include <stdio.h>
#include "freertos/FreeRTOS.h"
#include "esp_wifi.h"
#include "nvs_flash.h"
#include "esp_event.h"
#include "esp_netif.h"
#include "string.h"
#include "socket.h"
#include "connectWiFi.h"
void app_main(void)
{
    wifiConnect("Co", "SSID", "password", NULL, NULL);
    while (wifiStatus != 1010)
    {
        vTaskDelay(10 / portTICK_PERIOD_MS);
    };
    int sockfd = socket(AF_INET, SOCK_DGRAM, 0);
    struct sockaddr_in srvaddr;
    srvaddr.sin_family = AF_INET;
    srvaddr.sin_port = htons(8080);
    srvaddr.sin_addr.s_addr = inet_addr("192.168.253.73");
    int len = 1024 * 2;
    char buffer[1024 * 2] = "Hello UDP World";
    sendto(sockfd, buffer, strlen(buffer), 0,
                   (struct sockaddr *)&srvaddr, sizeof srvaddr);
}
```

If you run this particular client from folder UDOclient, on the machine with the correct IP address and a server, either the previous server on a ESP32 or the Python server given in the next section, when the server sends a datagram you will see:

Received Hello UDP World from ('192.168.253.68', 60713)

There is no limit on the number of datagrams that can be received. If you don't see the message when both client and server are running then the only possible reasons are that you are using the wrong IP address on the server or, and this is more likely, the firewall on the client is stopping the datagrams arriving.

If you want to receive data from the server after sending it some data you can simply use recvfrom without specifying an address. The sendto automatically binds the socket to the port:

```
int n = recvfrom(sockfd, buffer, len-1, 0, NULL,NULL);
```

A Custom Python UDP Server

While you can use another ESP32 to send UDP packets to a client, it is useful to have a Python program, UDPServer.py, that can run on almost anything:

It can be difficult to test UDP programs without a suitable client or server to connect to. Using Python it is very easy to create UDPServer.py, which can be used to test UDP servers:

```python
import asyncio
class ClientDatagramProtocol(asyncio.DatagramProtocol):
    def datagram_received(self, data, addr):
        message = data.decode("utf8")
        print("Received",message,"from", addr)

async def main():
    loop = asyncio.get_running_loop()
    transport, protocol = await loop.create_datagram_endpoint(
            lambda: ClientDatagramProtocol(),
                    local_addr=('0.0.0.0', 8080))
    await asyncio.sleep(100000)
    transport.close()

asyncio.run(main())
```

If you want to know more, this program is presented in *Programmer's Python: Async* by Mike James, (I/O Press), ISBN: 978-1871962595.

UDPLite

Usually a datagram includes a checksum computed on all of the data including the header. If the receiving client computes the checksum and it doesn't agree with the value included in the datagram then the whole packet is discarded and the application knows nothing about the server's attempt to send a packet. Often this is exactly what is required. Usually the client has some method of deciding when a datagram has gone missing. For example, a sequence number and a timeout can be used to trigger a request that the server send the datagram again. More often the loss of a datagram is simply tolerated.

For some applications, however, the use of a checksum is too sensitive. The whole datagram is discarded if even a single bit is in error. If the error is confined to a small number of bits and can be tolerated then a better option is to use UDPLite, which restricts the calculation of the checksum to a given number of bytes. The header always has to be in the checksum because if there was even a single-bit error in it then the datagram might not even be intended for the recipient.

At the time of writing, UDPLite is not supported by the IDF SDK even though it is supported by lwIP.

Broadcast UDP

You can use UDP to send a datagram to all of the machines on the network. Whether this is a good idea or not is debatable. IPv6 has abandoned broadcast UDP in favor of multicasting, which is just as simple from the program's point of view, but requires the network to be set up to use it and a router or managed switch that supports it. In short, broadcasting is simple, but not supported by IPv6.

You can set the client given earlier in folder UDPClient to broadcast with just some small changes:

```
srvaddr.sin_addr.s_addr = INADDR_BROADCAST;
char broadcast = '1';
setsockopt(sockfd, SOL_SOCKET, SO_BROADCAST,
                             &broadcast, sizeof broadcast);
int len = 1024 * 2;
char buffer[1024 * 2] = "Hello UDP World";
sendto(sockfd, buffer, strlen(buffer), 0,
               (struct sockaddr *)&srvaddr, sizeof srvaddr);
```

To enable broadcasting on the socket we have to set its SO_BROADCAST option. The specified address is treated as a mask to determine the subnet to transmit the broadcast on.

Nothing else has to change and the UDP client works as it did, but now any machine running it on the same sub-net will receive the datagram.

Using UDP

UDP is different from an TCP/IP connection in that it has no error correction and there is no guarantee that any packet will make it from client to server or vice versa. It isn't even guaranteed that packets will arrive in the order that they are transmitted. UDP is a lightweight fast protocol, but this means that you have to take care using it. Typically, UDP packets include a sequence number to indicate how they should be put back together and either the data is robust against packet loss or there is some way to make up for a lost packet. For example, you could implement an audio stream with UDP packets and simply miss out packets that didn't arrive. As long as there were few losses this would work. Similarly a sensor could send readings out to the world in UDP packets – again packet loss wouldn't be a huge problem.

Summary

- UDP is a lightweight protocol that can be used to exchange data between two machines.

- The sending machine specifies the address of the receiving machine and a port number.

- The receiving machine specifies the address and port number it wants to receive data from.

- UDP doesn't offer error correction or confirmation of receipt. Essentially packets or datagrams are sent into the network for other machines to pick up and if they are lost on the way that's something that has to be accommodated.

- There is error detection in the form of a checksum. Any datagram that has an error is automatically discarded.

- Implementing a UDP client or server follows the same lines as the use of TCP.

- There is a UDPLite protocol which allows you to ignore any errors in the data detected by the checksum.

- Datagrams can be broadcast to every machine on the local network, but only using IPv4.

Chapter 13

SNTP For Timekeeping

SNTP, Simple Network Time Protocol, is a network protocol for obtaining an accurate time and date and it is the obvious way to set the ESP32's clock without the need for additional hardware or user intervention. Knowing the correct time and date is particularly important if you are using certificates as these have to be checked to ensure they are still valid and not expired.

A full SNTP client is quite complicated and lwIP supplies a basic implementation as an application. However, for the purposes of setting the ESP32's RTC we can use a much simpler approach, which is also a good example of how to use UDP.

SNTP is an extensive topic of which we'll only cover a small fraction. You can find out about it in detail at https://www.ntp.org/, the website of the Network Time Protocol Project.

Unicast SNTP

There are two versions of SNTP, Multicast and Unicast.

The Multicast protocol broadcasts time packets that anyone can pick up and is useful for keeping a local network synchronized. The Unicast protocol is slightly more complicated from the client's point of view in that it has to request a packet, but it is the norm on the wider Internet.

To make use of SNTP we have to use UDP as described in the previous chapter. The basic transaction is simple.

1. The client sends an SNTP data structure as UDP packet using port 123 to the server.

2. The server then sends an SNTP data structure as a UDP packet back using the same port to the client.

The Structure of Time

The key to using SNTP is the SNTP data structure which consists of four 32-bit words followed by four 64-bit timestamps. There is also an optional 96-bit authenticator, which can be used to verify the server's identity, but this isn't used by publicly available time servers.

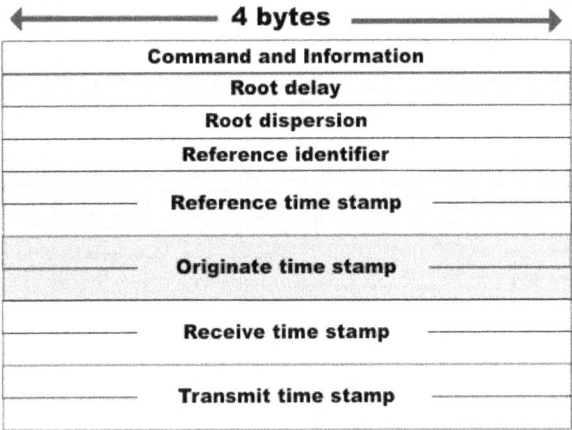

4 bytes
Command and Information
Root delay
Root dispersion
Reference identifier
Reference time stamp
Originate time stamp
Receive time stamp
Transmit time stamp

SNTP time packet

Each of the time stamps uses the same 64-bit format.

- The first 32 bits comprise an unsigned binary integer that gives the number of seconds since the so-called "fiducial date" - midnight on January 1, 1900.

- The next 32 bits is a pure binary fraction giving the fractional part of the seconds since the fiducial date.

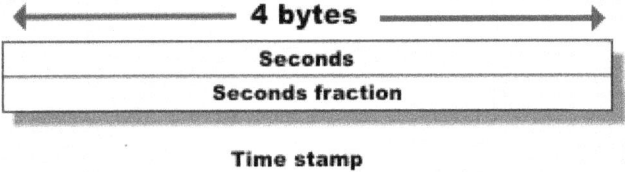

4 bytes
Seconds
Seconds fraction

Time stamp

Time Stamp format

The time stamp is always expressed using Coordinated Universal Time (UTC) and converting it to your local time zone is left to the client.

Interestingly there is a problem contained in this time stamp format that is very similar to the Millennium Bug, aka Year 2000 problem. Currently the high bit of the time stamp is set and it is heading to roll over in 2036, hence the "Y2036 bug problem".

SNTPv4, the latest version, appears to introduce a standard which uses a 128-bit date format: 64 bits for the second and 64 bits for the fractional-second. This has enough range to work until the end of the universe or 585 billion years. However, this isn't quite what it seems as even SNTPv4 uses the usual 64-bit format to send the current time and it is left to the client to expand this to a full 128-bit date by including "era" via other means.

The prime epoch, i.e. 00h on 1 Jan 1900, corresponds to an era of zero, i.e. the high-order 64 bits are set to zero. Once the date passes 00h on 1 Jan 2036 the era will be set to one and the timestamp will roll over to zero. That is, the full 128-bit date is given by

```
128-bit date = era x 2³² + timestamp
```

and it is for the client to determine the value of era.

Another way to look at this is that at the moment the timestamp measures the seconds from 00h on 1 Jan 1900 and after the rollover it will measure seconds from 00h on 1 Jan 2036 and so on.

As SNTP is used to set the current date and time, you can effectively ignore the problem and set the current date and time using the timestamp from the fiducial date that is appropriate for your era. Notice that this approach doesn't work for timestamps that are used to record when something happened in the past as the era cannot be deduced in the same way.

Time Commands

The first 32-bit word of the packet is an information and command word and from the specification it seems to be the only part of the structure you need to set before sending the request.

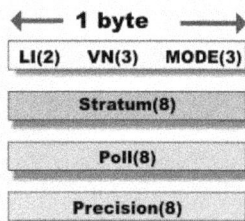

The first word

The first byte is most important. Its first two bits carry leap second information and can mostly be ignored if you are only interested in setting the RTC to a reasonably accurate time:

LI	
00	No warning
01	Last minute has 61 seconds
10	Last minute has 59 seconds)
11	Alarm condition (clock not synchronized)

The next three bits, VN, specify the SNTP version and can be set to 3 or 4 by a client.

The final three bits specify what should happen, i.e. the state. MODE should be set to 3 for a client request and the server will set it to 4 in the response packet.

Mode	
0	Reserved
1	Symmetric active
2	Symmetric passive
3	Client
4	Server
5	Broadcast
6	Reserved for NTP control message
7	Reserved for private use

The remaining three bytes provide information on the server's time keeper. Stratum gives the level of time precision.

Stratum	
0	Unspecified or unavailable
1	Primary reference (e.g., radio clock)
2-255	Secondary reference (via NTP or SNTP)

Poll gives the minimum time between packets that the server can send. This is a signed integer giving the nearest power of 2 in seconds. For example a value of 0 indicates 1 second, a value of 1 indicates 2 seconds, 2 indicates 4 seconds, -1 indicates 1/2 second and so on.

Precision is an 8-bit signed integer giving the clock's precision, again as a power of 2 in seconds.

The following two words are timestamps giving the root delay, i.e. the round trip delay to the server's primary time source; the root dispersion, i.e. the relative error of the server's time against the primary time source.

`Reference identifier`, i.e. a 4-byte ASCII code specifying the type of clock used as the standard.

The only problem with the reference identifier is that it isn't specified in the standard, but for stratum 1 servers you can look out for:

- ◆ `ATOM` Atomic clock
- ◆ `PPS` Precision Pulse Source
- ◆ `GPS` Global Positioning Satellite

and so on.

Radio clocks often quote their radio call sign. For a secondary reference, the four bytes are often the TCP/IP address of the primary server.

The Timestamps

When you get the time packet back it contains four timestamps that can be used to improve the estimate of the current time:

- ◆ Reference Time Stamp (`RefTS`) Time the server's clock was last set
- ◆ Transmit Time Stamp (`TTS`)   Time at server when the packet left
- ◆ Originate Time Stamp (`OTS`)   Time you sent the request packet
- ◆ Receive Time Stamp (`RTS`)   Time the server received the packet

These values can be used to estimate the round trip time and correct the final time to the last few tenths of a millisecond.

In practice, you can ignore all of this unless you really are trying for high accuracy. All that matters is `TTS`, which contains the time as measured at the server when the packet was transmitted. This will be accurate to a few milliseconds unless the conditions on the Internet are so bad that you would be well advised to use an alternative server.

So it looks as if we can ignore all the time stamps in the requesting package and only look at the TTS value in the return package.

The only problem is that some servers ignore packets with unreasonable values of `OTS` in the requesting packet, but when making the first request there is no reasonable way to set this value.

Simple SNTP Client

As we only want to set the RTC, we can greatly simplify the interaction with an SNTP server. You might think that the first thing we have to do is set up a struct suitable for holding the data, but there is no need as we are only interested in the first byte in the request packet and bytes 40-44 in the reply, which give the number of seconds from the fiducial date.

First, we need to set up a UDP connection on port 123, the standard SNTP port, to a suitable server. The first problem we have is determining which server to use. In principle, you should never hard-code the IP address of an SNTP server into a program. Instead you should allow DNS to select a suitable server from a pool of servers, but as this is a simple client we can start by hard-coding an IP address which you can find from www.ntp.org:

```
int sockfd = socket(AF_INET, SOCK_DGRAM, 0);

struct sockaddr_in srvaddr;
srvaddr.sin_family = AF_INET;
srvaddr.sin_port = htons(123);
srvaddr.sin_addr.s_addr = inet_addr("131.111.8.28");
```

The address used in this example is an NIST server and you should select a server geographically close to you for an accurate result and to spread the load.

Next we set up a suitable request buffer:

```
int len = 48;
char buffer[len];
memset(buffer, 0, len);
buffer[0] = 0x23;
```

Notice that all we do is zero the 48-byte payload and then set the first byte to 0x23, which specifies version 4 and client mode.

Sending the packet is trivial:

```
sendto(sockfd, buffer, 48, 0, (struct sockaddr *)&srvaddr,
                                            sizeof srvaddr);
```

Receiving the response is equally simple:

```
int n = recvfrom(sockfd, buffer, len, 0, NULL, NULL);
```

In this case, we don't have to specify the address of the server as sendto has bound the socket before we start the receive.

When recvfrom returns we can process the buffer to get the timestamp. As we only want the integer part of a single timestamp consisting of four bytes starting at buffer[40], we can put them together into a single 32-bit int:

```
int32_t seconds_since_1900 = (buffer[40] << 24 |
              buffer[41] << 16 | buffer[42] << 8 | buffer[43]);
```

The only complication is that the timestamp is in big-endian format and the ESP32 uses little-endian so we have to reverse the order of the bytes.

Setting the Date and Time

The EP32 has a Real Time Clock, RTC, but without battery backup it has to be set each time it starts.

The RTC supports the standard POSIX time and date functions. The two most important are:

- ♦ `int gettimeofday(struct timeval *restrict tv,`
  `                    struct timezone *_Nullable restrict tz);`

- ♦ `int settimeofday(const struct timeval *tv,`
  `                    const struct timezone *_Nullable tz);`

where `struct timeval` is a standard Linux time structure.

There are also some functions which allow you to manipulate an alarm and check to see if the timer is running.

We can now use the time returned by the previous program to set the RTC. The one difference is that we have to convert the `seconds_since_1900` that the SNTP server delivers into `seconds_since_1970`, which is what Unix/Linux, and hence the C library, uses.

```
time_t seconds_since_1970 = seconds_since_1900 - 2208988800;
```

Once you have the number of seconds from the correct starting point you can use this to set the RTC:

```
struct timeval tv;
tv.tv_sec = seconds_since_1970;
settimeofday(&tv, NULL);

gettimeofday(&tv, NULL);
struct tm *tm = localtime(&(tv.tv_sec));
char date[100];
strftime(date, 100, "%a, %d %b %Y %T", tm);
printf("date = %s\n", date);
```

The complete program can be seen in folder `SNTP1`.

A Better SNTP Client

The SNTP client that we have developed is very basic. It is suitable for setting the RTC clock at the start of an application, but it misses the ability to automatically refresh the time, use multiple time servers or take the round trip estimates into consideration to improve the accuracy. It also doesn't check for a wide range of error conditions.

All of this might be irrelevant to the application and trading sophistication for simplicity is often valid. However, if you do need something more robust then, rather than continuing to improve the very basic SNTP client, it is

223

more sensible to make use of the SNTP app provided by IDF. The only problem with this is that its documentation doesn't really help with getting started. The good news is that it is fairly easy to look up the time from an NTP (Network Time Protocol) server and to use it to set the RTC, see folder, SNTP2:

```
#include "esp_netif_sntp.h"
esp_sntp_config_t config=
                ESP_NETIF_SNTP_DEFAULT_CONFIG("pool.ntp.org");
esp_netif_sntp_init(&config);
if (esp_netif_sntp_sync_wait(pdMS_TO_TICKS(10000)) != ESP_OK) {
    printf("Failed to update system time within 10s timeout");
}
```

The host that you set should be one of the many NTP pool servers. A pool server has a list of time servers that it issues in response to a DNS request so as to spread the load. The sync_wait function simply waits until the update is complete. When an SNTP update is available the RTC can either be updated at once or the correction can be applied gradually according to the setting of:

```
void sntp_set_sync_mode(sntp_sync_mode_t sync_mode)
```

where sync_mode is SNTP_SYNC_MODE_IMMED or SNTP_SYNC_MODE_SMOOTH.

If the correction is more than 30 minutes the update is always immediate.

You can check on the status of the update using:

```
sntp_sync_status_t sntp_get_sync_status(void)
```

which returns one of:

- ◆ SNTP_SYNC_STATUS_COMPLETED   Update complete
- ◆ SNTP_SYNC_STATUS_RESET   Update not complete
- ◆ SNTP_SYNC_STATUS_IN_PROGRESS A smooth update is in progress

The SNTP app has two operating modes, polling and listening. In polling mode it queries the SNTP server at a set interval. In listening mode it simply waits for the server to send a packet.

To set up the mode for polling you have to use:

```
esp_sntp_setoperatingmode(ESP_SNTP_OPMODE_POLL);
```

Substitute ESP_SNTP_OPMODE_LISTENONLY for listening.

You can get the operating mode using:

```
u8_t esp_sntp_getoperatingmode (void)
```

You can set the polling time with:

```
void sntp_set_sync_interval(uint32_t interval_ms)
```

Notice that you cannot set this value to less than 15 seconds as the SNTP standard doesn't allow it.

The documentation only mentions being able to set servers by IP address:

```
void esp_sntp_setserver (u8_t idx, const ip_addr_t *server)
const ip_addr_t *esp_sntp_getserver (u8_t idx)
```

where idx is the index into the server array.

You can also use:

```
void esp_sntp_setservername(u8_t idx, const char *server)
const char *esp_sntp_getservername(u8_t idx)
```

Finally, when you have all this set up you can start the client running using:

```
esp_sntp_init();
```

and stop it using:

```
esp_sntp_stop();
```

Putting all this together gives a simple program for configuring and running the SNTP client:

```
esp_sntp_setoperatingmode(ESP_SNTP_OPMODE_POLL);
esp_sntp_setservername(0, "pool.ntp.org");
esp_sntp_init();
```

You can now poll for the update to be complete:

```
    const int retry_count = 15;
    int retry = 0;
    while (esp_netif_sntp_sync_wait(2000 / portTICK_PERIOD_MS) ==
                    ESP_ERR_TIMEOUT && ++retry < retry_count) {
        printf( "Waiting for system time to be set... (%d/%d)",
                                        retry, retry_count);
    }
```

You can configure the client to use multiple SNTP servers, accept SNTP server settings from the DHCP server, monitor the reachability of each server and so on. Of course, there is nothing stopping you from using the increased resolution, beyond one second, to set other hardware to a more accurate time.

Summary

- SNTP is a simple UDP-based protocol for acquiring the UTC time and date. The basic transaction is to send a UDP packet to port 123 and then wait for the server to respond with a packet that contains timestamps.

- Each time packet consists of four 32-bit words of general information followed by four 64- bit timestamps. The timestamps consist of four bytes giving the seconds and four bytes giving the fractional seconds since the fiducial date, which is midnight on January 1, 1900.

- The forthcoming time rollover in 2036 has be dealt with by adding a 64-bit era timestamp, which isn't transmitted along with the time data but is derived locally and added. This is, in essence, changing the fiducial date at each rollover.

- The four timestamps can be used to correct the received time to allow for network delays.

- The key timestamp is TTS, the last of the four, which gives the time at the server when the packet was sent. In many cases this is the only timestamp used.

- It is easy to set up an SNTP client as the request for a time update takes the form of a 48-byte buffer with its first byte set to 0x23. This has to be sent, using UDP, to port 123.

- The response is a 48-byte buffer in which the time in seconds at the server is stored in bytes 40 to 44 in big-endian format.

- The received timestamp can easily be converted to a Linux/Unix timestamp and used to set the RTC.

- The correct way to find a SNTP time server is to use DNS to query a pool server. This has a list of actual time servers which it supplies in rotation to even out the load.

- The IDF also provides an SNTP server module which has many additional features. It is easy to use provided you know how to configure it and how to use it to access the time or set the clock.

Chapter 14

SMTP For Email

Email is one of the simplest of protocols and potentially very useful. However, the need to deal with spam has added layers of protection that makes it very difficult to actually send an email using the standard mail transport, Simple Mail Transport Protocol, SMTP. Also, if you are planning to use email to send data back to a central server or to a user then you are going to have to find a suitable server that will accept the connection. This usually means setting up your own mail server or finding a hosted mail server that has suitable security settings.

SMTP Protocol

While SMTP originated as a simple protocol, it has become very complex due to the range of security measures that have been added to it over time. All SMTP commands and responses are text commands. You can even connect to an SMTP server using Telnet and conduct the session manually by typing in commands and reading the replies.

The first command is always:

`HELO` *domain making the connection*

The server will respond with a greeting message and the SMTP transaction has started. Of course, if the domain you specify is blacklisted or has other suspicious characteristics, the server will immediately terminate the connection. You can also use `EHLO`, the Extended HELO, for servers that implement more than just the basic SMTP commands.

Most servers will also respond with a list of optional commands that they support. For example:

- `250-PIPELINING`
- `250-SIZE 15728640`
- `250-ETRN`
- `250-STARTTLS`
- `250-ENHANCEDSTATUSCODES`
- `250-8BITMIME`
- `250-DSN`
- `250-SMTPUTF8`

Now we can send a batch of emails if we want to.

When SMTP first started you could deposit email into any SMTP server and expect it to be delivered to wherever it needed to go. That is, emails would be relayed mail from any user to any user.

Unfortunately spammers started to use arbitrary SMTP servers to send lots of emails to users who didn't want them. As a result most SMTP servers will not relay emails to other SMTP servers and as a result most will only accept email specifically direct to the domain that they serve, i.e. the one that the MX record corresponds to. You cannot just drop an email into any old SMTP server and expect it to be delivered to another SMTP server – in the early days of the Internet you could.

You will notice that this restriction effectively breaks the whole email system. How can a user send an email to a location remote from their local SMTP server and expect it to be sent on to its destination? After all, the server is usually set up to only accept emails destined for the local users. The solution is that SMTP servers which are expected to deliver mail to the wider Internet allow local users to login with a user name and password and if this is successful they will send, or relay, email to other SMTP servers. The alternative is to open the SMTP server and allow anyone to use it to relay mail. This is called an "open relay" and it will cause the server to be added to blacklists everywhere.

The next command you need is:
`MAIL FROM:` *from address*

The *from address* is used as a return address and it might even be looked up to see if it is on a white/black list if the server is performing spam filtering. Again, if the server doesn't like the *from address* the connection is closed.

To specify who the email is to you have to use:
`RCPT TO:` *to address*

As already noted, this generally has to be an address hosted by the server unless the server has been set up to relay emails to other servers.

After this you can send the body of the email as a multi-line text packet with the end marked by a line starting with a dot and nothing else.

To close the session you use the `QUIT` command.

All of the commands are accepted by the server, processed and a response is sent back.

The response can be more than one line and this complicates things just a little. Each line, however, starts with a code that indicates the status of the process - 250 means everything is fine and the command has been acted upon.

SMTP Ports

The standard SMTP port is 25, but many ISPs block this port to stop users running mail servers. This is a reasonably well-known fact and it is sometimes misinterpreted as meaning that port 25 is no longer used. This isn't the case as it is used by SMTP servers to connect to other SMTP servers to transfer mail, but to understand what is going on we need to consider things a little more generally.

There are two distinct roles that an SMTP server can play: submission and relay. Submission is where an email is sent by an SMTP client to a server – it is where an email gets into the system. Once into the system the SMTP server relays it to another SMTP server to get it closer to the delivery address. In the early days of the Internet, SMTP servers would relay multiple times, but today nearly all send the email to the SMTP server that hosts its address in one go.

- ◆ Port 25 is universally used for relay and it is also usually set up for submission, but it isn't recommended for this purpose and it is usually blocked by ISPs providing Internet connections to end users.

- ◆ Port 2525 is sometimes used in place of 25 as a way of getting round the blocking by ISPs.

- ◆ Port 587 is the port for encrypted submission using TLSstart.

- ◆ Port 465 is the standard port for encrypted submissions using TLS.

While SMTP email works perfectly well on an unencrypted connection, today the use of encryption is almost universal and almost always enforced. As a result we need to implement an SMTP client that connects using encryption.

There are two ways that SMTP can be used with encryption. The first, and currently the most common, is to use the StartTLS command. The idea is that the server and client first make a connection using plain text and then the client issues the StartTLS command to start a TLS handshake. After this is complete, assuming that the client and server can agree on a cryptographic suite to use, then the rest of the session is conducted using a TLS encrypted connection. SMTP servers can be set up to use StartTLS on any port including port 25, but for submission the standard port is 587.

The second way of encrypting SMTP is to establish an encrypted TLS to TCP connection before starting the SMTP connection. This is conceptually simple, but there is no plain text preamble to establish that the port supports encryption. The standard submission port for this approach is 465. This was briefly deprecated in favor of port 587, but it was later reinstated.

An additional problem is what do you call these two methods?

You will encounter port 587 being called the "StartTLS submission port" or confusingly the "TLS submission port". By contrast port 465 is often called the "SMTPS port for SMTP over SSL" or the "SSL port", even though, like port 587, it uses TLS. You will also encounter the StartTLS method referred to as "explicit TLS" and the alternative referred to as "implicit TLS".

What all of this means is that, in most cases, an IoT device operating in a home environment will have to connect to an SMTP server using either port 587 or port 465.

An Encrypted SMTPS Client App

SMTP uses TCP to make a reliable connection between two SMTP machines. One of the machines will play the role of the server and accept the connection and the other will play the role of a client and transfer mail to the server. Notice that SMTP provides no way for a client to download the email intended for it. To do this you need to implement either POP or IMAP.

The simplest SMTP client, from our point of view, is one that uses implicit TLS or SMTPS and this means it generally should connect on port 465. More importantly, it doesn't work with ports that only support StartTLS. The reason that SMTPS is easier is that we can use `esp-tls` to setup an encrypted connection and then send SMTP commands as if there were no encryption.

As an example we can create an SMTP client which can send mail using Gmail's SMTP server. This is a commonly suggested SMTP server to use, but it has its problems. The documentation states:

Gmail SMTP server address: smtp.gmail.com
Gmail SMTP name: Your full name
Gmail SMTP username: Your full Gmail address (e.g. you@gmail.com)
Gmail SMTP password: The password that you use to log in to Gmail
Gmail SMTP port (TLS): 587
Gmail SMTP port (SSL): 465

This makes it look easy – all we have to do is connect using TLS to port 465 and supply the Gmail user name and password. Notice that this isn't really a good idea in an IoT device as the password would be easy to find. To make use of this in a production environment you would have to set up a dedicated email account for use by the IoT device. Even then the fact that the password has to be in plain text in the program means that anyone with access to the device could start using the same server account to send spam.

There is another problem that the documentation doesn't refer to. If an application is connecting to the service it needs its own password – an application password. To create one you have to go to the Google account, select Security, and then under Signing in to Google, select App Passwords. From here you can use Select app to generate a Gmail password for your program. In other words, the fourth step in the documentation should read:

Gmail SMTP password: The password you generated for your app.

Setting up a TLS wrapped socket is as before but we set it up as a general socket on port 465:

```
esp_tls_t *tls = esp_tls_init();
esp_tls_cfg_t cfg = {
    .crt_bundle_attach = esp_crt_bundle_attach,
};
char mailserver[] = "smtp.gmail.com";
int err = esp_tls_conn_new_sync(mailserver,
                strlen(mailserver), 465, &cfg, tls);
```

If you don't want to use esp-tls you can follow the steps for the HTTPS client in Chapter 10 – it achieves the same result, but with more lines of code. In this example we are using Google's Gmail server, but as long as the server supports SMTPS on port 465 it should work.

Once we have the connection to the server we can send the first command but first we need to get the servers welcome message:

```
size_t BUF_SIZE = 512;
char buf[BUF_SIZE];

int ret = write_ssl_and_get_response(tls,
                        (unsigned char *)buf, 0);
```

The write_ssl_and_get_response function is going to be useful for all our interactions with the server and it simply sends what is in buf to the server and then reads all the data the server sends back and displays it. In a more advanced SMTP client, the respond code at the start of the line could be extracted and used to modify the flow depending on how the server responded:

```
static int write_ssl_and_get_response(esp_tls_t *tls,
                    unsigned char *buf, size_t len)
{
    int ret;
    const size_t DATA_SIZE = 128;
    unsigned char data[DATA_SIZE];
    while (len && (ret = esp_tls_conn_write(tls, buf, len)) <= 0)
    {
        if (ret != MBEDTLS_ERR_SSL_WANT_READ && ret !=
                                MBEDTLS_ERR_SSL_WANT_WRITE)
        {
            printf("mbedtls_ssl_write failed
                            with error -0x%x", -ret);
            return ret;
        }
    }
```

```
    while(true)
    {
        ret = esp_tls_conn_read(tls, data, DATA_SIZE - 1);
        if (ret == MBEDTLS_ERR_SSL_WANT_READ || ret ==
                                MBEDTLS_ERR_SSL_WANT_WRITE)
            continue;
        if (ret <= 0)
        {
            printf("mbedtls_ssl_read
                                failed with error -0x%x", -ret);
            break;
        }
        data[ret]=0;
        printf("%s", data);
        break;
    }
    return ret;
}
```

The send and receive loops are very similar to those encountered in earlier programs. Notice that if we send a buf with zero elements then the function simply reads the data from the server. For the Gmail server this is:

```
220 smtp.gmail.com ESMTP ffacd0b85a97d-429cab8575bsm13538797f8f.31 - gsmtp
```

Next we need to send EHLO:

```
    int len = snprintf((char *)buf, BUF_SIZE,
                                "EHLO %s\r\n", "ESP32");
    ret = write_ssl_and_get_response(tls,
                                (unsigned char *)buf, len);
```

to which the gmail server responds:

```
250-smtp.gmail.com at your service, [212.159.79.43]
250-SIZE 35882577
250-8BITMIME
250-AUTH LOGIN PLAIN XOAUTH2 PLAIN-CLIENT
```

At this point what servers want differs, but most want the client to sign in to their account. To do this the client email address and password generally have to be sent to the server base64-encoded. The encoding has nothing to do with security that is taken care of by the use of encryption:

```
    char senderemail[] = "sender email address";
    unsigned char base64_buffer[128];
    size_t base64_len;
    ret = mbedtls_base64_encode((unsigned char *)base64_buffer,
                                sizeof(base64_buffer),
                                &base64_len,
                                (unsigned char *)senderemail,
                                strlen(senderemail));
    len = snprintf((char *)buf, BUF_SIZE, "%s\r\n", base64_buffer);
    ret = write_ssl_and_get_response(tls,
                                (unsigned char *)buf, len);
```

```
char senderpassword[] = "sender password";
ret = mbedtls_base64_encode((unsigned char *)base64_buffer,
                            sizeof(base64_buffer),
                            &base64_len,
                            (unsigned char *)senderpassword,
                            strlen(senderpassword)));
len = snprintf((char *)buf, BUF_SIZE, "%s\r\n", base64_buffer);
ret = write_ssl_and_get_response(tls,
                                 (unsigned char *)buf, len);
```

As long as the user name and password are accepted we can now move on to actually sending an email. The first things we need are MAIL FROM and the client email address:

```
len = snprintf((char *)buf, BUF_SIZE,
                            "MAIL FROM:<%s>\r\n", senderemail);
ret = write_ssl_and_get_response(tls,
                                 (unsigned char *)buf, len);

char recipientemail[] = "recipient email";
len = snprintf((char *)buf, BUF_SIZE,
                            "RCPT TO:<%s>\r\n", recipientemail);
ret = write_ssl_and_get_response(tls,
                                 (unsigned char *)buf, len);
```

The start of the body of the email is signaled by DATA:

```
len = snprintf((char *)buf, BUF_SIZE, "DATA\r\n");
ret = write_ssl_and_get_response(tls,
                                 (unsigned char *)buf, len);
```

After the DATA command we can send almost anything, but generally it is a good idea to stick to the formatting of a standard email with a From and a To field:

```
len = snprintf((char *)buf, BUF_SIZE,
    "From: %s\r\nSubject: mbed TLS Test mail\r\n"
    "To: %s\r\n"
    "This is a simple test mail from the SMTP client example.\r\n"
    "\r\n"
    "\r\n.\r\n",
    "ESP32 SMTP Client", recipientemail);
ret = esp_tls_conn_write(tls, (unsigned char *)buf, len);
```

This is the absolute simplest email you can send. Notice that the end of the email is signaled by a single dot at the start of the final line. If you try this, folder SMTP1, you should discover that the email is sent and received. Of course, given the defensive nature of most email servers it could be rejected for a range of reasons far too numerous to detail here. You have no choice but to look at the error messages from the server and try and work out how to send it an email it is prepared to accept.

Also notice that the test email is unusually simple in that it contains no MIME header fields. MIME allows you to send a multipart message that can contain text, images and other binary attachments. However this usually isn't an issue for the SMTP server or client but rather for the email-reading software.

A STARTTLS Client

As its name suggests, STARTTLS is a protocol command used to switch an insecure plain-text connection to a secure one using TLS/SSL and is fairly easy to implement. The idea is that the initial connection is a standard unencrypted TCP/IP connection which is used for the preliminary interaction, mainly EHLO, and then the client issues the STARTTLS command to indicate that it is ready for encryption to begin. At this point the client and server begin a handshake sequence that settles on an encryption suite and after this the interaction is exactly the same as before, but encrypted.

We could implement STARTTLS using basic sockets by starting the connection with a standard socket and after issuing the STARTTLS command wrapping the socket using mbedTLS. However, a simpler approach is to use esp-tls and arrange to open a plain text connection and then convert it to an encrypted connection by taking advantage of the async mode of connection. This makes it easy to modify the previous example. After connecting the WiFi we simply make the connection using the esp_tls_plain_tcp_connect function:

```
esp_tls_cfg_t cfg = {
        .addr_family = ESP_TLS_AF_INET,
        .crt_bundle_attach = esp_crt_bundle_attach,
    };

    char mailserver[] = "smtp.gmail.com";
    int sockfd;
    struct esp_tls_last_error error;
    esp_tls_error_handle_t herror = &error;
    int ret = esp_tls_plain_tcp_connect(mailserver,
                strlen(mailserver), 587, &cfg, herror, &sockfd);
```

Now we need to send the EHLO command, but as cannot use the encrypted write_ssl_and_get_response, we need a new write_and_get_response function that works with unencrypted socket:

```
static int write_and_get_response(int sockfd, unsigned char *buf,
size_t len)
{
    int ret;
    const size_t DATA_SIZE = 128;
    unsigned char data[DATA_SIZE];
```

```
    if (len && (ret = send(sockfd, buf, len, 0)) <= 0)
    {
        printf("mbedtls_write failed with error -0x%x", -ret);
        return ret;
    }

    ret = recv(sockfd, data, DATA_SIZE - 1, 0);
    if (ret <= 0)
    {
        printf("mbedtls_read failed with error -0x%x\n", errno);
        return ret;
    }
    data[ret] = 0;
    printf("%s", data);
    return ret;
}
```

Using this we can send the EHLO and the STARTTLS commands:

```
ret = write_and_get_response(sockfd, (unsigned char *)buf, 0);
printf("\n\n");

int len = snprintf((char *)buf, BUF_SIZE,
                                "EHLO %s\r\n", "ESP32");
ret = write_and_get_response(sockfd,
                                (unsigned char *)buf, len);
printf("\n\n");

len = snprintf((char *)buf, BUF_SIZE, "STARTTLS\r\n");
ret = write_and_get_response(sockfd,
                                (unsigned char *)buf, len);

ret = write_and_get_response(sockfd, (unsigned char *)buf, 0);
printf("\n\n");
```

Next we need to convert the socket into a TLS encrypted socket. This can be done using the standard esp_tls_conn_new_sync function as long as we first setup the tls struct to specify the socket file descriptor and set the current state of the socket to be ESP_TLS_CONNECTING. This state skips the initial connection of the socket to the server and immediately starts the wrapping of the socket and the handshake:

```
esp_tls_t *tls = esp_tls_init();
esp_tls_set_conn_state(tls, ESP_TLS_CONNECTING);
esp_tls_set_conn_sockfd(tls, sockfd);
ret = esp_tls_conn_new_sync(mailserver, strlen(mailserver),
                                587, &cfg, tls);
```

When esp_tls_conn_new_sync returns the socket is encrypted and the program continues exactly as before. You can see the complete program in folder SMTP2.

This technique is generally useful when you need to convert an existing socket to an encrypted socket.

A more general SMTP client would attempt to connect to the sever using each port in turn until a successful connection was made.

Working With IoT Email

The SMTP clients given earlier are perfectly correct and adequate implementations. However, as already mentioned, the fact that they are correct doesn't mean they will work with any particular server. Defenses against spam email are so strong and complicated that it is hard to avoid triggering them even if you aren't sending spam. To do the job properly you would need a domain name for the client to use and you would have to implement the modern mechanisms for avoiding spam – DKIM (DomainKeys Identified Mail), DMARC (DomainKeys Identified Mail), and SPF (Sender Policy Framework). Even then there is no certainty that a cautious server will not reject your email because you are on one of the many blacklists or because it just doesn't like the color of the bits you are sending.

The only way to be sure that you can deliver an email from an IoT device to an SMTP server is to run and configure the server yourself. This isn't easy due to the precautions needed to avoid it being used for spam while serving your IoT devices. It is difficult to lock down a server that has to allow IoT devices to connect. The reason is that while you can use encryption to protect the data, and the username and password in particular, any attacker that has physical access to the device can quickly find out what these are. To stop the server from being used to send spam you have to also restrict recipients to the server's domain, i.e. no relaying even for logged in users. This limits the usefulness of the server to the IoT devices it serves.

If you do have a use case where sending emails from an IoT device is useful then you also need to be aware of what is missing from the SMTP client application. You can use it to send text-based emails, but if you want to send binary data or "file" attachments then you will have to implement your own MIME support. Email clients in more complete libraries build emails that include multiple headers and MIME types. The only header that the SMTP client adds to your email is the subject line.

Using email in an IoT context seems like a reasonable idea at first, if only because email is universally supported and human readable. However, once you start to contend with the need to reduce spam and maintain security, it becomes less attractive.

Summary

- SMTP is a simple protocol that has evolved to become very complex due to the need to add security.

- All SMTP commands are sent in human readable text and you can even communicate with a server using Telnet.

- Until a few years ago, SMTP servers used to accept mail from anyone and deliver it to anyone, but the need to fight spam has changed this so that a server will accept outgoing email only from users on its local network or users that are authenticated and will only accept incoming mail addressed users on its local network.

- Port 25 used to be the only port used by SMTP, but today it is mainly used for connections between SMTP servers delivering mail. If you want to submit mail to an SMTP server then you might well find that port 25 is blocked to you.

- Port 465 is used for SMTP over a TLS connection which is set up before the SMTP transaction starts. Often called implicit TLS, it is used by lwIP and so you should connect using port 465.

- Port 587 is used for encrypted TLS connection mediated using TLSstart. It is also called the SMTPS port or just the SSL port.

- You can connect to the Gmail SMTP server on port 465 or 587, but you need to obtain a special password for your applications.

- Hard coding an SMTP password into your program is a big security risk.

- The problem with using SMTP is that the majority of servers will reject your attempt to submit email without authentication.

Chapter 15

MQTT For The IoT

So far we have been exploring protocols that haven't been invented specifically for the Internet of Things. A simple device can make use of HTTP to send data to a server or email, but neither of these have characteristics that make them suitable for IoT use unless you add additional processing to the server.

Consider the simple application of a sensor that reads the temperature and needs to make this available to other devices. You can use HTTP to send data to the server and save it in a file, but you will have to make sure that the data is saved in a suitable format to allow clients to process it. For example, you will need to make sure that it is dated and fed to clients in the correct order. An IoT-specific protocol would make tasks such as these much easier and MQTT – originally standing for Message Queue Telemetry Transport – is exactly this. It is lightweight, easy to use and popular so let's take a look at how to use the MQTT client included in the IDF SDK.

Principles Of MQTT

MQTT is a publish-and-subscribe messaging system. What this means is that there are clients which submit messages to a server, or broker, which sends them on to clients that are subscribed to the topic. Messages are organized by topics and clients can be subscribed to messages on multiple topics.

The connections between client and server are via TCP and optionally TLS-encrypted TCP. The data packets are binary-encoded and not human-readable and there is no standard for the payload data that they carry. There is a mechanism for specifying the format of the payload data in MQTT 5, but most servers and clients, including lwIP, use MQTT 3.1. The advantage of using binary data is that MQTT packets can be small. However, TCP is not good at working with small packets and so it is generally important to keep the TCP connection alive while the client and server exchange packets.

This all sounds useful, but there are some important subtleties that you need to be aware of before you can see the sorts of things that MQTT can easily be used for. The first important point is that a client has to be subscribed to a topic to receive any published data. If a client publishes data, then the server sends it to all of the clients that are currently connected and subscribed to the topic. MQTT has no memory of clients that were subscribed and are now disconnected – it is a stateless protocol. After it has been sent to all of the active subscribed clients, the data is deleted from the server. Again, by default, MQTT has no memory of what happens. The exception is that the server can set a retain flag on a message which causes the server not to delete it after sending it to subscribed clients. If another client connects before another message is published then it is sent the retained message as soon as it has subscribed. Notice that the server keeps only one retained message per topic. This is intended to allow clients to receive the most up-to-date message immediately after they subscribe rather than having to wait for the next published message.

It is also possible to set up a default message, humorously called the last will and testament, which is delivered if the publisher of a topic goes offline unexpectedly.

The key ideas are:

- MQTT is mostly a memoryless and stateless protocol.
- Messages are published and subscribed to under topics.
- A published message is sent to all currently connected clients subscribed to the topic and then it is deleted unless set to be retained.
- A message that has no current subscribers is immediately deleted.
- Messages can be set to be retained to be sent to new subscribers but are still deleted when a new message arrives.
- A publisher can also set a default message to be sent if the server becomes unavailable.

What all this means is that MQTT is an intermediary between clients and other clients. It allows a client to acquire data from an IoT device without the IoT device having to take on the responsibility and overheads of being a server. MQTT doesn't do anything about data aggregation, i.e. it doesn't store a time series of sensor data. Also notice that there is no sense in which MQTT operates as a queue of messages. Each message is distributed to the subscribed clients in the order that it was submitted, but the messages are not retained in a queue for new subscribers to examine.

There are many online services that make use of MQTT as a communications method and add to this storage and analysis features of the data that is published.

An MQTT Server

Before we can start implementing an MQTT client we need to have access to an MQTT server. There are two ways of achieving this - you can host your own or you can use a cloud-hosted server.

If you decide to host your own server the problem is reliability and access. One of the important characteristics of an MQTT server is that it has to be available 24/7 for IoT devices to send data to and for subscribers to read data from. Usually this means using a custom server in the cloud to pass the problem to a third party. This makes using a cloud-provided MQTT server attractive. On the other hand, if you don't need 24/7 availability, then hosting MQTT on local hardware isn't difficult and it is the lowest cost option with maximum flexibility.

If you want to host your own MQTT server then the two programs most commonly used are Mosquitto and HiveMQ.

Mosquitto is open source and the project is hosted by Eclipse. It runs on Linux, Windows and Mac and is very easy to install and configure. You can also make use of a sandbox public server to try out your MQTT client, but this isn't suitable for anything but limited experimentation.

The commercial product HiveMQ has a trial version limited to 25 connections and not for production use. This isn't particularly attractive for testing purposes, but HiveMQ cloud provides a free to use public server which is suitable for very low volume use. The downside is that there is no uptime guarantee and you are limited to 100 devices and 10 GB of traffic per month. The HiveMQ Cloud also insists on TLS encryption.

For simplicity, the examples in this chapter make use of the Mosquitto sandbox at test.mosquitto.org. It provides a range of differently configured servers on different ports:

- 1883 unencrypted, unauthenticated
- 1884 unencrypted, authenticated
- 8883 encrypted, unauthenticated
- 8884 encrypted, client certificate required
- 8885 encrypted, authenticated
- 8886 encrypted, unauthenticated
- 8887 encrypted, server certificate deliberately expired
- 8080 WebSockets, unencrypted, unauthenticated
- 8081 WebSockets, encrypted, unauthenticated
- 8090 WebSockets, unencrypted, authenticated
- 8091 WebSockets, encrypted, authenticated

Even with encryption you need to keep in mind that your data is not private – this is a testing facility.

A Simple MQTT Client

In general, there are two sorts of MQTT clients, publishers and subscribers, and e a client generally doesn't implement both. To make things as simple as possible we can start with a client that publishes a message to the server without using any encryption.

The main struct used by the MQTT client is `esp_mqtt_client_config_t` and the most important field is `broker`, which has two fields, address and verification. For a simple unencrypted client, we only need to use the address field:

```
esp_mqtt_client_config_t mqtt_cfg = {
    .broker.address.hostname = "test.mosquitto.org",
    .broker.address.port = 1883,
    .broker.address.transport = MQTT_TRANSPORT_OVER_TCP};
```

You can also set the `uri` field with a full url and path to the server.

Once you have the `config` struct set up you can create the client:

```
esp_mqtt_client_handle_t client = esp_mqtt_client_init(&mqtt_cfg);
```

Following this you can start the client:

```
esp_mqtt_client_start(client);
```

and stop it:

```
esp_mqtt_client_stop(client);
```

You can also use:

```
esp_mqtt_client_reconnect(client);
```

and

```
esp_mqtt_client_disconnect(client);
```

The client uses the ESP event handler framework to signal when messages are sent and arriveThe events are:

- ◆ `MQTT_EVENT_BEFORE_CONNECT`
  Client is initialized and about to start connecting to the broker
- ◆ `MQTT_EVENT_CONNECTED`
  Client has successfully established a connection to the brokerand is now ready to send and receive data
- ◆ `MQTT_EVENT_DISCONNECTED`
  Client has aborted the connection due to being unable to read or write data
- ◆ `MQTT_EVENT_SUBSCRIBED`
  Broker has acknowledged the client's subscribe request
- ◆ `MQTT_EVENT_UNSUBSCRIBED`
  Broker has acknowledged the client's unsubscribe request and the event data contains the message ID of the unsubscribe message

- ◆ MQTT_EVENT_PUBLISHED
  The broker has acknowledged the client's publish message
  (This is only posted for QoS level 1 and 2, as level 0 does not use
  acknowledgments)
- ◆ MQTT_EVENT_DATA
  Client has received a publish message to a topic it has subscribed to
- ◆ MQTT_EVENT_ERROR
  The client has encountered an error and the event handlers are
  passed data concerning the message

Sending a Message

Now that we have a connection we can call the function that sends a
message:

```
esp_mqtt_client_publish(client, "MyTopic", "Hello MQTT World",
                                                    0, 1, 0);
```

The second parameter sets the topic and the third is the payload. The next
parameter gives the length of the payload or, if it is zero, the payload is a
null terminated string. This is a blocking function. The fifth parameter, qos,
sets the quality of service which determines how often the subscriber will
receive messages:

- ◆ 0   At most once
- ◆ 1   At least once
- ◆ 2   Exactly once

Obviously, ensuring even a single delivery takes more resources. The final
retain parameter simply asks for the server to keep the message until the
next message is received or to discard the message after the last delivery.

The function:

```
int esp_mqtt_client_enqueue(esp_mqtt_client_handle_t client,
     const char *topic, const char *data, int len,
                          int qos, int retain, bool store)
```

is non-blocking and places the payload into an internal buffer to wait for the
server to be available. One difference is that this will run in the task of the
MQTT client rather than the task that it is in.

Receiving a Message

Receiving a message is slightly more complicated in that you have to first
subscribe to a topic.

The function to subscribe is simple enough:

```
esp_mqtt_client_subscribe(client, "MyTopic", 1);
```

The actual reception of the message is handled by the DATA event:

```
case MQTT_EVENT_DATA:
    printf("DATA  msg_id=%d\n", event->msg_id);
    printf("    TOPIC=%.*s\n", event->topic_len, event->topic);
    printf("     DATA=%.*s\n", event->data_len, event->data);
    break;
```

The actual message data is in `event->data`.

The Program

We can now put all this together to create a single program (in folder `MQTT1`) that connects to the MQTT server, sets up a subscription and then publishes data to it every few seconds. We are making an unencrypted connection with no authentication. It is natural to use a polling loop approach and a status global variable:

```
#include <stdio.h>
#include "freertos/FreeRTOS.h"
#include "esp_wifi.h"
#include "nvs_flash.h"
#include "esp_event.h"
#include "esp_netif.h"
#include "string.h"

#include "mqtt_client.h"
#include "esp_event.h"

#include "connectWiFi.h"

bool mqttOnline = false;
void mqtt_event_handler(void *handler_args, esp_event_base_t base,
                              int32_t event_id, void *event_data)
{
    esp_mqtt_event_handle_t event = event_data;
    switch ((esp_mqtt_event_id_t)event_id)
    {
    case MQTT_EVENT_CONNECTED:
        mqttOnline = true;
        printf("connected\n");
        break;
    case MQTT_EVENT_DISCONNECTED:
        mqttOnline = false;
        printf("disconnected\n");
        break;
    case MQTT_EVENT_SUBSCRIBED:
        printf("subscribed\n");
        break;
    case MQTT_EVENT_UNSUBSCRIBED:
        printf("unsubscribed\n");
        break;
```

```c
        case MQTT_EVENT_PUBLISHED:
            printf("PUB, msg_id=%d\n", event->msg_id);
            break;
        case MQTT_EVENT_DATA:
            printf("DATA  msg_id=%d\n", event->msg_id);
            printf("    TOPIC=%.*s\n", event->topic_len, event->topic);
            printf("     DATA=%.*s\n", event->data_len, event->data);
            break;
        case MQTT_EVENT_ERROR:
            if (event->error_handle->error_type ==
                                    MQTT_ERROR_TYPE_TCP_TRANSPORT)
            {
                printf("Last errno string (%s)",
                    strerror(event->error_handle->
                            esp_transport_sock_errno));
            }
            break;
        default:
            break;
    }
}
void app_main(void)
{
    wifiConnect("Co", "SSID", "password", NULL, NULL);
    while (wifiStatus != 1010)
    {
        vTaskDelay(10 / portTICK_PERIOD_MS);
    };
    esp_event_loop_create_default();
    esp_mqtt_client_config_t mqtt_cfg = {
        .broker.address.hostname = "test.mosquitto.org",
        .broker.address.port = 1883,
        .broker.address.transport = MQTT_TRANSPORT_OVER_TCP};
    esp_mqtt_client_handle_t client =
                    esp_mqtt_client_init(&mqtt_cfg);

    esp_mqtt_client_register_event(client, ESP_EVENT_ANY_ID,
                                mqtt_event_handler, NULL);

    esp_mqtt_client_start(client);
    while (!mqttOnline)
    {
        vTaskDelay(10 / portTICK_PERIOD_MS);
    }
    esp_mqtt_client_subscribe(client, "MyTopic", 1);
    while (true)
    {
        esp_mqtt_client_publish(client, "MyTopic",
                        "Hello MQTT World", 0, 1, 0);
        vTaskDelay(2000 / portTICK_PERIOD_MS);
    }
}
```

If you run this you will see:

```
DATA  msg_id=128
   TOPIC=MyTopic
    DATA=Hello MQTT World
PUB, msg_id=30951
DATA  msg_id=129
   TOPIC=MyTopic
    DATA=Hello MQTT World,,,  . .
```

repeated every two seconds.

MQTT TLS

Adding TLS security to the MQTT client is very easy, let's add TLS to the previous client using the certificate bundle.

In this case all we have to do is add:

```
#include "esp_crt_bundle.h"
```

and change the configuration to:

```
    esp_mqtt_client_config_t mqtt_cfg = {
        .broker.address.hostname = "test.mosquitto.org",
        .broker.address.port = 8886,
        .broker.address.transport = MQTT_TRANSPORT_OVER_SSL,
        .broker.verification.skip_cert_common_name_check = true,
        .broker.verification.crt_bundle_attach =
                                        esp_crt_bundle_attach};
```

Notice that we are now using port 8886 which uses a certificate that can be checked using the certificate bundle. You can try the program, in folder MQTT2 and you will discover it works in exactly the same way as the non-encrypted example.

Using a complete certificate bundle to verify a single server could be seen as a waste of resources. Port 8883 supports encryption without the need to log in, but with a self-signed certificate. The Mosquitto website provides a certificate that you can use to verify the server's certificate:

https://test.mosquitto.org/ssl/mosquitto.org.crt

The certificate is in PEM format and can be converted to C code using the Python program given earlier and included in folder MQTT3. Using this you can verify the server's certificate by adding:

```
char serverCert[] = "-----BEGIN CERTIFICATE-----\n"
"MIIEAzCCAuugAwIBAgIUBY1hlCGvdj4NhBXkZ/uLUZNILAwwDQYJKoZIhvcNAQEL\n"
...
"LdUdRudafMu5T5Xma182OC0/u/xRlEm+tvKGGmfFcN0piqVl8OrSPBgIlb+1IKJE\n"
"m/XriWr/Cq4h/JfB7NTsezVslgkBaoU=\n"
"-----END CERTIFICATE-----\n";
```

and change the configuration to:

```
esp_mqtt_client_config_t mqtt_cfg = {
    .broker.address.hostname = "test.mosquitto.org",
    .broker.address.port = 8883,
    .broker.address.transport = MQTT_TRANSPORT_OVER_SSL,
    .broker.verification.certificate = serverCert,
};
```

Notice that for a PEM-format certificate you don't need to specify the number of bytes, but if you do it has to include the NULL at the end of the string.

Summary

- MQTT makes use of a central server to allow clients to exchange messages.

- Publishers connect to the server and send messages labeled by topic. The server sends each message to all of the clients subscribed to the topic and then, by default, deletes the messages.

- Clients do not see messages that occur while they are offline, but publishers can set a message to be retained until the next message is sent. Clients that connect to the server see the latest retained message.

- A publisher can also set a default message to be sent if the server becomes unavailable.

- There are a number of MQTT servers, but two of the best known are the open source Mosquitto and the commercial HiveMQ. Both provide free to use services that are suitable for testing and low volume use.

- MQTT communications can be via TCP or TLS encrypted TCP.

Chapter 16
Advanced WiFi and AP Mode

Most of the time the ESP32 is used as a client to an AP and it engages in simply transferring data. However the WiFi hardware can be used in other ways. The most direct is the software implementation of an Access Point, AP. In this chapter we look not only at how to use this, but what it can be used for.

Beyond the simple AP, the ESP32 can be used in a long range mode and it can implement a direct point-to-point network in the form of ESP Now. Going beyond this it can implement a complete mesh network using ESP WiFi Mesh.

AP Mode

Access Point (AP) mode on the ESP32 allows other devices to connect but, as in general the ESP32 doesn't have access to the Internet when in AP mode, this only allows the connected device to talk to the ESP32. The basics of implementing an AP follows the rough outline of creating a client STA.

The AP is event driven and uses non-volatile storage by default which has to be initialized:

```
nvs_flash_init();
esp_event_loop_create_default();
esp_event_handler_register(WIFI_EVENT, ESP_EVENT_ANY_ID,
                                    wifi_event_handler, NULL);
```

Next, we have to create a suitable net interface:

```
esp_netif_init();
esp_netif_create_default_wifi_ap();
```

An AP netif automatically includes a DHCP server.

The WiFi subsystem has to be initialized:

```
wifi_init_config_t wificonfig = WIFI_INIT_CONFIG_DEFAULT();
esp_wifi_init(&wificonfig);
```

Configuring the AP is easy and a minimal configuration is something like:

```
wifi_config_t APconf = {
    .ap = {
        .ssid = "ESP32",
        .password = "mypassword",
        .channel=5,
        .authmode=WIFI_AUTH_WPA2_PSK,
        .max_connection=2
    }};
```

and this can now be used to get the AP up and running:

```
esp_wifi_set_mode(WIFI_MODE_AP);
esp_wifi_set_config(WIFI_IF_AP, &APconf);
esp_wifi_start();
```

If you run this, folder **AP1**, you will be able to connect to the AP, but it will not be very useful as it doesn't provide Internet access and the AP isn't running any servers for the client to connect to.

When managing connections, the function

```
esp_err_t esp_wifi_ap_get_sta_list(wifi_sta_list_t *sta)
```

returns a list of clients MAC addresses that are connected to the AP.

You can remove any client using:

```
esp_err_t esp_wifi_deauth_sta(uint16_t aid)
```

and you can get the clients aid using:

```
esp_err_t esp_wifi_ap_get_sta_aid(const uint8_t mac[6],
                                  uint16_t *aid)
```

DHCP Server

The DHCP server is automatically included with the netif when you use:

```
esp_netif_create_default_wifi_ap();
```

The functions which allow you to control its operation are very similar to those used with the DHCP client.

You can start and stop the server using:

- ◆ `esp_err_t esp_netif_dhcps_start(esp_netif_t *esp_netif);`
- ◆ `esp_err_t esp_netif_dhcps_stop(esp_netif_t *esp_netif);`

and get the current status with:

- ◆ `esp_err_t esp_netif_dhcps_get_status(esp_netif_t *esp_netif,`
  `esp_netif_dhcp_status_t *status);`

Where status is one of:

ESP_NETIF_DHCP_INIT	Client/server in initial state (not yet started)
ESP_NETIF_DHCP_STARTED	Client/server has been started
ESP_NETIF_DHCP_STOPPED	Client/server has been stopped

You can list the clients' IPs by looking up their MAC address using:

```
esp_err_t esp_netif_dhcps_get_clients_by_mac(
        esp_netif_t *esp_netif, int num,
                esp_netif_pair_mac_ip_t *mac_ip_pair);
```

The esp_netif_pair_mac_ip_t struct is:

```
typedef struct {
    uint8_t mac[6];          /**< Clients MAC address */
    esp_ip4_addr_t ip;       /**< Clients IP address */
} esp_netif_pair_mac_ip_t;
```

It lets you fill in the MAC addresses in the array you want to look up and it returns the IP addresses in the same array.

The most important of the DCHP functions is:

```
esp_netif_dhcps_option(esp_netif_t *esp_netif,
                    esp_netif_dhcp_option_mode_t opt_op,
                    esp_netif_dhcp_option_id_t opt_id,
                    void *opt_val,
                    uint32_t opt_len);
```

Where opt_op is one of:

```
    ESP_NETIF_OP_START
    ESP_NETIF_OP_SET
    ESP_NETIF_OP_GET
```

The option that is modified is specified by opt_id and is one of:

- ◆ ESP_NETIF_SUBNET_MASK   Get/Set
- ◆ ESP_NETIF_DOMAIN_NAME_SERVER   Get/Set
- ◆ ESP_NETIF_ROUTER_SOLICITATION_ADDRESS   Get/Set
- ◆ ESP_NETIF_REQUESTED_IP_ADDRESS   Get/Set
- ◆ ESP_NETIF_IP_ADDRESS_LEASE_TIME   Get/Set
- ◆ ESP_NETIF_CAPTIVEPORTAL_URI   Set

In addition we can set the IP address and net mask of the AP using the same method as for the STA i.e. using esp_netif_set_ip_info. Notice that the address pool has to make sense in terms of the AP's address and its netmask.

For example, to set the address of the AP and the size of the address pools that the DCHP server manages, we could use:

```
esp_netif_init();
esp_netif_t *esp_netif = esp_netif_create_default_wifi_ap();

esp_netif_ip_info_t ip_info;
esp_netif_str_to_ip4("192.168.253.2", &ip_info.ip);
esp_netif_str_to_ip4("192.168.253.1", &ip_info.gw);
esp_netif_str_to_ip4("255.255.255.0", &ip_info.netmask);
dhcps_lease_t dhcpPool = {
        .enable = true};
```

```
IP4_ADDR(&dhcpPool.start_ip, 192, 168, 253, 240);
IP4_ADDR(&dhcpPool.end_ip, 192, 168, 253, 243);
esp_netif_dhcps_stop(esp_netif);
esp_netif_set_ip_info(esp_netif, &ip_info);
int err = esp_netif_dhcps_option(esp_netif, ESP_NETIF_OP_SET,
     ESP_NETIF_REQUESTED_IP_ADDRESS, &dhcpPool, sizeof(dhcpPool));
printf("dchp error %X\n", err);
esp_netif_dhcps_start(esp_netif);
```

This sets the AP to 192.168.253.2, with a net mask of 255.255.255.0 and the DCHP address pool is 192.168.253.240 to 192.168.253.241. If you run the complete program, folder AP2, you will see that the first client that connects is assigned the IP address 192.168.253.240.

An Initialization Server

A very obvious problem is how do you allow a user to configure an IoT device. The traditional solution is to add a physical user interface, but this is often too expensive for a small device. A growing number of devices use a more modern alternative – web-based configuration. This moves the emphasis from hardware to software.

The idea is that the device configures itself as an access point and the user connects using a WiFi-enabled device, usually a mobile phone. This can be done without any configuration as the access point can be set up to be open. Once the connection has been made, the user can download a webpage, configure the settings for the device and send it back to the server. The device then configures itself, switches to client mode and disables the server. To make this approach look "polished" to the user you generally have to implement a mobile app that makes the connection without the user having to do anything. However, there is no technical reason why a mobile browser wouldn't work.

The novel part of an initialization server is that it is running in access point mode. The next example is the start of an initialization server and shows how this can be done.

We first need to setup the AP with no password

```
wifi_config_t APconf = {
    .ap = {
        .ssid = "ESP32",
        .channel = 5,
        .authmode = WIFI_AUTH_OPEN,
        .max_connection = 2}};
```

Once the client connects it uses a browser to download the root page that is a form to be filled in. You can use any of the server types described earlier but the easiest is the HTTP module. There is no obvious need to apply any security to the HTTP or the WiFi connection as everything is local.

In this case we do need to process the request because the server will respond differently according to the request's type. If the request is GET / then we need to send a page of HTML that sets up the configuration form:

```
esp_err_t get_handler(httpd_req_t *req)
{
    printf("GET %s\n",req->uri);
   if (strcmp(req->uri, "/") == 0)
    {
    const char resp[] =  "<!DOCTYPE html>"
     "<html><head>"
     "<meta http-equiv=""content-type"" content=""text/html"" />"
     "<title>Setup</title></head><body>"
     "<form name=""Form"" action=""/"" method=""POST""
                                    enctype=""text/plain"">"
     "<p>SSID of the AP</p>"
     "<input name=""SSID"" style=""width: 6cm;
                                    height: 1cm""></input>"
     "<p>Password </p>"
     "<input name=""Password"" style=""width: 6cm; height: 1cm"">
                                    </input>"
     "</br></br>"
     "<button>Ok</button>"
     "</form></body></html>";
     httpd_resp_send(req, resp, HTTPD_RESP_USE_STRLEN);
    }else{
        httpd_resp_send(req, "", HTTPD_RESP_USE_STRLEN);
    }
    return ESP_OK;
}
```

As long as the file requested is "/" the function sends the client the HTML defining a simple form:

```
<!DOCTYPE html>
<html>
<head>
    <meta http-equiv="content-type" content="text/html" />
    <title>Setup</title>
</head>
<body>
    <form name="Form" action="/" method="post" enctype="text/plain">
        <p>SSID of the AP</p>
        <input name="SSID" style="width: 6cm; height: 1cm"></input>
        <p>Password </p>
    <input name="Password" style="width: 6cm; height: 1cm"></input>
    </br></br>
    <button>Ok</button>
    </form>
</body>
</html>
```

This defines two input boxes and a submit button:

SSID of the AP

Password

Ok

Clicking on the button causes the browser to make a POST request with the form data encoded as key value pairs:

SSID = *value*/r/nPassword = *value*/r/n

in the body of the request. You could use a GET and specify the file to return, but in this case the form data is encoded into the URL as a query string. The POST is easier to process, but either approach works.

When the user enters the data and presses the Ok button the browser sends a POST request and this can be processed by the server:

```
esp_err_t post_handler(httpd_req_t *req)
{
    char buffer[50];
    int n = req->content_len;
    int i = 0;
    while (n != i)
    {
        int m = httpd_req_recv(req, buffer + i, n - i);
        i = i + m;
    }
    buffer[i] = 0;
    char ssid[20];
    char password[20];
    getField(buffer, "SSID=", ssid);

    getField(buffer, "Password=", password);
    printf("ssid\n %s\n", ssid);
    printf("password\n %s\n", password);

    char html[] = "<html><head><title>Thanks</title></head>"
                  "<body><p>The new WiFi connection will now be
                                                made</p>"
                  "</body></html>\r\n";
    httpd_resp_send_chunk(req, html, strlen(html));
    return ESP_OK;
}
```

This extracts the data that the user entered into the form and sends back a page that informs the user that everything worked.

Of course, in a real initialization server the data would be used to make a connection to an AP and the access point and server would be deactivated.

The complete program, folder InitServer, is:

```
#include <stdio.h>
#include "nvs_flash.h"
#include "esp_wifi.h"
#include "esp_netif.h"
#include "dhcpserver/dhcpserver.h"
#include "dhcpserver/dhcpserver_options.h"
#include "esp_http_server.h"
int retry_num = 0;
static void wifi_event_handler(void *event_handler_arg,
esp_event_base_t event_base, int32_t event_id, void *event_data)
{
    switch (event_id)
    {
    case WIFI_EVENT_AP_STACONNECTED:
        printf("STA CONNECTING....\n");
        break;
    case WIFI_EVENT_AP_STADISCONNECTED:
        printf("STA DISCONNECTED\n");
        break;
    }
}
esp_err_t get_handler(httpd_req_t *req)
{
    printf("GET %s\n", req->uri);
    if (strcmp(req->uri, "/") == 0)
    {
        const char resp[] = "<!DOCTYPE html>"
                            "<html><head>""<meta http-equiv="
                            "content-type"
                                content=""text/html"" />"
                            "<title>Setup</title></head><body>"
                            "<form name=""Form"" action=""/"""
                                method=""POST"
                            " enctype=""text/plain"">"
                            "<p>SSID of the AP</p>"
                            "<input name=""SSID"" style="
                            "width: 6cm; height 1cm"">
                                </input>""<p>Password </p>"
                            "<input name=""Password"" style="
                            "width: 6cm; height: 1cm""></input>"
                            "</br></br>""<button>Ok</button>"
                            "</form></body></html>";
        httpd_resp_send(req, resp, HTTPD_RESP_USE_STRLEN);
    }
```

```
else
    {
        httpd_resp_send(req, "", HTTPD_RESP_USE_STRLEN);
    }
    return ESP_OK;
}

int getField(char buffer[], char name[], char value[])
{
    char *myPtr1 = strstr(buffer, name);
    if (myPtr1 == NULL)
        return -1;
    char *myPtr2 = strstr(myPtr1, "\r\n");
    if (myPtr2 == NULL)
        return -2;
    int c = myPtr2 - myPtr1;
    strncpy(value, myPtr1, c);
    value[c] = 0;
    return 0;
}

esp_err_t post_handler(httpd_req_t *req)
{
    char buffer[50];
    int n = req->content_len;
    int i = 0;
    while (n != i)
    {
        int m = httpd_req_recv(req, buffer + i, n - i);
        i = i + m;
    }
    buffer[i] = 0;
    char ssid[20];
    char password[20];
    getField(buffer, "SSID=", ssid);

    getField(buffer, "Password=", password);
    printf("ssid\n %s\n", ssid);
    printf("password\n %s\n", password);

    char html[] = "<html><head><title>Thanks</title></head>"
                  "<body><p>The new WiFi connection will now be
                                                        made</p>"
                  "</body></html>\r\n";
    httpd_resp_send_chunk(req, html, strlen(html));
    return ESP_OK;
}
```

```c
void app_main(void)
{
    nvs_flash_init();
    esp_event_loop_create_default();
    esp_event_handler_register(WIFI_EVENT, ESP_EVENT_ANY_ID,
                                wifi_event_handler, NULL);

    esp_netif_init();
    esp_netif_t *esp_netif = esp_netif_create_default_wifi_ap();

    wifi_init_config_t wificonfig = WIFI_INIT_CONFIG_DEFAULT();
    esp_wifi_init(&wificonfig);

    wifi_config_t APconf = {
        .ap = {
            .ssid = "ESP32",
            .channel = 5,
            .authmode = WIFI_AUTH_OPEN,
            .max_connection = 2}};
    esp_wifi_set_mode(WIFI_MODE_AP);
    esp_wifi_set_config(WIFI_IF_AP, &APconf);
    esp_wifi_start();

    httpd_config_t config = HTTPD_DEFAULT_CONFIG();
    httpd_handle_t server = NULL;
    httpd_uri_t uri_get = {
        .uri = "/",
        .method = HTTP_GET,
        .handler = get_handler,
        .user_ctx = NULL};

    httpd_uri_t uri_post = {
        .uri = "/",
        .method = HTTP_POST,
        .handler = post_handler,
        .user_ctx = NULL};
    if (httpd_start(&server, &config) == ESP_OK)
    {
        httpd_register_uri_handler(server, &uri_get);
        httpd_register_uri_handler(server, &uri_post);
    }
    while (true)
    {
        vTaskDelay(100 / portTICK_PERIOD_MS);
    };
}
```

If the initialization server is developed any further then using an existing HTTP and HTML parsing library would be a good idea. This example gives you the basic principles, but the UI needs a great deal of work.

An ESP32 Internet Access Point

As well as STA and AP mode, the ESP32 can be placed in a APSTA mode where the ESP32 behaves as a client and an access point. At this point you might expect this to be a way to connect a client of the ESP32 AP to the network that the ESP32 is connected to. The simplest way of doing this would be to use the same IP addresses for both networks and simply pass packets with an IP address on the same network between the AP and STA. However this isn't a standard option.

An alternative way of connecting the AP client to the "outside world" is to configure the AP as a NAT router. This appears more complex, but it is easier to actually implement as there is a NAT router module included as standard. Using a NAT router might be more complex, but from the user's point of view it delivers the same result – the ESP32 client is effectively connected to the network that the ESP STA is connected to. There is one drawback. The ESP32 client has a different IP network address from the STA network and NAT allows it to exchange packets with the STA network, but a device on the STA network cannot initiate communication with a client connected to the ESP32. The STA network can only see the ESP32 as all of its clients use its IP address on the STA network and on the connected internet.

The program needs to support both STA and AP modes and these have to work together. We first have to establish an STA connection and then use this to configure the AP server correctly. First, we need an event handler that works for both STA and AP mode and we need to register it for the events:

```
int wifiStatus = 1000;
int retry_num = 0;
static void wifi_event_handler(void *event_handler_arg,
                               esp_event_base_t event_base,
                                   int32_t event_id, void *event_data)
{
    switch (event_id)
    {
    case WIFI_EVENT_STA_START:
        printf("Got STA START\n");
        break;
    case WIFI_EVENT_STA_CONNECTED:
        printf("Got STA Connect\n");
        break;
    case WIFI_EVENT_STA_DISCONNECTED:
        if (retry_num < 5)
        {
            esp_wifi_connect();
            retry_num++;
        }
        break;
```

```
        case IP_EVENT_STA_GOT_IP:
            printf("Got IP\n");
            wifiStatus = 1010;
            break;
        case WIFI_EVENT_AP_STACONNECTED:
            printf("STA CONNECTING....\n");
            break;
        case WIFI_EVENT_AP_STADISCONNECTED:
            printf("STA DISCONNECTED\n");
            break;
    }
}
void app_main(void)
{
    nvs_flash_init();
    esp_netif_init();

    esp_event_loop_create_default();
    esp_event_handler_register(WIFI_EVENT, ESP_EVENT_ANY_ID,
                                wifi_event_handler, NULL);
    esp_event_handler_register(IP_EVENT, IP_EVENT_STA_GOT_IP,
                                wifi_event_handler, NULL);}
```

As always, we need to initialize the WiFi hardware:

```
wifi_init_config_t wificonfig = WIFI_INIT_CONFIG_DEFAULT();
esp_wifi_init(&wificonfig);
```

Now we need to set the mode and create a netif for both the STA and the AP:

```
esp_wifi_set_mode(WIFI_MODE_APSTA);
esp_netif_t *esp_netif_ap = esp_netif_create_default_wifi_ap();
esp_netif_t *esp_netif_sta = esp_netif_create_default_wifi_sta();
```

Of course, we have to configure both the STA and AP:

```
    wifi_config_t staconf = {
        .sta = {
            .ssid = "SSID",
            .password = "password",
            .threshold.authmode = WIFI_AUTH_WPA_PSK,
        }};
    esp_wifi_set_config(WIFI_IF_STA, &staconf);

    wifi_config_t APconf = {
        .ap = {
            .ssid = "ESP32",
            .authmode = WIFI_AUTH_OPEN,
            .max_connection = 2}};
    esp_wifi_set_config(WIFI_IF_AP, &APconf);
```

Don't set the channel number as it will be automatically set when the STA connects.

We are now ready to make the STA connection:

```
esp_wifi_start();
esp_wifi_connect();
while (wifiStatus != 1010)
{
    vTaskDelay(10 / portTICK_PERIOD_MS);
}
```

Any client connecting to the AP will be supplied with the default IP address, gateway and mask, but not a DNS server. This has to be the DNS server used by the network that the STA is connected to and so we have to get the DNS server from the STA netif and set it on the AP netif:

```
esp_netif_dns_info_t dns;
esp_netif_get_dns_info(esp_netif_sta, ESP_NETIF_DNS_MAIN, &dns);
uint8_t dhcps_offer_option = 0x02;
esp_netif_dhcps_stop(esp_netif_ap);
esp_netif_dhcps_option(esp_netif_ap, ESP_NETIF_OP_SET,
            ESP_NETIF_DOMAIN_NAME_SERVER,
                &dhcps_offer_option, sizeof(dhcps_offer_option));
esp_netif_set_dns_info(esp_netif_ap, ESP_NETIF_DNS_MAIN, &dns);
esp_netif_dhcps_start(esp_netif_ap);
```

Notice that this is a matter of using the DHCP option function as in the previous example.

Now we can set the STA netif to be the default and start the NAPT running:

```
esp_netif_set_default_netif(esp_netif_sta);
int err = esp_netif_napt_enable(esp_netif_ap);
```

To use the NAPT module you need:

```
#include "lwip/lwip_napt.h"
```

and you need to enable it using the SDK configuration editor:

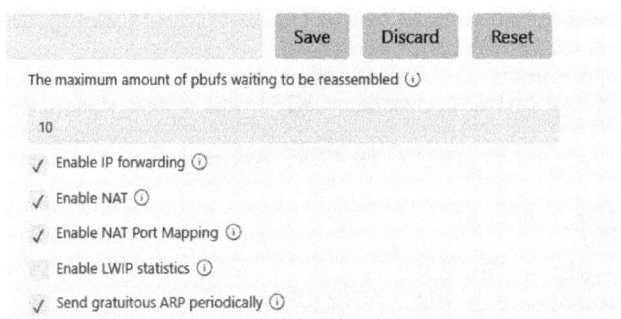

If you compile and run the program in folder NAP1, you will find that a client device can connect to ESP32 and browse the Internet and the local network. However, devices on the local network will not be able to see devices connected to ESP32.

Promiscuous Mode

Normally you only see data that is intended for the IP address of the device. Promiscuous mode lets you view all of the packets on the network including management packages. This is, in principle, really useful as a diagnostic tool and for reverse engineering. In practice it isn't so useful, unless you go to a lot of trouble. you will miss many packets and the format of the packets isn't well documented. In most cases you would be better off using WireShark or similar sniffer programs.

Using promiscuous mode is easy; all you have to do is setup an event handler:

```
esp_wifi_set_promiscuous_rx_cb(promiscuous_rx_cb);
```

and then set the promiscuous mode:

```
esp_wifi_set_promiscuous(true);
```

The event handler receives the packet data and its type.

A complete demonstration program, to be found in folder sniffer, is:

```
#include <stdio.h>
#include "freertos/FreeRTOS.h"
#include "esp_wifi.h"
#include "nvs_flash.h"
#include "esp_event.h"
#include "esp_netif.h"
#include "string.h"

static void promiscuous_rx_cb(void *buf,
                        wifi_promiscuous_pkt_type_t type)
{
    switch (type)
    {
    case WIFI_PKT_MGMT:
        printf("Received packet: management\n");
        break;
    case WIFI_PKT_CTRL:
        printf("Received packet: control\n");
        break;
    case WIFI_PKT_DATA:
        printf("Received packet: data\n");
        break;
    case WIFI_PKT_MISC:
        printf("Received packet: misc\n");
        break;
    }
}
```

```
char header[6000] = {"1"};
void app_main(void)
{
    nvs_flash_init();
    esp_event_loop_create_default();

    wifi_init_config_t cfg = WIFI_INIT_CONFIG_DEFAULT();
    esp_wifi_init(&cfg);

    esp_wifi_set_mode(WIFI_MODE_NULL);
    esp_wifi_set_promiscuous_rx_cb(promiscuous_rx_cb);
    esp_wifi_set_channel(10, WIFI_SECOND_CHAN_NONE);
    esp_wifi_set_promiscuous(true);
}
```

This simply prints the type of each packet received on channel 10. . You can also apply a filter to the packets so that you only see packets of a given type. For example if you add:

```
wifi_promiscuous_filter_t mask;
mask.filter_mask = WIFI_PROMIS_FILTER_MASK_MGMT;
esp_wifi_set_promiscuous_filter(&mask);
```

you will only see management packets.

Long Range Mode

The ESP32 family of processors supports a special WiFi mode, Long Range or LR. This only works between ESP32 devices so you need at least one AP mode using LR and a number of STA clients also using LR. Notice that routers and other WiFi devices cannot use LR mode, but it doesn't interfere with them and they can share the same radio frequencies. The advantage of LR is that it can achieve a 1km line of sight range with a suitable external antenna and around 500m with the standard on-board antenna. The downside is that transmission rates are slower, but for IoT applications this isn't usually a problem.

Using LR is easy and the good news is that all of the networking functions that you have encountered so far work in LR mode so you can use the HTTPS client and server and any `net-tls` or socket applications you care to write. The only thing you have to do is use the function:

```
esp_err_t esp_wifi_set_protocol(wifi_interface_t ifx,
                                uint8_t protocol_bitmap)
```

For example, if you are in STA mode you would enable LR using:

```
esp_wifi_set_protocol(WIFI_IF_STA,WIFI_PROTOCOL_LR)
```

before you made the connection with the ESP32 in AP mode.

Notice that the AP using LR is not visible to devices not using LR. Also notice that LR is not compatible with other long range protocols such as LoRa.

ESP Now

The ESP Now module implements a very simple packet network between ESP32 devices. It makes use of the standard WiFi connection and the ESP32 devices can either be in AP or STA mode. It is a two-way protocol and a given ESP32 can send packets to other ESP32 devices and receive them from those devices.

It is a connection-less protocol which makes it easy to use, but it has no error correction or delivery guarantees and is restricted to 250 bytes of data per packet. In this respect it is more like UDP than TCP and if you need secure communication you need to implement error detection/correction and acknowledgment and if you need to send more than 250 bytes it you will need to package it and serialize it. This said there are many applications that don't need these extras.

It implements optional encryption based on AES with a 128-bit key. Another key difference is that MAC addresses are used to specify the device that the packet is intended for. This is much simpler than using an IP address, but as there is no DNS for MAC addresses you have to invent a way to automatically find the MAC address of the target.

To use ESP Now all you have to do is turn WiFi on. You can do this by connecting to an AP or setting up an AP, but all you really have to do is start the WiFi:

```
void app_main(void)
{
    esp_event_loop_create_default();
    nvs_flash_init();
    esp_netif_init();
    wifi_init_config_t cfg = WIFI_INIT_CONFIG_DEFAULT();
    esp_wifi_init(&cfg);
    esp_wifi_set_mode(WIFI_MODE_STA);
    esp_wifi_set_channel(3,WIFI_SECOND_CHAN_NONE);
    esp_wifi_start();
```

Notice that we haven't connected the WiFi to an access point and this means we have to set the channel that it is working on. For devices to communicate using ESP Now they have to be on the same channel.

As this program, which is in folder `ESPNowReceive`, is implementing a receiver, the transmitter needs to know its MAC address so the first thing to do is print it so that it can be transferred to the transmitter program:

```
uint8_t mac[6];
    esp_wifi_get_mac(ESP_IF_WIFI_STA, mac);
    for (int i = 0; i < 6; i++){
        printf("%2X ", mac[i]);
    }
    printf("\n");
```

Next we can start ESP Now and simply listen for incoming packets:

```
esp_now_init();
esp_now_register_recv_cb(example_espnow_recv_cb);
while (true)
{
    vTaskDelay(10 / portTICK_PERIOD_MS);
};
}
```

The recv callback simply prints the data that has been received:

```
static void example_espnow_recv_cb(
                const esp_now_recv_info_t *recv_info,
                const uint8_t *data, int len)
{

    for (int i = 0; i < len; i++)
    {
        printf("%2X", data[i]);
    }
    printf("\n");
    fflush(stdout);
}
```

If you run ESPNowReceive nothing happens until another ESP32 sends some data.

We now need to create a program, ESPNOWTransmitter, that sends data to the receiver and this is very slightly more difficult. It starts off in the same way by starting the WiFi without making a connection:

```
void app_main(void)
{

    esp_event_loop_create_default();
    nvs_flash_init();
    esp_netif_init();

    wifi_init_config_t cfg = WIFI_INIT_CONFIG_DEFAULT();
    esp_wifi_init(&cfg);

    esp_wifi_set_mode(WIFI_MODE_STA);
    esp_wifi_set_channel(3, WIFI_SECOND_CHAN_NONE);
    esp_wifi_start();
```

Notice that this ESP32 is also set to channel 3. Now we initialize ESP Now and register a send callback:

```
    int err = esp_now_init();
    err = esp_now_register_send_cb(example_espnow_send_cb);
```

The main difference between this program and `ESPNowReceive` is that we need to setup a peer struct:

```
esp_now_peer_info_t peer = {
    .peer_addr = {0x08, 0xB6, 0x1F, 0x29, 0xBE, 0x7C},
    .encrypt = false,
    .ifidx = ESP_IF_WIFI_STA,
};
```

This is where you have to enter the MAC address of the receiving ESP32. If you run `ESPNowReceive`, you can read the MAC address and enter it into this program.

Now we add the peer:

```
err = esp_now_add_peer(&peer);
```

and send some data:

```
uint8_t data[] = {1, 2, 3, 4, 5, 6};
err = esp_now_send(NULL, data, 6);
```

If the first parameter is NULL the data is sent to all of the peers that we have included in the list. If the first parameter is a MAC address the the data is only sent to that device. You can have up to 20 unencrypted peers set at any time.

If you run this program, folder `ESPNOWtransmitter`, while the previous program is running you will see:

```
 8 B6 1F 29 BE 7C
I (663) ESPNOW: espnow [version: 2.0] init
 1 2 3 4 5 6
```

If you want to use encryption, set the `peer.encrypt` field to `true` and set the `lmk` field to the 128-bit key to use. Of course, both the sending and receiving devices have to use the same key and the receiving device has to add the sending device as a peer. A receiving device with no peers set can only receive broadcast packets and unencrypted packets addressed to it. Different pairs of devices can use different keys up to a maximum of six. The problem to be solved is how to distribute or agree upon a key.

If you want to broadcast a message to all ESP32s listening on the same channel, you can do so using the broadcast MAC address `FF,FF,FF,FF,FF,FF`. This address has to be added as a peer and you also have to specify its address in the send function:

```
esp_now_peer_info_t broadcast = {
    .peer_addr = {0xFF,0xFF,0xFF,0xFF,0xFF,0xFF},
    .encrypt = false};
err = esp_now_add_peer(&broadcast);
uint8_t data[] = {1, 2, 3, 4, 5, 6};
err = esp_now_send(broadcast.peer_addr,data,6);
printf("error= %x\n", err);
```

Also notice that due to the difficulty of managing keys, you cannot broadcast an encrypted message.

The broadcast mechanism can be the key to distributing the MAC address. To enable this one of the ESP32s needs to broadcast a "Join" message which contains its MAC address. Any new ESP32s can receive the Join message, extract the MAC address and then send its MAC address back to the broadcasting ESP32. It can then extract the MAC address and be added to the peer list.

You can see that, using mechanisms like this, it is fairly easy to build up a network of peers that can exchange data in a very general way.

ESP WiFi Mesh

ESP Now is a simple point-to-point communication network and it suits many applications. The next step is a full mesh network. The IDF contains an ESP WiFi Mesh module which implements a mesh network in which all the devices are capable of acting as intermediaries passing packets to their final destination.

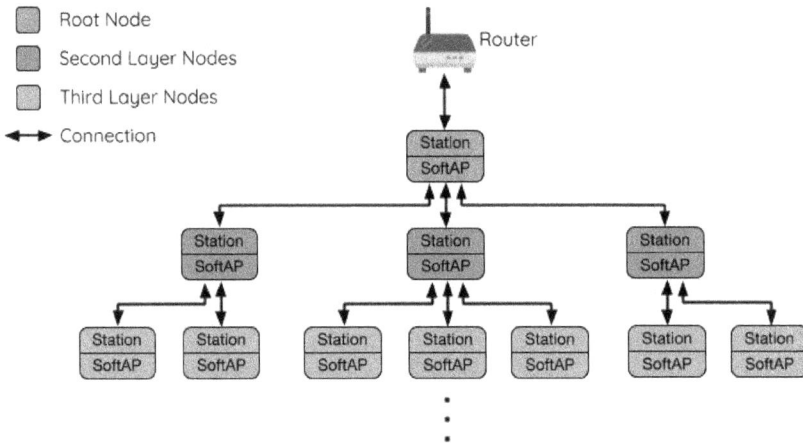

This architecture really only makes sense if at least two of the devices in the network are so far apart that they cannot communicate using a single WiFi AP. The only downside of this module is that it only works with ESP devices.

The idea is that some of the devices are within the range of an AP that has a router connection to the outside world. One of the ESP32 devices is close enough to connect and this is the root device. The ESP WiFi Mesh has only one root device and other ESP32 devices, nodes, can connect to it. All of the nodes, with the possible exception of terminal nodes, run an AP which other nodes can connect to. Terminal nodes are devices that other nodes cannot connect to and these obviously do not need to implement an AP.

The default is that the mesh self-configures. One of the devices, the one with the highest signal strength from the router AP, is selected as the root device. The other devices then connect to their closest device. If the mesh is disrupted by a device failing or being removed, then they reconfigure to maintain the connection. The mesh is said to be self-configuring and self-healing.

You can find more information about ESP WiFi Mesh in the documentation, but this is all you need to know to get started. Our example, in folder Mesh, is going to be the simplest possible example of a mesh. A single root node will receive data from a number of connected nodes. As each node has to be configured with the same Mesh Network ID, router configuration and SoftAP, the only difference between the program that runs on any of the nodes is what happens after the network has been configured. As there is also a function that can be used to discover if the node is the root node or not, we can write a single program for all the nodes.

The first thing we need to do is configure the WiFi. As with ESP Now we don't have to make any connections – the mesh code does this for us. In fact if you have a self organizing mesh you shouldn't use the WiFi at all unless you disable the self organization. Initializing the Wifi follows the standard steps:

```
void app_main(void)
{
    esp_event_loop_create_default();
    nvs_flash_init();
    esp_netif_init();
    wifi_init_config_t config = WIFI_INIT_CONFIG_DEFAULT();
    esp_wifi_init(&config);
    esp_wifi_start();
```

Next we need to configure the mesh. We need to set a mesh id that is unique and that is common to all of the nodes. This is an arbitrary set of six bytes which is often selected to be the MAC address of the router just to ensure that it is unique:

```
    mesh_cfg_t cfg = MESH_INIT_CONFIG_DEFAULT();
    uint8_t MESH_ID[6] = {0x77, 0x77, 0x77, 0x77, 0x77, 0x77};
    memcpy((uint8_t *)&cfg.mesh_id, MESH_ID, 6);
```

The other elements of the configuration struct that we need to fill in are the ssid and password of the router AP, the password of the node's AP and the number of connections it will support. The channel that the mesh uses is determined by the AP router:

```
char ssid[] = "SSID";
char password[] = "password";
char APpassword[] = "APpassword";
cfg.router.ssid_len = strlen(ssid);
memcpy((uint8_t *)&cfg.router.ssid, ssid, cfg.router.ssid_len);
memcpy((uint8_t *)&cfg.router.password, password,
                                        strlen(password));
memcpy((uint8_t *)&cfg.mesh_ap.password, Appassword,
                                        strlen(APpassword));
cfg.mesh_ap.max_connection = 5;
esp_mesh_set_config(&cfg);
esp_mesh_start();
```

Once we have the configuration, we can start the mesh. If the mesh is started on more than one ESP32 then one of them will be the root node. We can now write a short section of code that will send some data to the root node or, if it is the root node, receive data.

To send data we use:

```
esp_err_t esp_mesh_send(const mesh_addr_t *to,
                        const mesh_data_t *data,
                        int flag,
                        const mesh_opt_t opt[],
                        int opt_count)
```

The to parameter specifies the MAC address of the node that the data is for. If this is the root node you can set it to NULL. If it is to an external destination, i.e. on the connected network or even out on the Internet, then you can specify the IP address and port. The address is specified using a struct:

```
typedef union {
    uint8_t addr[6];     /**< mac address */
    mip_t mip;           /**< mip address */
} mesh_addr_t;
```

The MAC address is specified in the usual six-byte format. The IP address is specified by a mip struct:

```
typedef struct {
    esp_ip4_addr_t ip4;    /**< IP address */
    uint16_t port;      /**< port */
}  mip_t;
```

The second parameter is the data to be sent, but this is a struct that also specifies the type of the data and how it should be sent:

```
typedef struct {
    uint8_t *data;          /**< data */
    uint16_t size;          /**< data size */
    mesh_proto_t proto;     /**< data protocol */
    mesh_tos_t tos;         /**< data type of service */
} mesh_data_t;
```

The proto field specifies the protocol:

```
typedef enum {
    MESH_PROTO_BIN,      /**< binary */
    MESH_PROTO_HTTP,     /**< HTTP protocol */
    MESH_PROTO_JSON,     /**< JSON format */
    MESH_PROTO_MQTT,     /**< MQTT protocol */
    MESH_PROTO_AP,       /**< IP network mesh communication of
node's AP interface */
    MESH_PROTO_STA,      /**< IP network mesh communication of
node's STA interface */
} mesh_proto_t;
```

In most cases BIN is the best choice and its the default. The tos field sets the type of service:

```
typedef enum {
    MESH_TOS_P2P,      /**< provide P2P (point-to-point)
retransmission on mesh stack by default */
    MESH_TOS_E2E,      /**< provide E2E (end-to-end) retransmission
on mesh stack (Unimplemented) */
    MESH_TOS_DEF,      /**< no retransmission on mesh stack */
} mesh_tos_t;
```

Your only choice is between P2P, which implements a reliable blocking transmission, and DEF, which doesn't.

The flag parameter can be any combination of:

- MESH_DATA_P2P   Send to an internal node
- MESH_DATA_FROMDS   Send to root node or external IP
- MESH_DATA_TODS   Send from root to internal root

You can ignore the final two parameters.

For example, to send a message to the root:

```
mesh_data_t data;
data.data = (u_int8_t *)"Hello mesh world";
data.size = strlen((char *)data.data);
data.proto = MESH_PROTO_BIN;
data.tos = MESH_TOS_P2P;
esp_mesh_send(NULL, &data, MESH_DATA_P2P, NULL, 0);
```

To receive data you use the function:

```
esp_err_t esp_mesh_recv(mesh_addr_t *from,
                        mesh_data_t *data,
                        int timeout_ms,
                        int *flag,
                        mesh_opt_t opt[],
                        int opt_count)
```

The from parameter is the address structure given earlier which is filled in when some data is received. The data is the mesh_data_t struct also given earlier. Notice that, even though it is an opt parameter you will have to supply the data field as an array. Setting timeout_ms to 0 makes the call non-blocking. The flag field is as for send, but in this case it is set to indicate that data has been received. You can ignore opt and opt_count.

So to receive data you would use:

```
mesh_addr_t from;
mesh_data_t datarx;
uint8_t rxbuf[100] = {0,};
datarx.data = rxbuf;
datarx.size = 100;
int flag;
esp_mesh_recv(&from, &datarx, 0, &flag, NULL, 0);
```

Using the function:

```
esp_mesh_is_root()
```

you can discover if the device is a root node or not. If it is a root node we simply see if there is anything to read. If it isn't a root node we send some data to the root node:

```
    mesh_addr_t from;
    mesh_data_t datarx;
    uint8_t rxbuf[100] = {
        0,
    };
    datarx.data = rxbuf;
    datarx.size = 100;
    int flag;

    mesh_data_t data;
    data.data = (u_int8_t *)"Hello mesh world";
    data.size = strlen((char *)data.data);
    data.proto = MESH_PROTO_BIN;
    data.tos = MESH_TOS_P2P;
```

```
while (true)
    {
        vTaskDelay(1000 / portTICK_PERIOD_MS);
        if (esp_mesh_is_root())
        {
            esp_mesh_recv(&from, &datarx, 0, &flag, NULL, 0);
            printf("%d\n", flag);
            if (flag != 0)
                printf("%s\n", datarx.data);
        }
        else
        {
            esp_mesh_send(NULL, &data, MESH_DATA_P2P, NULL, 0);
        }
    };
}
```

If you put all of this together (folder Mesh) and run it on two ESP32s, one of them will be a root node and it will display the message sent to it by the non-root node.

To enable encryption use:

```
esp_err_t esp_mesh_set_ie_crypto_funcs(
                const mesh_crypto_funcs_t *crypto_funcs)
```

to specify an AES encrypt and decrypt function.

This is just the start of what you can do. You can opt to manually configure the mesh – which node is the root, and which node each one connects to. You can also control the way the mesh configures itself and fine tune its operation. Of course its main problem is that it is specific to the ESP32 family of devices. Platform independent networks like Zigbee and Thread are more complicated and usually need special hardware. They are supported in software but only for the ESP32 C6 and H2.

Summary

- AP mode allows a small number of clients to connect to an ESP32.
- A DHCP server is automatically added to an AP net interface (netif) to assign IP addresses to clients.
- One application of AP mode is to allow the user to connect to an ESP32 using a browser or a custom mobile app and configure the ESP32.
- You can set an ESP32 into AP and STA modes, but clients are not able to connect to the AP and use the STA to communicate with the local network or the Internet.
- It is possible to give clients Internet and local network access using a NAT router module.
- In promiscuous mode the WiFi will pass any packets it receives to the program, even if they are not addressed to the device.
- Two or more ESP32 devices can connect using long range mode and achieve a range of up to 1 kilometer.
- The ESP Now module provides a very simple point-to-point network without access points or connections.
- ESP WiFi Mesh can be used to connect ESP32 devices to each other and to a router, even if some of the devices are too far away to communicate directly.

Appendix I
Advanced WiFi Configuration

The ESP32 family of devices makes use of a proprietary WiFi implementation and the Espressif IDF has many more functions for working with the basic hardware than other WiFi implementations. In other words you can customize much more of the operation of the ESP32's WiFi than is generally possible. However most of the time you don't want to or need to. The whole point is to interoperate with other WiFi hardware and as such you generally need the defaults that have been automatically set.

Here we list the rest of the functions with minimal annotation, just in case you encounter them or need to use them. Most of them have names and parameters that make their purpose and use obvious. All of them return esp_err_t unless otherwise indicated.

Transmission Mode

Functions which control the transmitter and receiver basic operation:

- `esp_wifi_set_bandwidths(wifi_interface_t ifx,`
                          `wifi_bandwidths_t *bw)`
- `esp_wifi_get_bandwidths(wifi_interface_t ifx,`
                          `wifi_bandwidths_t *bw)`

- `esp_wifi_set_channel(uint8_t primary,`
                       `wifi_second_chan_t second)`
- `esp_wifi_get_channel(uint8_t *primary,`
                       `wifi_second_chan_t *second)`
  If the device doesn't support a second channel set to NULL

- `esp_wifi_remain_on_channel(wifi_roc_req_t *req)`
  Sets how long to lock the channel number

- `esp_wifi_set_max_tx_power(int8_t power)`
- `esp_wifi_get_max_tx_power(int8_t *power)`

- `esp_wifi_set_band(wifi_band_t band)`
- `esp_wifi_get_band(wifi_band_t *band)`
  where band is 2.4GHz or 5GHz

- `esp_wifi_set_band_mode(wifi_band_mode_t band_mode)`
- `esp_wifi_get_band_mode(wifi_band_mode_t *band_mode)`
  Selects exclusive 2.4GHz or 5GHz or both

- `esp_wifi_set_rssi_threshold(int32_t rssi)`
- `esp_wifi_sta_get_rssi(int *rssi)`
  Triggers event if RSSI goes below threshold

WiFi Standard

You can configure the WiFi standard that is used:

- `esp_wifi_config_11b_rate(wifi_interface_t ifx, bool disable)`
  enable/disable 11b rate

- `esp_wifi_config_80211_tx_rate(wifi_interface_t ifx,`
  `                              wifi_phy_rate_t rate)`
- `esp_wifi_config_80211_tx(wifi_interface_t ifx,`
  `                         wifi_tx_rate_config_t *config)`

- `esp_wifi_set_vendor_ie(bool enable,`
  `  wifi_vendor_ie_type_t type, wifi_vendor_ie_id_t idx,`
  `                              const void *vnd_ie)`
- `esp_wifi_set_vendor_ie_cb(esp_vendor_ie_cb_t cb, void *ctx)`

- `esp_wifi_80211_tx(wifi_interface_t ifx, const void *buffer,`
  `                         int len, bool en_sys_seq)`
  end raw 802.11 data.

- `esp_wifi_register_80211_tx_cb(`
  `                         esp_wifi_80211_tx_done_cb_t cb)`
  Callback for tx data event

- `esp_wifi_disable_pmf_config(wifi_interface_t ifx)`
  Configures PMF Protected Management Frames.

- `esp_wifi_sta_get_aid(uint16_t *aid)`
  Gets Id assigned by AP. Zero if not connected

- `esp_wifi_set_dynamic_cs(bool enabled)`
  Sets dynamic carrier sense

- `esp_wifi_action_tx_req(wifi_action_tx_req_t *req)`
  Sends an action frame

State Functions

- `esp_wifi_set_csi(bool en)`
- `esp_wifi_set_csi_rx_cb(wifi_csi_cb_t cb, void *ctx)`
- `esp_wifi_set_csi_config(const wifi_csi_config_t *config)`
- `esp_wifi_get_csi_config(wifi_csi_config_t *config)`

  Work with the Channel State Information CSI.

- `int64_t esp_wifi_get_tsf_time(wifi_interface_t interface)`

  Returns time synchronization from the AP in use in microseconds

- `esp_wifi_ftm_initiate_session(wifi_ftm_initiator_cfg_t *cfg)`
- `esp_wifi_ftm_end_session(void)`
- `esp_wifi_ftm_resp_set_offset(int16_t offset_cm)`
- `esp_wifi_ftm_get_report(wifi_ftm_report_entry_t *report,`
  `                                   uint8_t num_entries)`

  Works with a Fine Time Measurement provided by AP.

- `esp_wifi_set_inactive_time(wifi_interface_t ifx,`
  `                                        uint16_t sec)`
- `esp_wifi_get_inactive_time(wifi_interface_t ifx,`
  `                                        uint16_t *sec)`

- `esp_wifi_statis_dump(uint32_t modules)`

  Dumps WiFi statistics

- `esp_wifi_connectionless_module_set_wake_interval(`
  `                                     uint16_t wake_interval)`

Configure Antenna

- `esp_wifi_set_ant_gpio(const wifi_ant_gpio_config_t *config)`
- `esp_wifi_get_ant_gpio(wifi_ant_gpio_config_t *config)`

- `esp_wifi_set_ant(const wifi_ant_config_t *config)`
- `esp_wifi_get_ant(wifi_ant_config_t *config)`

Configure Power Management

- `esp_wifi_set_ps(wifi_ps_type_t type)`
- `esp_wifi_get_ps(wifi_ps_type_t *type)`

- `esp_wifi_force_wakeup_acquire(void)`
- `esp_wifi_force_wakeup_release(void)`

Index

279

Programming The ESP32 In C Using The Espressif IDF
ISBN: 978-1871962918

C is the ideal choice of language to program the ESP32, ensuring that your programs are fast and efficient, and here it is used with the Espressif IoT Development Framework, ESP-IDF and VS Code, a combination which makes it simple to get started and provides a wealth of functions not found elsewhere.

The purpose of this book is to reveal what you can do with the ESP32's GPIO lines together with widely used sensors, servos and motors and ADCs. After covering the GPIO, outputs and inputs, events and interrupts, it gives you hands-on experience of PWM (Pulse Width Modulation), PWM for Motor control, the SPI bus, the I2C bus and the 1-Wire bus, the UARTs and of course WiFi. To round out, it covers direct access to the hardware, adding an SD Card reader, sleep states to save power, the RTC, RMT and touch sensors. It also devotes a chapter to FreeRTOS which takes us into the realm of asynchronous processing.

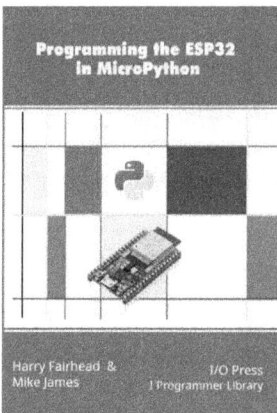

Programming the ESP32 in MicroPython
ISBN: 978-1871962826

Although MicroPython is slower than C, most of the time this doesn't matter and it is much easier to use. It is based on Python 3 and is fully object-oriented.

Another good thing about MicroPython on the ESP32 is that it is very easy to get started. After a simple installation procedure you have a working MicroPython machine which you can program almost at once using the Thonny IDE or PyCharm which has more extensive syntax checking and input prompting.

The purpose of the book is to reveal what you can do with the ESP's GPIO lines together with widely used sensors, servos and motors and ADCs. After covering the GPIO, outputs and inputs, events and interrupts, it gives you hands-on experience of PWM (Pulse Width Modulation), the SPI bus, the I2C bus and the 1-Wire bus. We also cover direct access to the hardware, adding an SD Card reader, sleep states to save power, the RTC, RMT and touch sensors, not to mention how to use WiFi.

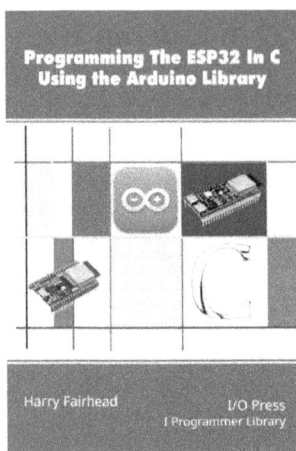

Programming the ESP32 In C Using the Arduino Library

ISBN: 978-1871962291

C is the ideal choice of language to program the ESP32, ensuring that your programs are fast and efficient, and here it is used with the customized ESP version of the Arduino library and its associated IDE which makes the device as easy to use as possible. The Arduino library runs on top of the official Espressif ESP32 IoT Development Framework as a simplifying layer and you can always drop down a level and make use of its additional features when required.

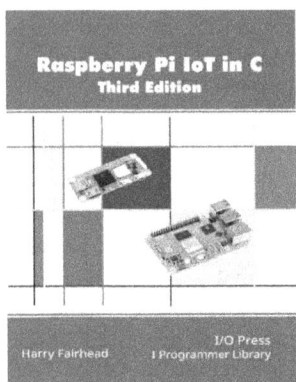

Raspberry Pi IoT In C, 3rd Edition
ISBN: 978-1871962840

This book takes a practical approach to understanding electronic circuits and datasheets and translating this to code, specifically using the C programming language. The main reason for choosing C is speed, a crucial factor when you are writing programs to communicate with the outside world. If you are familiar with another programming language, C shouldn't be hard to pick up. This third edition has been brought up-to-date and focuses mainly on the Pi 4, Pi5 and the Pi Zero.

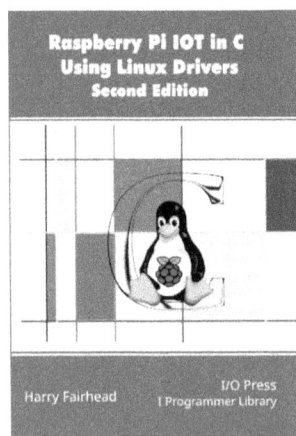

Raspberry Pi IoT in C With Linux Drivers, 2nd Edition
ISBN: 978-1871962857

This second edition has been updated and expanded to cover the Raspberry Pi 5 and the Raspberry Pi Zero W/2W. There are Linux drivers for many off-the-shelf IoT devices and they provide a very easy-to-use, high-level way of working. The big problem is that there is very little documentation to help you get started. This book explains the principles so that you can tackle new devices.

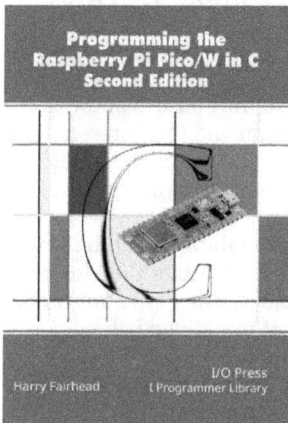

Programming The Raspberry Pi Pico/W In C, Second Edition
ISBN: 978-1871962796

This book explains the many reasons for wanting to use C with the Pico, not least of which is the fact that it is much faster. This makes it ideal for serious experimentation and delving into parts of the hardware that are otherwise inaccessible. Using C is the way to get the maximum from the Pico and to really understand how it works.

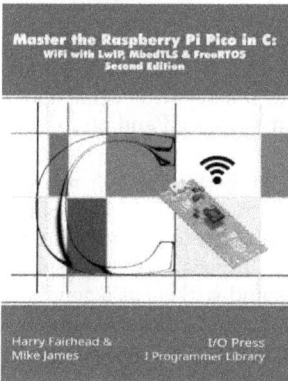

Master the Raspberry Pi Pico in C: WiFi with LwIP, MbedTLS & FreeRTOS, Second Edition
ISBN: 978-1871962390

Adding WiFi to the Raspberry Pi Pico turns this low-cost, small form factor device into a true IoT device. The extra capabilities added to the Pico W open up loads of opportunities, but only if you are prepared to do battle with the two libraries that provide networking and security – Lightweight Internet Protocol (lwIP) and Mbed Transport Layer Security (mbedTLS), respectively. This second edition has been updated to cover the second generation Pico 2W as well as the original Pico W and has been extended to cover FreeRTOS, which offers significant advantages when working with lwIP and mbedTLS.

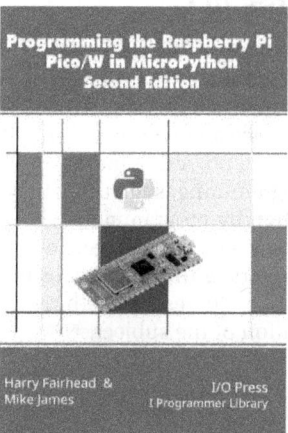

Programming the Raspberry Pi Pico/W in MicroPython, Second Edition
ISBN: 978-1871962802

MicroPython is a good choice of language to program the Pico. It isn't the fastest way, but in most cases it is fast enough to interface with the Pico's hardware and its big advantage is that it is easy to use.

The purpose of the book is to reveal what you can do with the Pico's GPIO lines together with widely used sensors, servos and motors and ADCs. One of the key advantages of the Pico is its PIO (Programmable I/O) and while this is an advanced feature, it is introduced in this book. After finding out how the PIO works, we apply it to writing a PIO program for the DHT22 and the 1-Wire bus.

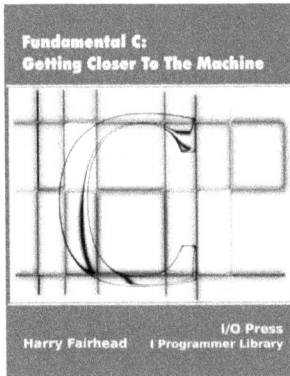

Fundamental C: Getting Closer To The Machine
ISBN: 978-1871962604

For beginners, the book covers installing an IDE and GCC before writing a Hello World program and then presents the fundamental building blocks of any program - variables, assignment and expressions, flow of control using conditionals and loops.

When programming in C you need to think about the way data is represented, and this book emphasizes the idea of modifying how a bit pattern is treated using type punning and unions and tackles the topic of undefined behavior, which is ignored in many books on C.

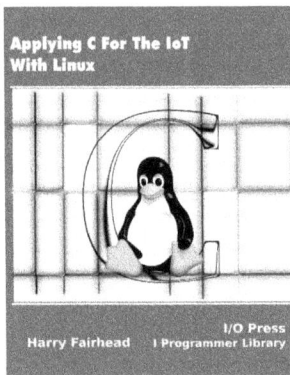

Applying C For The IoT With Linux
ISBN: 978-1871962611

If you are using C to write low-level code using small Single Board Computers (SBCs) that run Linux, or if you do any coding in C that interacts with the hardware, this book brings together low-level, hardware-oriented and often hardware-specific information.

It starts by looking at how programs work with user-mode Linux. When working with hardware, arithmetic cannot be ignored, so separate chapters are devoted to integer, fixed-point and floating-point arithmetic. It goes on to the pseudo file system, memory-mapped files and sockets as a general-purpose way of communicating over networks and similar infrastructure. It continues by looking at multitasking, locking, using mutex and condition variables, and scheduling. It rounds out with a short look at how to mix assembler with C.

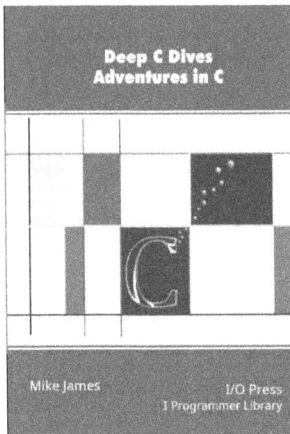

Deep C Dives: Adventures in C
ISBN: 978-1871962888

This book provides in-depth exploration of the essence of C, identifying the strengths of its distinctive traits. This reveals that C has a very special place among the programming languages of today as a powerful and versatile option for low-level programming, something that is often overlooked in books written by programmers who would really rather be using a higher-level language. To emphasize the way in which chapters of this book focus on specific topics, they are referred to as "dives", something that also implies a deep examination of the subject.

www.ingramcontent.com/pod-product-compliance
Lightning Source LLC
Chambersburg PA
CBHW061348210326
41598CB00035B/5919